One Man's Happiness

Other Books by Lord Tweedsmuir

Hudson's Bay Trader
Always a Countryman

ILLUSTRATED BY B. S. BIRO F.S.I.A.

ONE MAN'S HAPPINESS

Lord Tweedsmuir

ROBERT HALE · LONDON

230

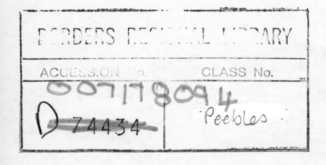
Printed and bound in Great Britain by
C. Tinling and Co. Ltd,
Liverpool, London and Prescot

To
Priscilla

Contents

Acknowledgements

I have drawn upon a number of books and other written sources in the course of this volume and have acknowledged them where they occur in the text. I would, however, express a special appreciation of the following:

The Great Storm by J. Lennox Kerr (George Harrap & Co., 1954) without which I should not have been able to relate our own experiences of "The Great Gale" (Chapter 8) to what was going on elsewhere round the shores of Britain;

The North-east of Scotland (Central Press, Aberdeen, 1963) for "Animals" (Chapter 16);

The Aberdeen Journal for the account, in two issues of January 1850, of the York Buildings Company referred to in "The Parish in Pawn" (Chapter 18);

Glyn Mills & Co. for details from their archives, of the Financial Crisis of 1772, in which Alexander Fordyce was involved (Chapter 19);

The Minister of Belhelvie, the Rev. David Forsyth, who lent me an invaluable transcript of the records of our Kirk Session;

And to many helpers, amongst them my mother who gave me a great deal of good advice.

Foreword

There are those, and I am one of them, who claim that the Scots are the most influential small race since the ancient Greeks. If that is true it is because so many of us go abroad to seek our fortunes. We have always done so and we always will do so. And our particular gifts are the more marketable the more distant our destination. But, however long we are absent, and it may be for several generations, we never lose our love of Scotland. It is our home, just as the world is our opportunity.

Twenty years ago I married and made a home in Scotland after a generation's absence. We settled down in Aberdeenshire, where my wife, and her forbears, had always lived. We spent our first four years in a little castle among the high mountains, and the next sixteen years within sight and sound of the northern sea. Our home is a base for further wandering, but it is also a refuge from the fret of the furious cities, where we have had to spend so much of our time.

If you have had the good fortune to have a country childhood you may hope to grow up with one of the greatest ingredients for a happy life, the ability to take pleasure in small things. If you share the feeling for romance, which most Scots possess, you have another ingredient equally as great. As in Scotland the past is always within easy reach we have naturally enjoyed ourselves exploring it, and following the adventures of the Scots that have gone over the centuries from these few square miles of our parish to seek their fortunes as we do to this day.

I had returned from my wandering with no fortune but a rare collection of people and places. We have lived for twenty years among those things that we both learned to love in our country childhoods and this book has been put together in the hope that it may be of some interest and enjoyment to those who find happiness in these same things.

I *Braemar*

JULY 27th was one of the very few hot days in the summer of 1948. The shadows were lengthening as Priscilla and I drove over the Bridge of Dee at Invercauld. The heat of the day, and the cool of the dusk, brought out the smell of the heather on the lower slopes and of the pines along the river. We basked in it. It was of the magic of that moment. All Britain had been drowsing in the sun that day. We knew, for we had spent several contented hours gazing down upon it from a small aircraft. The noise of the engines was out of our ears by now, and the sound of the river crept into them. But even its strong soothing sound could not drown the beat of the bells, pealing from an old tower in a Southern city. Once over the bridge the road follows the windings of the river along its right bank. A mile or so upstream it rounds a steep bluff, and the rapids wash the rocks not many feet below. To them cling a line of larches, almost down to the water's edge, forming a screen. Then road and river go their separate ways, and between them is rough pasture in the flat of the valley. We looked across it to the old castle of Braemar standing on its green hillock amidst its guard of lanky and leaning larches. A thin plume of smoke was rising from one square chimney, straight up into the still evening air. This was to be our home. We had been married in London that morning.

Any ordinary prudence would have dictated that we took a small flat in London and departed, for inexpensive holidays, with Priscilla's two small daughters, at appropriate times. But we had chosen a home five hundred miles by rail and sixty more by road from our work. There are times when you feel entitled to dodge prudence. Not to shun it, but to side-step it.

The next day and the next were hot, with that crisp northern sunlight that burns your bare skin. The river sank still lower among its boulders. Salmon jumped petulantly in the tepid water. And then the sun left us and we only saw it again in snatches. Winds set the larches sighing round the castle, and the mountains lost their lines in the mist, as rain marched down the valley and the river ran full and dark with peat flood.

We were possessors of a lease of the castle for several years. We had neither of us ever cherished any ambition to live in a castle, but we had seen this one and had known instantly that we wanted to live there, and to live there more than anywhere else in the world. Only a parcel of land went with it, but we had some three and a half miles of salmon fishing from both banks. It was set on a green knoll to guard the pass, and within comfortable musket range of the road that runs between the river and the steep mountain side. It faces southwards to a belt of trees that hides the road, not a hundred yards away. That road runs on through Braemar and, up and over the Devil's Elbow, to Perth. Beyond the road and the trees you look upwards past heather and scree and rock, and single scattered birch trees and clumps of pines, to a stony peak, crowned by a little rounded cairn. The English put it there when they finally moved their garrison out, at the beginning of the last century.

The castle is of L-shaped design with a round tower which contains the staircase in its inner angle. It is curtained by a star-shaped defensive wall, with embrasures and loop-holes for musketeers, which was built on more than a century later to extend the castle's defences. This was built later—it owes its design to Vauban, the fortification builder of the eighteenth century, whose effective concept was so widely copied.

We came out of the small front door, at the bottom of the tower, next morning. A flagged path took us to the door in the loopholed wall. From there the drive circled down the castle knoll to join the road away to the right, at the end of the belt of trees. But, the shortest cut to the gate, was down a steep grassy slope. At the top of this slope, in the 1840s, Queen Victoria had sat and presided over what was the first Royal Braemar Gathering. On the sward beneath her four of the young Farquharsons of Invercauld did the foursome reel. Then there was a ghillies race up to the cairn at the top of the craig. The winner returned an astonishingly fast time, and paid the penalty by being an invalid from that day to his death.

We turned back and looked at the castle itself with four square windows, one above the other in the roundness of the tower, covered by iron bars. Those iron bars were riveted red-hot into place as a defence against cannon balls. They contrasted with the narrow slits of windows in the turrets, each just big enough for a musketeer to take aim. Most of the ground floor rooms had barrelroof ceilings to give them greater tensile strength against bombardment. We chose the room at the bottom of the circular staircase as our rod room, and another, along a short flagged passage as our gun room. Beside the flagstones, in an alcove, was a bottle-shaped dungeon after the French style. There was a rusty iron clasp to keep the lid on it. If prisoners climbed on each other's shoulders, and tried to push it up from beneath, they could easily reach it for the dungeon was only just over eleven feet deep, and there were once seventeen men in it at the same time. Turning right-handed our feet echoed on the flags, passing doors that had once been servants bedrooms, and our storeroom and larder, then a scullery, a boiler room and a small bedroom, and we emerged into the light of day again, at the back door. All this took quite a lot of exploring. All this extra space came about from the joining of the tower to the perimeter of the wall at the back, and the clamping, like a limpet, of a tiny cottage against the outside of the wall beside the back door. It somewhat spoiled Vauban's star-shaped symmetry.

Domestically the boiler room was the only one of these rooms in really active use, and the smell of drying clothes vied with the smell of coal dust and met you in the passage. For we and our wonderful cook and housekeeper, Ella Gold, lived on the first floor and above. There were two big rooms one above the other and identical in dimension. Each was big enough to support a grandfather clock in its right perspective. The lower one was the dining-room. Our living room above, being that much higher, had a splendid view across the valley to the rapids of the river. The windows on that side were much bigger and were not barred, because it was thought unlikely that enemy cannon would be directed to that quarter, as the ground falls down steeply to the valley below, and it was the side opposite to the road that might have to be denied to an enemy. Above were the bedrooms, on two top floors, and from there we could climb to the top of the round tower and see all that we wanted to see of the world.

The winding stone staircase was like a lighthouse. We grew used to the unyielding touch of flag stones, naked stone walls or a cold stone staircase; it was a part of life in a castle. The thread of that staircase puzzles antiquaries. It gives a swordsman mounting the stairs the advantage of the full sweep of his sword, it favours the attacker against the defender. This is always supposed to be the sign of church property, on whose staircases swords were not meant to clash. It was probably built in this way to give colour to the claim that this was not meant to be a fighting castle, but rather to be a lodge from which to hunt the deer on the Braes of Mar.

The staircase does not take you to the roof of the tower. That is reached by creeping through a space under the pitch of the roof, where the cistern sits among its water pipes, muffled in felt and deep in dust. From there the trap-door gives on to the leads, and a rickety set of steps used to take us up the few feet or so that remained of the outside of the tower, to creep through an embrasure and stand cob-webbed and triumphant beside the flag pole.

We did this on the morning after our arrival. It was going to be a hot day, and the stonework was already warm to the touch. The skyline of the castle was grouped around us. We were above the tops of the turrets, but below the tops of those big square chimneys, which the jackdaws were still trying to occupy. There was no breeze to stir the lanyard on the flag pole. The whole mountain world was in one of its rare moods of drowsy warmth. In a pool of shade among the pines, that marched up the mountain side of Craig Choinnich beyond the road, a blackcock called, and called again. In the stillness we could hear the murmur of the river. We stood for a long time letting the sun warm our faces, while we revelled in the smell of the sun-warmed hillsides. We were sixty miles from Aberdeen, half of which city Priscilla represented in Parliament, and of whose university I was to be Rector for the next three years. London and the Houses of Parliament, which was our principal place of work, were five hundred miles beyond that. We had several weeks of holiday to which to look forward. Our time was our own and our world was around us.

Summer slipped into autumn with the frosts on the morning grass when August was barely out. As in most Scottish seasons the most delectable days came in September. There were days when the crisp hot sunshine dried the diamonds of dew on the spiders' webs and there was stillness except for the buzzing of bees. As the river grew chill, so the reddening salmon threw off their lethargy to snatch at a hook. The autumn colours were vivid to the point that, if they could not match it, they put you in mind of the Canadian fall. The days shortened. When Christmas came the sky was overcast, and the air was muggy and still, and then came the frosts. After the New Year the snow began to fall. Sometimes it was driven down the wind. Sometimes it fell slow and unhurried in those big flakes that we call, in the north, "Snowing Hudson's Bay blankets". Some of it would last, up in the corries, through the whole of the following summer. The stags that had filled the valley with their roaring had fallen silent, and the only steady sound was from the running of the river, for nearly all the birds, among them the duck and the oyster-catcher and the curlew had headed towards the coast when they smelled the onset of winter. The silent time had come.

We were not much at home in January as the Parliamentary recess, at that time, gave us both a chance to travel abroad on matters connected with business and politics. And we had no intention of going abroad during the summer recess. We had spent too long looking forward to that short northern summer to be away from Scotland at its most wonderful moment, the blend of warmth and running water and the smell of heather and bog myrtle, when Jo and Anne, my step-daughters, would be back for their school holidays, and other members of our families come to join us. Winter was slow in going. At last the ice floes bumped and ground their way down stream, leaving an empty torrent,

B

Thames-coloured with snow water. In April we fished in fierce snow showers, but the world did not quicken until May when the birds came back, and the cuckoo and the curlew were with us, and the lifeless water was broken by the moving salmon.

We never quite believed that this was our home. Coming back from an evening engagement in Aberdeen we would turn the bend of the road above the boat pool and see the line of lights, one above the other, through the barred windows in the tower. And we would wonder if we were not looking at some elfin castle, that might fade away into the mountains. Sometimes, in a rainy misty afternoon, it would look like a great rock, and the hawks and the hoodie crows would seem to take it for some grey outcrop and fly close past the windows or sit upon the square chimneys. Deer came up close to the walls and shed their horns beside them in summer, and the rutting stags roared beside them in the autumn.

The village of Braemar is the capital of the Commonwealth on the day of its Gathering. But in the winter there are none but its own people, and their chimneys smoke and their lights twinkle cheerfully in the winter dusk. The feeling that we were cut off we greatly enjoyed. One of the tradesmen used to order his supplies by carrier pigeon. It was a wonderful place to do one's shopping, and had a friendliness and a cosiness all of its own. Divided by the river Cluny, dashing down to join the Dee, it is one of those old and remote villages which the Reformation hardly touched and so, to this day, a fair proportion of its people are Roman Catholics. When we lived there there were six churches of varying denominations, although not all were in use. We made many friends there. Almost the first that we met was a man who came, unbidden, to the castle and marched about from room to room. We stalked him, and found that he was winding up all the clocks. Rather shamefacedly, in the pressing needs of economy, we told him that we would do it ourselves.

The drawing room was our main room. On the panelling and on the window sills the English Garrison had carved their names. We created their likeness in our imagination. The biggest and boldest lettering on the flat of a window sill ran "John Chestnut, sergeant XXII Regiment 1797." We saw him as black-moustached and red faced and burly. The top button of his scarlet uniform would have been undone as he stared out through the rain and the mist of the valley to the round flank of Ben a Bhuird, and took out his knife to pass the time by carving his name.

The castle was fully furnished. The pictures were in keeping. In the drawing room was a painting of Italian ruins and had probably been brought back from the "Grand Tour" a century earlier. There was a print of Queen Victoria as a girl, and two of eighteenth-century military leaders. We were cold in that room, of an evening, sitting in front of a tiny Victorian grate. And then we discovered that there was a splendid square stone fireplace behind it. We got leave from the laird to restore it to its original form. Across the lintle ran a continuous slab of stone, at least five feet long. The fireplace stood nearly five feet from the floor and was probably seven feet deep. If we looked up the chimney we could see, just above our heads, a great iron bar which runs across it where the garrison hung their cooking pots. We were never cold any more, in that room. Instead of a wretched little scuttle of coal, one complete birch tree a day went up that chimney thereafter. But in winter time, guests were given the chance to wear their overcoats at meal times in the dining room below.

During our married life, home has been something that has had to be enjoyed at the intervals of weekends and Parliamentary recesses. Sunday has always been a day when, from lunch time onwards, we could not escape from the depressing thought that by evening we had to be at Aberdeen station, to be in London next morning. The sixty-mile drive to the station we somehow managed in those days without minding. In contrast returning at the end of the week was wildly exciting. We have always celebrated Saturday nights, knowing that we would wake at home on Sunday morning.

The Castle had stood for more than three hundred and twenty years. It had seen Montrose come there, in the rain, to be deserted by his fair-weather friends after the battle of Philiphaugh. It had been burned in Dundee's Rebellion by the Black Colonel— Farquharson of Inverey. There had been no loop-holed wall round it then, and the soldiers' horses had been tethered to the castle walls. He had stampeded them, with some shots, and the soldiers had rushed after them, giving him the chance to pile up faggots and fire them. Its blackened walls had seen the Standard of the 1715 Rebellion raised by the Earl of Mar not many hundred yards away. It had been rebuilt by the War Office who had garrisoned it with musketeers. They had been put there to guard the upper end of the Dee valley, to disarm the Highlanders and carry out the most un-British of all policies, the prohibition of the wearing of the plaid. That garrison stayed there until the turn of the last century having done nothing for a long time except keep a check on smuggling. It was the Earl of Mar who had built it and lost it to the Farquharsons, when the 1715 Rebellion failed and Mar was attainted after the Battle of Sheriffmuir. It is still firmly in Farquharson hands. That Earl of Mar was the first colonel of what became the Royal Scots Fusiliers in which my father had served and with whom my uncle, Alastair, had been killed. From this valley a large part of the original regiment had been raised. And now, for four years, it was our home. Here we entered our new world.

Among the Scots the points of the compass mean a great deal. A map of the world on Mercator's projection, has the Mediterranean as its centre. A Scotsman usually carries a world map in his head, with his home in the middle of it. My father enjoyed repeating the story of the wounded Jock, in the 1914 War, who, when asked where he received his wound, replied, "Twa miles on the Rothiemurchus side of Baghdad."

Both Priscilla and I had the good fortune to travel widely, and I had lived outside the country for most of the five years between leaving Oxford and going off to the War, starting as a district officer in East Africa and ending as a Hudson's Bay Company fur trader in Baffin Island. But now this old stone dwelling was the centre of our world. For us East meant the Far East. West meant to us the plains of Western North America. North meant to us the Canadian Eastern Arctic. South meant London. Unlike Mercator's globe ours was not quite round, but a peculiar shape of its own.

In the castle we enjoyed our own separate existence. Animals and birds did not seem to suspect the existence of human beings inside that mass of stone, even if the Union Jack straining and fluttering on its flag pole, deterred them somewhat on windy days. And that flag flew all the time for, even when we were in London, the castle was lived in by the person who made our tenure of it possible. She was called Ella Gold. She lived there in all weathers and in all seasons, and cooked and housekept for us. She was surrounded by dogs, two Corgis, a Scottie and a Sealyham. Every day she took them for a walk and for the rest of the day they kept her company indoors. She knew a lot about dogs, and from all angles, for she had been a lady postman on Speyside. She was a wonderful cook, and we looked forward to our welcome when we got home for the weekends. She would stand waiting for us at her kitchen door, white aproned and welcoming and knee deep in dogs. Her sense of humour was explosive. She cherished a strange and interesting piece of demonology regarding the people of Fife, whom she held to be the repository of all wickedness. When she had reason to refer to the Devil she always called him the Earl of Fife. When a particularly shocking assassination took place in the Middle East, her comment on the murderers was that, "it seems there's warse about than the Fifers." She rarely went to the village. The castle and the valley and the dogs were her world.

We were joined by Jo and Anne, my two stepdaughters, about a month after our marriage, and thereafter they were with us for all of every school holidays. They were going to school in Aberdeen at the time, and were aged 13 and 11. They had one big turret room as a sitting-room, which was full of their possessions, and one of the rooms on the ground floor beside the stone-flagged passage which contained probably every toy that they had ever possessed, quite regardless of its state of repair. No armless doll or headless teddy bear seemed ever to have been thrown away. On one of our many picnics before the autumn, they each caught their first trout in a little river that flows out of Loch Callater. The next year they both caught their first salmon and soon after were going fishing by themselves, as salmon fishers in their own right.

It was on August 22nd of our second summer in the castle that Susie was born. As far as any of us has ever been able to make out she was the only child ever to be born in that castle since it was built in the 1620s. According to our Scottish custom she was christened in the castle itself, by the minister of Crathie. The christening vessel was placed on the window sill on which "John Chestnut, Sergeant" had so laboriously carved his name more than one hundred and fifty years before. Round the top of the mountain above us, two ravens circled and croaked. In any fairy story their presence would have been at least as unwelcome as that of a witch or a wicked fairy. But here they were welcome. Susie prospered. The days of rationing were still with us and we received from a Caribbean island, which we had recently visited on a political mission, the gift of a sack of the purest brown sugar. As the sack grew smaller so Susie grew bigger.

Susie was soon joined by Nannie, who was with her for some seven years and has remained a close family friend ever since.

These two joined Jo and Anne on the top floor, with its superb view over the mountains, and completely filled it. Priscilla and I slept on the floor below, and any guests below that. Susie's advent meant a pleasantly restrained summer's holiday that year; Gatherings and Games, and such gregarious goings-on, being out of the question. This enlarged garrison of the castle had been reinforced by James Thom and his wife and a small daughter. He had been a petty officer in the Navy and was our gardener and general helper.

By the year following, which was 1950, Susie was being pushed down the short drive and out of the gate and past the graveyard and leftwards up the long steep slope to Braemar village. Often James Thom's small girl accompanied them on foot. More rarely Ella went too, with a fist full of leads, controlling a four-in-hand of dogs.

We seemed never to be able to enjoy home for long enough. We always seemed to be having to leave for somewhere. In that year Priscilla had to give up a substantial part of her summer recess to attend the Council of Europe as a delegate. She had been with the European Movement from its beginning in the Hall of Knights at The Hague. Jo and Anne helped me to prepare a tremendous welcome home for her. We decided that we must get some game, to add to the salmon which we could depend on catching but which would be well past its best at that time of year. I was only able to shoot one old and tough cock grouse. But coming back from fishing next day we put up a covey of partridges and one flew into a wire fence, broke a wing and we pounced on it like retrievers. We left catching the salmon to the last and had a splendid dinner starting with grouse soup.

The next year, 1950, started with a General Election in the fog and sleet and darkness of February. Our party ended up still in opposition, but only just.

Then life settled down. Susie had become an articulate being, and was taken to the Braemar Gathering, to stare round-eyed at the pipers and the dancers and the huge hairy men who put shots and tossed cabers. She and Nannie now had a round of calls to make when they went to the village. Susie was invited to sit on the counters of various shops. But the highlight of the trip was a visit to the jeweller, and she would go round to his garden at the back to see the tortoise that lived there.

We saw a lot of sun in the autumn of the next year. The General

Election we had been expecting for months took place in October sunshine and our Party were back in power, with a very modest majority. It involved my departure to Paris for the whole winter, as a delegate to the U.N. which met there for that Session. When we came to leave the castle in the autumn of 1952 it took two complete afternoons for Nannie and Susie to say their goodbyes, and on each occasion they came back from the village laden with gifts. Susie was three when she left the castle where she had been born, christened and brought up. She was too young for the memory of it to last. But our memories of it will never fade.

When we moved down the river to set up our new home within sound of the sea we brought with us a memory of four years of happiness in that stone tower among the high mountains, and hardly a detail of it has faded.

The jackdaws returned to the chimneys that no longer smoked, and the quiet of the mountains enfolded to the castle.

2   *Upper Deeside*

IF YOU have ever ridden on the North American prairies, or on the grassy plains of the Argentine, it will come back to you in your dreams. But plains seem just to happen to be there and not to have been created with a purpose, while mountains seem to have been set up, moulded into their present shape and parted by running rivers, all very deliberately.

The minister of Crathie and Braemar, in 1842, wrote that this parish contained "a far richer display of what may be styled the grand and sublime, than any other district in Aberdeenshire." And you may come to agree with him, as you follow the road from the tides at Aberdeen upwards along the windings of the Dee to Braemar. The fields grow fewer and the hills grow higher, until at Ballater you look across mountain country. This was our rail-head when we lived at Braemar. A railway that coined money for three months, and lost heavily for the other nine. It was said that Queen Victoria forbade the further passage of the rail up the glen, and at the same time made it clear to the people of Ballater that she did not wish to look into the peoples' backyards. Houses must be made to look as though they fronted on the principal road, even if they were facing the other way. Here Priscilla's great-great uncle, Peter Thomson, had a house in his later years. He was born the year before Waterloo, and he and his many brothers and sisters grew up in a croft that is still lived in at Forgue, in the north-western end of the county. He, and his great brother George, harnessed a boundless energy to the early days of railway building. Peter died, distant and distinguished, as Mayor of Liverpool. George died in a large and comfortable house at Cheltenham, supported by a massive bank account, and surrounded by a garden of Ilex trees and greenhouses full of grapes. But they never forgot Forgue and the croft beside the road there. Their father was a mason of renown. That croft is a craftsman's building. You can tell by the pointing of its stones.

From Ballater to Braemar you leave the hills for the mountains, with the rushing river in the valley beneath you. Road and river come together beside the old stone tower of Abergeldie Castle, one of the many in this shire which is still habitable and inhabited. Not far upstream the towers of Balmoral rise above the trees on the other side of the river. It is a splendid example of the exuberance and robustness of Victorian Gothic romanticism. It was not an alien cult, for Sir Walter Scott had much responsibility for it. Almost everything in the castle is of that period. The tartan cushions and the carpets, the candle holders of silver stag's horns, and Landseer pictures of the ghillies, drawn to look like the Apostles. Pure Victorian decoration has its own very real charm, but it will marry with no other. It commemorates a great era of British history which, as Walter Elliot used to say, started with Napoleon and ended with Bernard Shaw. It is modish today to discount the virtues of that century and harp only upon its vices, whose relict is the maze of mean and grimy streets in so many of our cities. Future historians will rediscover it.

The road crosses the river at the gates of Invercauld, beside the old Brig of Dee. It was built after Culloden by troops of two infantry regiments, clearly under skilled direction. Some say that ugliness is merely a matter out of place. This bridge must be one of the most beautiful engineering works of art in the world.

It is so clearly matter in its right place that it seems not to have been built, but to have grown out of its banks to span the river.

You have not finished with Scots' baronial architecture as you move up-stream. You see it in the castle of Invercauld, away to your right on the north side of the river. As a style it would be hideous south of the border or in any low country, but it has its place in a cradle by high mountains and hanging forests. It is, after all, hewn of the local rock, and nowhere could it be as ugly as most modern building. The Victorians happily left Braemar Castle alone, but there exists a picture of the castle painted by Gustave Doré. It is shown amidst the lowering darkness, with a storm about to break. It might have served as a frontispiece for Dracula, and although you cannot actually see vampires, they are heavily suggested, together with the distant howling of were-wolves.

On the road that goes past the entrance to it, you find a hundred yards further on on your right, the graveyard with the mausoleum of the Farquharson family. Beyond that, is a farm road which goes down to a long slow pool with a stalker's cottage on the far side of it. Beside this little road there is a cottage from which as we passed, rod in hand, we could hear the clicking and clacking of a hand loom turning out tartan cloth, in the way they did it in the old days. Then the road bends steeply leftward and runs straight uphill into Braemar. If you follow the fork to the left you make your way up the valley of the Cluny to the pass above the Devil's Elbow, where the road angles down the far side of the watershed to Perth. The right fork over the Cluny Bridge goes through the village and seems as big as the left one. But you have only just got to the far end of the village to discover that your road has lost heart, and is very much a country lane, as it runs through the birch trees. It climbs high up the hillside, until you are looking at the Dee far below you, curving through the flat bed of the valley among fields that gradually become sparser. The clear waters of the Quoich join it from the far bank, through a stony delta. If you drove off this road here you would fall a long way before you reached those rapids.

Ahead of you on the far side of the valley, Mar Lodge stands in its flat park, and beneath mountains bald from the axes which sheared away the forests during the wars. Patches of forest still hang from the slopes. Through one such stand of tall timber the road runs down to the river. It is a real forest. Only in a natural forest are the dead trees allowed to stand among the living until they totter and fall, instead of being tidily removed. And in summer it smells, as the Canadian forest smells, of hot pine needles. Beside the river a little stone lodge of Victorian Palladian, faces an ugly iron bridge with a locked gate. Armed with permission and the key, you rumble across and the gate clangs behind you. The drive winds between clumps of tall trees, pine and spruce, and suddenly in front of you is a building that has no kinship with Scotland, past or present, but it strikes no discord. You are staring at a large German hunting lodge, perfect in every detail in the style of a century ago. In this up-ended mountain world its Teutonic shape is set in an expanse so green and so flat that, were it not for the clumps of trees, would seem like Lord's Cricket Ground. It is now a hotel for those who follow those same mountain sports to which they add ski-ing in the winter. But when we saw it first it stood empty, while its clocks ticked away in the silence, and the Winterhalter portraits peered through the dim light of a northern dusk at the dark woodwork and heavy brocade. Its owner was bedridden far to the south, with a crippling malady, and could only enjoy the silence of that valley and the lines of those mountains in memory.

Up and along the valley road again you pass the hamlet of Inverey at the bottom of the glen of that name. On your right, if you look carefully, you will see the ruins of the old Farquharson castle of Inverey, the home of the Black Colonel, as they called that sturdy Jacobite who had burned Braemar Castle and given General Mackay, commanding Dutch William's forces, so much trouble in 1689. Mackay sparring with Claverhouse decided to occupy Braemar Castle to keep Upper Deeside in check. He sent a strong detachment in June, to occupy the castle with orders to push on at top speed to Inverey to lay hands on the Laird of Inverey and various other Jacobite gentlemen. The detachment was a fast mobile column of fifty horse, fifty of Barclay's Dragoons and sixty foot. Leaving twenty dragoons to hold Braemar Castle, they halted just too long to refresh their horses. It was almost day and the light of the June morning was breaking when they reached Inverey Castle. The Black Colonel and his friends just got away in time, their night shirts flapping as they ran helter-skelter into the forest where the horses could not follow, amidst a shower of musket balls that thudded and sang amongst the tree trunks. The Colonel raised the country against them and when they returned crestfallen to Braemar Castle, a day or so later, he opened fire with a few supporters from Craig Chonnich, and stampeded the horses tethered outside. The horses bolted and were pursued down the glen by their riders, and the whole of Mackay's force disappeared down the valley. There was a great coming and going and carrying of faggots and fire roared up the winding staircase and the castle burned. Back thundered Mackay and burned Inverey Castle as a reprisal, and put a garrison of his men into the castle of Abergeldie, as Braemar was now a blackened ruin. No sooner had he swept off to face Claverhouse again than the Black Colonel laid seige to Abergeldie, so that in August Mackay was forced to return to raise the seige as his garrison were near to their last gasp. The Black Colonel escaped from under the feet of Mackay's horsemen, and fled into the hills with a price on his head. As a fugitive he had hidden himself in an enormous cave in a cleft of the Ey, about two or three miles further upstream. His wife was said to have taken food to him every day. They cannot have searched for him very hard, for he had chosen a very obvious place in which to hide.

There are deer right down to this road on a spring day and in the dusk of the autumn. And in the darkness at night their eyes will shine in your headlights. Along that road you start to see the signs that, if you know the Canadian forests, tell you that lumber operations have been afoot in the recent past. We first took this road when we had just become engaged and were exploring the country, and that was three years after I had laid aside my Canadian uniform. At a bend or two later in the road we came on the now shrunken river running over a clear stony bed, spanned by a Canadian lumber bridge of that simple timeless construction of a wooden cantilever, supported by two hollow square pillars of logs filled with rocks. A few years later, one of the lumberjacks who had built it, was in Montreal, and rang us up at our hotel there, and asked whether it was still standing. It was built in the '40s, so he told us, to carry the timber from the mountain sides of Mar Lodge beyond, across the river to the road. It was meant to last only a few months. In fact it lasted until it was swept away in a heavy spate in the '60s. Those lumber jacks must have felt Canada close to them in this country, with the Luie tumbling down to join the Dee as clear as any of those streams in British Columbia where the rainbow trout revel in the clear cold water at the foot of the glaciers. And then you are at the Lynn itself, and the road ends in a pine needle track beyond the bridge beneath which the river roars in the narrow trough to which it has been confined. Full of foam and thunder, at the bridge, it falls silent and dark below and flows through a deep and widening cleft until it opens out to murmur again, over its shallow staircase of pools and rapids, on its journey to the sea. The road, now a gravel track, retraces its steps down stream on the far bank. Looking up the glen you will follow the windings of the river until they are lost in the huddle of the hills. In a hot sun, after rain, you can fall into a trance, drugged with the smell of the pines, watching the waters converge into the race at the head of the Lynn. Or you may lose the line of the river in the mist and the march of rain. Up that glen runs the track that passes through the Larrig Gru and on to Speyside. You will not see much sign of human life there. There are the ruins of a few cottages and a wall standing beside the river that was part of an advance post, of about an infantry section in strength, from the English garrison at Braemar. It must have been a dreary business being quartered in that glen, keeping those awkward and impractical uniforms up to parade ground standard in cramped and uncomfortable quarters in the eerie silence of those hills. And, lest you think that they are not eerie, listen to those who claim to have encountered the "grey man of Ben Macdhui."

It will not be long before a road is built across this noble wilderness which has four of Scotland's five highest peaks in it. But that should still leave plenty of wilderness, because modern man buzzes along such roads seldom leaving them. Robbed of the use of his car he is like Samson robbed of his locks.

There are some who hate the idea of a wilderness in Britain. As there are many publicists among them they speak with a penetrating voice. They probably do not realize that they dislike almost everything to do with the countryside. The silence is distasteful to them. They would like to see a motor road in every valley and the nights bright with neon signs. But if you are going to overcrowd parts of an industrial country as parts of ours are overcrowded, and will steadily become more so, more desperately do you need areas of wilderness where there is silence, except for the sound of birds and of running water, a range for the eagle and the red deer, and the sour smell of wet moorland or, on a hot day, the blend of heather and bracken and bog myrtle instead of the smell of asphalt and petrol and industrial smoke. A wilderness where man can become human again.

Until a road is built through the Cairngorms, Braemar will be the frontier on this wilderness of mountains. The road to the Lynn now runs to the wilderness, but no further.

It is too often said of old Scottish roads that they were built by General (later Marshal) Wade. This gallant, but inept, Irish soldier was in fact an extremely indifferent builder of roads. He built 260 miles of them but only a relatively small stretch of the roads that he built are in use today. He took little account of contours and less of drainage and his roads lacked foundation. They were rather a matter of marking out a line, then clawing back the turf on either side until the gravel or stones were reached and giving that some rough levelling. Naturally they filled up with snow in the winter and usually became water courses in the summer. As a road-builder he could not compare with Thomas Telford of a generation later. But he was a great bridge-builder and was responsible for the construction of forty stone bridges. Faced by the Jacobite Army in 1745, in spite of his wide experience of soldiering, he was completely out of his depth. He has been charged with pacifying the Highlands after the 1715 rising, by disarming the Highlanders and breaking up their solitudes with the military roads. When the 1745 Rebellion came his roads were used to great advantage by those very Highlanders to speed them on their march south.

But if you had chosen to take the left fork of the road from Aberdeen you could have gone up the valley of the Cluny and down to Perth and beyond. A well-known Braemar figure told me that the only time that he ever caught a big salmon was in the early summer and at the beginning of the century, quite far up the Cluny. When it was safely landed he looked up in time to wave to the stage coach making its last trip to Perth. It must have called for skid pans and formidable braking power to have gone down those bends at the Devil's Elbow, and all the power of its horses to climb it on the way back. As it is the powerful buses of today have to treat the Elbow with respect.

Braemar village is largely Victorian. The advent of Queen Victoria at Balmoral naturally transformed it and its name became known all over the English-speaking world. There are almost certainly more streets and farms and villas in the New World called after it than after any other place in Scotland. The old Gatherings had been simple country festivals. There had been sports and prizes and a parade called the Wrights' March, when craftsmen marched past in groups according to their trades, all the blacksmiths together and all the wheelwrights and so on. Mar Lodge was built, replacing an older building, and there was the ring of the stonemasons' tools as shooting lodges and stalkers' cottages took shape in lonely glens. The Braemar Gathering became a world event, and the wearing of tartan assumed a place in Scottish life which had no earlier precedent.

The village expanded on both sides of the ravine which divides it, where the Cluny tumbles under the bridge and, in the autumn, you can see the shapes of lean dark salmon making their way up its rapids on their way to its head waters. Comfortable houses were built, well protected against the cold of those long dark winters. In 1896, when my father and his fellow undergraduates at Oxford were roasting an ox on the frozen Isis, Braemar had the lowest temperature ever recorded in Britain, of minus 17° Fahrenheit on February 11th of that year.

In one of the substantial houses which stands close beside the road to Perth, Robert Louis Stevenson laid the foundation of his literary fame. He wrote part of an essay about his time there, and he says of himself "I was 31; I was head of a family; I had lost my health, I had never yet paid my way, nor yet made £200 a year." He liked his dwelling in Braemar well enough, though he found it very hard to get used to, it being always referred to as the "late Miss McGregor's Cottage". He shared it with a schoolboy who, with a pen and ink and a shilling paint box produced an endless series of little pictures. Stevenson probably spent quite a lot of time indoors because he says of the climate, "there it blew a great deal and rained in proportion," and one day he borrowed the pen and the ink and the paint box from the schoolboy. Just for the fun of it he made a map of an imaginary island. He then decided to write a book to fit the map. It had been his intention to call the book *The Sea Cook*. He wrote fifteen chapters in fifteen days and then stuck. But he finished later, having migrated to Davos, and called it *Treasure Island* after the map, and stepped straight into immortality.

People came to Braemar to retire. Some of them built very large houses. To this day the incomers form a strong contrast to the people of the glens. These last defy any very clear authentic category. The Gaelic tongue has long gone from Upper Deeside*, but they have something of the traditional Highland softness of speech. Sometimes attending some small and all-male gathering such as a British Legion meeting, you were surrounded by people, almost every one of whom Goya would have enjoyed painting.

Old men could tell of a very different life. There was one of them who, well into his seventies, did a full day's work at putting up fences in all weathers, and all weathers in those mountains is no figure of speech. He had married very young and remembered his father-in-law, who was even then an old man. And from him he had heard reminiscences of the first half of the last century. Those were days when very hard winters often brought death in their train, when there were whole communities in some of the glens, living in little turf-roofed crofts. Most of them lived by cattle, a short-legged and hardy breed, which they drove over the hills to sell at the cattle trysts. They also distilled illicit whisky in the little conical depressions that you can still see, beside the scattered stones in the glens. It had always been the popular drink in the Highlands among all conditions of men. But elsewhere in Scotland ale had been the popular drink until a tax on malt, in the mid-eighteenth century, drove men to drink whisky which, up to that time, few had tasted. Of all the whisky distilled in Scotland only a relatively small quantity paid duty. There were said to have been at one time, no fewer than two hundred illicit stills at work in Glenlivet. It has taken a long time and the perfection of a ruthlessly efficient fiscal machine to get the Scots to pay taxes on their liquor.

During one very hard winter, so the old man told us, it was assumed that two old women who lived together in a distant and tiny croft, would have died of starvation. But when spring came they were found to be alive and in splendid health. They explained that they lived almost entirely on slugs. They must have meant snails which often winter in large colonies, but they must have had other food as well. Famine, as well as pestilence could carry you off in those days, and the lairds kept famine supplies of oatmeal and peats for their people.

The coming of the sheep, and the preservation of the deer, he used to say, was the reason for the desertion of the glens. But these

*There was one Gaelic church left in Aberdeen in 1839. When I first went to Canada in 1936 there were more sermons in Gaelic on a Sunday in Cape Breton, Nova Scotia, than in all Scotland.

factors only hastened a trend which would have begun to work later and ended with the same result.

Scotland is always supposed to have more churches and more banks than its people can possibly use.

There were six churches in Braemar, as has been mentioned earlier, though not all of them were open. There was one bank. As you went in at the front door you found the room that was the Bank on your right, and on your left, if the door was open, you looked at the fire burning in the bank manager's comfortable living room. Thus it is that we Scots have the habit of taking off our hats when we go into a bank, because it is part of somebody's private house. The Bank house at Peebles, lived in by five generations of Buchans, ending with my Uncle Walter in 1954, was an example on a larger scale. The habit is a strong one, and most of us find ourselves uncovering in the great echoing temples of Lombard Street. But in spite of their respectful approach to banks and bankers, only one in six of the people of Scotland has a banking account.

With the mountains above you, you feel the edge of the wilderness at Braemar, at the limits of the village. It is a wilderness which draws the hill climbers from all over Britain. The mountains take a steady toll of them. The Braemar policeman, with some long-legged stalkers and a pony or two, sets off to quarter the hills when a climber is reported as missing.

The victims are those who have not taken this wilderness seriously, who do not understand that you can perish here from exposure and exhaustion as surely as you can in the Arctic tundras. The Commandos who trained there during the war, and whose business was life and death, soon learned to respect them.

With winter the climbers withdraw and at Braemar the procession of cars ceases, the hotels fall empty and the holidays are over for another year. Snow blocks the road to Perth, and is only kept open to Aberdeen by the regular attention of snow ploughs. The village is now no longer on the way to anywhere. The road stops there. The hills are as white and empty as the Arctic and hungry deer drawn down to the valley bottoms, indifferent to the nearness of mankind. And the chimneys of the village smoke cheerfully by day and its lighted windows beam comfortably in the darkness.

3 *Among the Mountains*

IN PLACES where almost anyone can sail, almost everybody tries their hand at sailing. This is also true of those who grow up with shooting or fishing or riding within their reach. You then find out the sports to which you have a natural leaning. It was towards shooting and fishing, and falconry, in my case. But I could enjoy sailing and riding.

As a Hudson's Bay fur trader in Baffin Land, before the war, I journeyed perhaps a thousand miles in summertime in a Peterhead schooner. It was a useful craft that had mainsail, jib and an auxiliary engine, and smelt of petrol, seal oil, cordite and Eskimos. We usually had a great many Eskimos aboard because we were always going somewhere to do something that mattered, such as hunting walrus for winter dog feed, which was three weeks' work. And then at times we would be looking at the blue seas of

Hudson Strait through black spectacles, to shield our eyes from the blinding blink of the northern sun on the fields of ice. At other times we would be chasing the walrus herds through the long cold rollers, with the crack of rifles and the thud of harpoons in the gale-ridden seas of autumn. It was almost always exciting, with an excitement that anyone would have shared. But having a real love for the sea and true understanding of it is a totally different thing from simply enjoying it as a passenger. It is that deep feeling that makes men, who must earn their living in the cities, think about ships and the sea all week long, and get afloat at the first possible chance at the weekend. It explains Sir Francis Chichester, and those like him down the ages. But all of us can feel in some degree, the freedom of the seas.

Riding has its own feeling of freedom, particularly in the cattle country of the West, whether at a nodding walk or a steady canter, or simply listening to the movement of the tethered horses beside a dying camp fire before dropping off to sleep. This was a world my brother Alastair knew well when he was a cowboy in the Porcupine Hills, in Alberta, before the War. He was the only one of us, beside my father, who understood and always enjoyed horses. Perhaps you find that freedom most strongly on the plains of the Argentine, which Cunninghame Graham called the "greatest galloping ground on earth." And you feel it there even if you are the merest dilettante at riding. One may never be a real horseman, or have a vision of Trapalanda, the horse-heaven of the gauchos. But equally one can feel part of that world astride a Mexican saddle, cushioned by the softness of a sheep's fleece, smelling that warm wind that has billowed the grasses and stirred the manes of horses across hundreds of miles of that great sea of level land beyond the Equator.

Fishing and shooting and falconry all carry with them their own peculiar feeling of freedom. They call for a close concentration under the open sky. There is no need to throw off the dusty, workaday indoor world. It vanishes by itself, and leaves no trace. Instead there is a world of fresh air, which is bounded by what you can see around you and the distance that your feet can carry you.

Oxfordshire, where we grew up, was not a good shooting country. Pheasants and partridges disliked the cold clay soil. But rabbits and pigeons were in plenty, and sometimes snipe. The habit of solitary shooting came naturally to a lover of solitude, of wandering alone with a gun in landscapes which have varied from Africa to the Canadian Arctic. This is what the Canadians call "hunting", as opposed to the accepted meaning of the word "shooting" in Britain. The latter implies a large party of shooters. They return with correspondingly larger bags and have helpers to pick up and to carry whatever has been killed. Such shoots are much more humane as the guns are good shots, and there are plenty of men and dogs to prevent wounded quarry escaping. Although I have seldom taken part in a big shoot, I hope that they will always continue. Without them there will never be first-class shots. And this is a form of artistry in which Britain has always excelled. And without them gamekeepers would disappear who are not only the best field naturalists and, to some of us, the best company in the country, but are above all other the repository of the lore of the countryside.

The shortcoming of big shoots is that your movements are ordered and thus you lose your freedom, as well as the excitement of planning with regard to sun and slope and wind and season, which alone means that you can get plesaure out of a blank day. As a solitary shooter it is unlikely that you will ever be more than a very moderate shot. For you will never shoot more than you can carry. You can only hope to be a good marksman if you fire your gun a great many times in the same day.

There are some men in Britain who, several times in the season, will fire at a very hot stand as many cartridges as some of us fire in a year, but they do not enjoy their sport any more than we enjoy our own chosen form. We know different degrees of the same pleasure. And the whole object of sport is pleasure. That is why sportsmen get on so well with each other.

Not the least of the excitement of going to live among the mountains was the prospect of carrying a gun up and along the slopes. Living in the middle of our shooting ground, we could load our guns on our own doorstep when we set out.

I had a golden autumn in 1945, of this kind of shooting, on which to look back. It was among the hills of Tweedsmuir in the Scottish Borders, with the war in Europe just over.

In the summer of 1939 there had been grouse in plenty all over the Border counties. Few people could remember there being more, or even as many. But the world went to war and everybody dropped their guns. The grouse were left largely undisturbed, and with the consequent overcrowding, disease set in, and they lay dead beside the burns in thousands. As the war years passed the moors were left untended, and heather either grew too long or was set on fire and allowed to burn for days. And so it was in the autumn of 1945 that the grouse population was at a very low ebb.

Recently released from the Service, four of us took up our abode at the Crook Inn at Tweedsmuir. It had been rebuilt several times, but had been a hostelry since before 1600, and had been patronised by Robert Burns. We moved on after a week or so to an eighteenth-century house which took in shooting guests. Our host there was Andrew Lorimer, a remarkable, but by no means unduly rare, example of a Scottish schoolmaster, historian, first-class sportsman and naturalist.

From these bases we took the hill for three delightful weeks. None of the moors had been let that year: there were too few grouse. Thus we were able to take about twenty-four thousand acres for the price of a farthing for every four acres, and we set about to enjoy ourselves. The war had dictated widely varying forms of service to us four friends. We found that we tired very quickly on the hills, although we believed ourselves to be very fit. The one who had been a spy and had not long before been released by the Allied advance after a year and a half in Buchenwald preceded by a year in Fresnes, was still in the process of fining down to his normal build, after being swollen with starvation. He moved slowly on the hills at first, but at the end of a fortnight he was a different man. We came back delightfully weary in the evening and fell asleep in front of a wood fire after dinner. We gradually gave up talking about the war, and talked of birds and beasts on the hills instead. The cure was working.

There were a few pheasants and partridges on that low ground bordering the Tweed. But we spent most of our time quartering the hills for grouse. We hunted the heather every inch of the way. We walked two hundred and seventy miles, and shot a grouse every eleven miles. It was a wonderful Indian summer, and the bracken turned bronze and the birch trees bright gold. These steep hills were a great contrast to the easy inclines of Oxfordshire, and the dead flat of the Lombardy plains, where a few of us, who had been able to lay hands on a shotgun, used to vary the war by tramping after snipe and woodcock, and waiting for duck, with the Italian partisans. We had been lucky if we could find anything to lighten those five dreary years.

That insatiable sportsman, Colonel Peter Hawker, has a word

to say in his diary about shooting in the Peninsular War, in 1809, until a ball shattered his hip bone at Talavera, on July 28th of that year. Of Portugal he wrote, "the only birds I killed there which I had never shot before were two storks and a Portuguese owl." He therefore left his gun behind with the heavy baggage, "which I had afterwards reason to regret, as I found that Spain not only abounded with game, but curious foreign birds of every description."

Our sport at Braemar was fishing, and splendid fishing. And it absorbed us for half the year. It partly overlapped the shooting season. The laird was very kind in allowing us to shoot in the big flat field beside the castle, and the slopes of Craig Choinnich. There were, as well as that flat field three fields beyond it, between the river and the road, at least one of them in roots every year, which we also had his permission to walk over. They held as many as three or four coveys of partridges in a good year. Down on the flat we would occasionally find one or two big brown hares, a rarity among the mountains that are the home of the blue hare. In the autumn a few duck would come flighting up the river, and pitch at dusk into whatever field was in stubble.

Otherwise we had the slope of Craig Choinnich rising, level after level, above us and alive with rabbits. You could almost always see the jerky movement of a white powder-puff tail, and sometimes a flurry of them, as when you looked up that steep slope. The mountain and its slopes formed a salient. Its base was a hill road which wound up and across a saddle, called the Queen's Drive. Queen Victoria and her children, and the faithful if peppery John Brown, would ride over it in a dog cart from time to time. They must have had a very strong pony to get it up those steep zig-zags and a good brake to hold it on the far side. In the ragged pines and spruces on one side of Craig Choinnich there were often a fair number of black-cock when we got a late outburst of hot sun, which you sometimes get in that high country, at the beginning of September. There was an occasional woodcock in the bracken, and one or two grouse, to be found in those patches of heather which had not been burnt off in the fire of a year or two earlier. These grouse were feathered Methuselahs, horny and ancient, and seemingly outcasts from their race. We enjoyed hearing them croaking their challenges from the high slopes. They had more to offer alive than dead.

In addition to this we rented the low ground round Mar Lodge, several miles upstream. On the green expanse round that German hunting lodge, protected by green ramparts against river spates, there were always some rabbits feeding, and sometimes there were scores of them. There was generally a flight of mallard up the river who were tremendously wily. They were wary of the big hill foxes who would come down to stalk them, so that they always put out a sentinel. Where the firm sward gave way to marsh there were snipe, sometimes a good number of them. And, last of all, there were a few partridges in the half dozen fields that were farmed along the low ground.

When we came to leave Braemar in 1952, our game book showed that we had shot 339 head of thirteen varieties of game. But subtracting 243 rabbits and 22 red deer from that total, we shot only 74 head of eleven varieties. Of no species, except grouse and ptarmigan, had we shot more than a dozen. A wretched shooting record for four years, but mightily enjoyable walking with a gun.

Walking with a gun for ordinary quarry in any such country, you never need more than a belt of twenty-five cartridges. A belt has a great many advantages, and does not bang against you when you are climbing hills, or pull down your shoulder when you shoot. And climb we did, on summer days after rabbits on Craig Choinnich, or up to the stony levels where the ptarmigan live at Gleney. On winter days, moving silent with our footsteps muffled by the snow, we would pause to look down from Craig Choinnich at the tops of the castle tower and turrets far below us, with a thin spiral of smoke rising from the square chimneys to lose itself in the cold stillness, while our panting breath rose like steam in the frost. Whatever the season we managed to leave London a long way away.

The first calendar year that we were at Braemar, which ended in July 1949, we devoted ourselves almost entirely to fishing. Our bag with the gun was a score of rabbits and one or more each of five other varieties. But the year following we did a fair amount of shooting. Priscilla never cared for a shot gun, always preferring a rifle, but James Thom, our handyman, used to come out with a repeating 20-bore shotgun which had belonged to my brother Alastair's Canadian in-laws. James Thom, like so many ex-petty officers in the Royal Navy, could turn his hand to almost anything. He used to make very fair shooting with this complex little weapon. Thus, in 1950 we succeeded in shooting one hundred and fourteen rabbits and about half a dozen, or less, of nine other varieties. This very large number of rabbits sustained our four very hungry dogs. Ella believed in feeding them, and occasionally us, on rabbits. In fact, she would send me up the hill to get rabbits when the supply ran low. The rest were marketed in the village.

The varied armament of the family made a combined shooting expedition rather difficult. Priscilla had a repeating .22 rifle which we had bought secondhand and which, seventeen years later, still shoots extremely straight. Joanna and Anne had short and inexpensive air guns, which fired small and slow-moving crumbs of lead for a very short distance. My 12-bore was an old non-ejector which my Uncle Willie had acquired in 1898 and shot with it in his Indian Civil Service days. My father had used it, and passed it on to me when I was a boy. It fell off a truck on safari in East Africa, in my Colonial Service days, and had to be fitted with a new pair of barrels. It still retained its excellent balance.

The problem was this. The rifles needed a stationary target and so, at some stage, we had to divide our forces and meet up later on. I had to go far enough away so as not to stampede the game into motion by the sound of my own shooting.

In the early autumn of 1950 Priscilla was a delegate to the Council of Europe. We gave her a great welcome when she returned, and insisted on going on a family shooting party at Mar Lodge, the day following, in spite of the fact that international conferences are very poor training for the glens.

It was an afternoon of early autumn sunlight, and Priscilla and the two girls, rifles in hand, tiptoed into the strip of forest that divided the green glass levels from the marshy ground. I started off into the marsh, and returned about an hour and a half later with a mallard and a couple of snipe. A very large part of that time had been spent in looking for the mallard, in long marsh grass, with no dog to help. Starting back to the forest I picked up four rabbits, and found the three ladies sitting on a tree trunk, exhausted but radiant with triumph. Priscilla had got two rabbits and Anne had contrived to get one with her tiny rifle. It was her first and for a very long time her last. And that was a fair sample of our family shooting expeditions, although they were not usually so successful. We managed to enjoy ourselves wildly, while exacting only a very modest toll from nature.

In 1951 we shot a great many rabbits, four partridges and a hare. Our season was brought to an abrupt end by an autumn election, which brought our Party back into power, with a modest majority, and swept me off to the corridors of the Palais de Chaillot in Paris, as a delegate to the United Nations, for the session that covered the autumn and winter months. The meetings were held in Paris at that time because the United Nations Headquarters in New York was at that time being built.

So guns and rifles slumbered in their cases that winter. Except for one winter afternoon, when Gladwyn Jebb and I, having placed an unwilling deputy in the British seat in the Assembly, slunk away from Paris. For a whole afternoon under purple black snow clouds, we fruitlessly but happily pursued mallard on the formal waters, beside the elegant terraces of Chantilly.

When some years afterwards Priscilla represented Britain, for two successive years, in the United Nations at New York, there were no such outlets.

The year following was our last year at Braemar. And so we determined that we were going to enjoy ourselves as much as possible to blunt the sadness of parting, and in the autumn of 1952, we took the stalking beat of Gleney, which was part of the Mar Lodge estate.

There was a gravel road up the glen, that ended at a ruined stalker's cottage at its head, and was barred by a locked gate at its foot. For a month we had the key to that lock and the freedom of the glen. Beside that gate was a keeper's cottage, and a large and elaborate game larder. It was here that we would meet our stalker, Willy Grant. He was a wonderful companion on the hills. He was also a famous piper and had piped a battalion of the Gordon Highlanders into battle at Alamein. With him we would set off up the glen. It was a murderous road for a car. It began with a misleadingly good gravel stretch and crossed over a plank bridge just below where the burn tumbles over a fall into a big pool, where the salmon lie waiting for autumn spates. Then it was a matter of climbing and turning and twisting, sometimes skidding on boiler plates of rock, and sometimes throwing up sprays of peaty puddles, with little opportunity to look at the glen unfolding before and above us. Its sides ran up steep to the high stony levels where the ptarmigan live. Big glens open out on either side down which tumble burns which would have delighted the eye of Sir Edward Landseer. It is strange that until the days of Sir Walter Scott few people agreed that this kind of Highland scenery was beautiful. We crossed another plank bridge, a good deal higher up, and the road ended in a stand of tall spruce, an island of trees in the level stretch of glen, with a ruined stalker's cottage in the middle of them. The deer came to shelter in those trees during the winter blizzards. They had been planted there for that very purpose. And there we would stop, miles from anywhere, with nothing but the sound of falling water. We could not hear that sound until we had turned off the engine of the car, and got out and banged the doors shut. Then, and not till then, did we feel that we were in the embrace of the hills.

Some time that day we would be sure to see the slow wheeling of an eagle and its mate quartering the slopes. If it was a warm morning, a cock grouse would scold from the heather, and then another, and another. We could see that the valley had once been lived in, and that it had not always been wilderness. For there were stones that were laid out in a way that was not the work of nature, and beside them were little patches of green grass. Old people in Braemar remembered hearing from their grandfathers how a score of families would come down that glen, in their Sunday best, to kirk every Sabbath. They made a living, as the people of the glens did in those days, by raising short-legged skinny cattle and driving them over the mountains to sell them at the cattle trysts. The illicit distilling of whisky was their other industry.

The little river Ey divided the glen which was big enough for a rifle to be out on each side of it. More often Priscilla would go out with a rifle and Willy Grant. I would quarter the hills alone, on the opposite side, with my gun. There were a great many deer there, far too many in fact, as we could tell from the number of switch horns and scraggy beasts. But there were some splendid heads. Priscilla allowed herself one 12-pointer, but for the rest we shot only the very worst that we could find as a contribution to the principle of the survival of the fittest. I killed five altogether. Two were switch horns and three were poor beasts with growths on them. In that short span of a few weeks at Gleney, every day's expedition was wonderful in its own way, but the most memorable was on September 9th that year. There is a sporting distinction in Scotland, whose origin goes deep back into the mists of the past, called the Hunter's Badge. It means, quite simply, that you have killed a stag, a salmon, and an eagle by your own hand on the same day. That, in the modern day, is varied to a stag, a salmon and a brace of grouse. It may sound easy, but there are not very many places where it is even possible, unless you have a very great deal of luck.

It was the last thing that we had in mind on that warm morning, as on that September 9th, Priscilla and I set off in opposite directions high up the glen, with the river dividing us. She went on up the glen and leftward: I went right-handed up a broad tributary glen which, high as it was, was well clad with heather. I had been there before, when we were still exploring our new kingdom. A week ago we had been up that glen with Francis Crossley, Priscilla's nephew, who was to die tragically two years later. We had done well according to our modest ambitions. We had got five grouse in the heather, and three ptarmigan among the stones, and Francis with a very high shot had got a golden plover, while away on the other side of the valley, high up towards the ridges, Priscilla had got a stag. And then three days before, Gladwyn Jebb and his family had motored a prodigious distance to shoot with us, and we had got two grouse and eight ptarmigan. That was ten more head than we had got at the last time that we had shot together, and had pursued the mallard at Chantilly. Not perhaps a very prodigious bag, but a very great deal of walking and quite a lot of shooting. While he was having his bath, his son went down to the Boat pool with me and got an eleven-and-a-half pound salmon. He returned in time to take his turn for the bath, and greatly surprise his father.

Now that particular day was near the end of the Summer Parliamentary Recess of 1952 and there were a lot of places where we should have been, and a lot of other things that we ought to have been doing. But this was the end of an era, our life at Braemar, and we were going to enjoy the last minutes of this wonderful wilderness. We motored up, skidded and slithered about on the road, on the boiler plates of rock and pools of water, and got to the bottom of this tributary valley where Willy Grant was waiting for us, together with the pony boy, who wore his usual equable smile of lethargic expectancy. And I had watched them all go off together and had taken my gun and gone by myself, with a full cartridge belt and bag empty except for my sandwiches.

One of the limiting factors of solitary shooting is that you have to carry what you kill. Therefore, as you become progressively weighted down, you become progressively less accurate in your shooting. It was hot as I set off up the left bank of the burn. The heathery slopes rose steeply ahead, then the burn they contained turned leftward and was lost to sight, though it clearly had its genesis in the stony slopes far above me. The sun shone warmer. It had melted the last of the mist. Big buzzing bees blundered by. The smell of the heather was intoxicating. It was hot walking, even walking very slowly. Nothing happened for about perhaps twenty minutes. Looking back the main glen seemed to have fallen far below. Then, quite suddenly, a covey got up at my feet, and I got a right and left. In the next half-mile I got another three grouse and was beginning to start to feel their weight. The sun had that crisp warmth that you find in high country. The steepness of the slope was making itself felt. When I had commanded an Ontario battalion, in the War, we had done our commando training, at the last phase before going to Sicily, at Inverary. The Ontario farmers, who overwhelmingly made up the men of that battalion, were vastly intrigued to find what they described as "a swamp on a slope." That, I think is a peculiarly Scottish phenomenon. Trampling over the rocks and the dry heather along a steep slope that day from one of these hanging swamps rose a single snipe, at a greater height than you would expect to find one of his race. I fired at it a long way out and it folded up like a ping-pong ball. Then gradually the heather was thinning. The glen turned upward and leftwards to the source of the burn. Two more grouse were added and my load was starting to get rather heavy as the stony ridges got closer and a breeze stirred to windward. Just near the top there was an overhanging patch of heather and out of it got a covey, right beside me. I fired two shots and got one bird, so that gave me a load of six grouse and a snipe, and a half-empty cartrigde belt, a tremendous appetite, and still half a day on the hills ahead.

There was a different world above the heather, a ptarmigan world, among the stony ridges rocks split with the frost, and that short tundra growth that is such a familiar environment to those of us who have lived in the Canadian Eastern Arctic. This is the point of a climb when you exchange one world for another. Being now rather heavily laden, and puffing a good deal, I sat down for a moment near a little rill of water which was the well from which this burn came. There was little wind, and happily no flies. This was a world in which to revel in the smell of moorland, the sharper smell of tundra, and the feeling of being separate from the whole of the rest of creation. The sky was hazy blue. Then, like a sound of a knock on a nearby door, came a shot from Priscilla's rifle. It sounded a long way off. I ate my few sandwiches and smoked a cigarette. The whole of the world was at my feet and the day only half done. It had been a long climb and I had all the game that I needed. I laid my gun beside me on the stones. The smoke of a cigarette, and then of another cigarette, brought that peace that makes you disinclined to move. But I got on to my feet and climbed the last slope on to the flat stony ridges that ran right out to stop short at the trough of the glen, and started again on the other side of the valley. Here was the old familiar summer landscape of the Arctic. The rock split by the frosts, plants growing like pincushions, with a single root sticking into a pinch of earth in a crack in the stone. This was a place of few birds but it was the home of the ptarmigan. It is hard to know why the ptarmigan is so difficult to shoot. He often gets up at your feet, but flies away with a curious wavering flight which means that your shot so often wastes itself in the air. He goes along on the ridge in front of you then turns and passes below you. You may see the flash of wings among the boulders as he goes. But you will be lucky if you get a second shot at him.

The afternoon wore on. I saw ptarmigan. I shot at ptarmigan. I missed them all except one. When I picked it up it was white, and curiously dovelike, and I was more than a little sorry that I had shot it. I picked it up and added it to the bag. Then I tucked my gun under my arm and thought that I would not shoot again unless a particularly enticing shot should come my way. I sauntered along slowly, in silence except for hobnails grinding on the stones of the plateau. The valley opened beneath me as I picked my way slowly down to the heather, disregarding a few grouse who got up chattering at a distance. From here I made my way slowly down to the little river Ey, took off the game bag, and sat down on a boulder and smoked another cigarette. From the high ridges I had noticed that the pony and the pony boy had deserted their stance, so I knew that somewhere among the hills Priscilla had got a stag, and, at that moment there came the sound of another shot, from not far distant, that reverberated among the hills. I hoped that she had got another stag. She had. Not long afterwards the pony appeared carrying the first stag whose antlered head nodded slightly to his gait. Evening was on us when Willy appeared and Priscilla appeared. The pony boy was carefully informed as to where to find the other stag. We bumped down the valley and got back to the castle in time to have some tea, and then felt one could not forsake such a lovely day. For lovely days are rare in the far north, and every minute of daylight must be enjoyed. And so I set off with my rod to the boat pool. If I go to Heaven the Boat pool will be there waiting for me. I went down the right bank. The water was fairly clear. I could see the bottom and the shapes of the stones through the weaving of the swirls. I put on a fairly strong nylon cast, and a big fly and began to fish. And when it was getting very near dinner-time, and light was fading, I had three salmon. They were not particularly big ones. The biggest was just nine pounds. With the six grouse, two stags and three salmon we had cumulatively got the Hunter's Badge twice and almost three times, except, of course, that the Hunter's Badge cannot be cumulative.

That was one of the happiest days with a gun that I ever remember. Our life in the mountains was at an end. When the duck and the oyster-catcher and curlews went down the valley to the sea, at the onset of winter, we went down that valley with them and took our memories with us.

4   *Beside the River*

THE DEE at Braemar winds in a long, lazy circle round the low ground out of which the castle mound rises. We were the temporary possessors of about four miles, counting one bank with the other, of this fairy river. And we had the added excitement, if that were possible, of living right beside our own water. It was only a few minutes walk, with a rod over your shoulder, across a flat field, to reach the bank of our nearest pool.

Our beat had an uncertain number of pools, as silting and unsilting is a continuous evolutionary process in the Dee. The preference of the salmon for different pools can change from year to year. The best of all, the Boat pool, was beside the road at the bottom of the beat. Then there was a fast narrow pool which bordered the flat field beside the castle. A quarter of a mile above that, upstream again was a long still pool, with a boat on it, in which the stalker used to ferry himself backwards and forwards to his cottage on the far bank. Beyond Braemar, where road and river again come together, there were two pools, one below the other, where salmon lay late in the season. Except for these last two, the pools were anything from a quarter of a mile to three-quarters of a mile apart. At certain seasons, and heights of water, salmon lay in odd places in the lengths between, and could be caught there.

This part of the river had little shade from trees, to fend off the glare of the afternoon sun. It flooded quickly, due to the cutting of the forests above. In spring the flood water seemed to be much clearer than it was from late summer onwards, when it ran like black coffee with peat flood, so that it had no precise height or colour of water that could be said to be its normal.

When we went to live at Braemar Castle Priscilla was a seasoned salmon fisherman, having caught many a salmon in the Don. Although having had the luck to catch great numbers of trout in Kenya and Canada, as well as Scotland, I had had far fewer opportunities for salmon fishing. For the fourteen years of peace and war since I had left Oxford, had been spent in the salmonless world of East Africa, Canada's landward spaces and her Eastern Arctic, and then Southern England and the Italian peninsula. The salmon that I caught in a loch in Sutherland, at the age of eleven had only been joined by one other, caught in a loch in Mull, six years later. There had been other wonderful moments, but it had been a matter of much travelling and never arriving. One of them was on the Petit St. Jean in Quebec. It was on a blinding hot afternoon, when the burning sun of an Eastern Canadian summer was beginning to slant and the trees to throw their shadows, that I set a big yellow-winged English mayfly floating down a pool below a logging dam. Up from the bottom a 20-pound salmon climbed to the surface and took it like a chalkstream trout, ridding himself of it an hour later and a mile further downstream. A fortnight on the Deveron at Rothiemay just after the last war, brought four others, and that was the total of the salmon that had come my way after nearly thirty years of fishing.

Our salmon gear was Priscilla's light spliced greenheart rod with which she had killed quite a few salmon on the Don at Monymusk. The rest had belonged to my father, and some of it went back to the beginning of the century. The great greenheart

rod which, together with its massive reel, weighed 4½ pounds
he had used in Norway before the 1914 War. With them was a
splendid collection of fly books and tin boxes containing every
kind of shaggy salmon fly, many with gut loops instead of metal
eyes. From the rod cases and fishing bags came a strong aroma of
citronella, which was what Canadian fishermen used to put on
their faces in those days to keep off the black flies.

And now all these things were carefully arranged in our rod
room, with the low doorway and the barrel-roofed ceiling. We
were some four hundred yards from the nearest pool on our own
beat and one of the great salmon rivers of the world.

But if neither of us had an earlier chance to fish the Dee my
father's big salmon rod had done so several times, for he had
fished with Arthur Wood down at Cairnton when that remarkable
man was developing his theory of fishing for salmon with a
greased line. My father had actually stayed at Invercauld, with the
tenant of an earlier laird, sometime in the thirties. He had arrived
with my mother and sister sometime in the late afternoon to find
the whole household out on the hills. He easily yielded to a
suggestion that he should try a cast on the river, and had walked
some half mile from the house to a pool on a big bend that lies
right beside the main road. Somewhere in the course of that walk
he had dropped his gaff without noticing it. He fished for an hour
or so, and was preparing to reel in, when he had hooked a big
salmon. Time passed, the shadows lengthened, and the salmon was
still on. He was in a place where there was no convenient beach
on which to bring it ashore, and he had never mastered the art of
tailing a fish. A tourist stopped his car on the road opposite and
strolled down the opposite bank. My father appealed to him to
get a gaff from somewhere and throw it across to him. The man
replied that he did not know what a gaff was, and took himself off.
A few minutes later the fish did the same thing, and my father
returned dishevelled and disappointed to meet his host and
hostess and their guests, who were by now half way through their
evening meal.

We had four delectable years of that castle. We lived close
enough to the river to leave our fly rods up in the long rod box
at the foot of one of the castle walls. From my dressing-room I
could see a bend in the river, and watched it while my fingers
fumbled with braces and buttons, being in such a desperate
hurry to get into country clothes and throw off everything to do

with cities. We knew already how high the river was, as the road follows it for the last mile and there is a rock, at the top of the Boat pool, from which can be gauged its exact level. After that, it was a matter of tumbling down the spiral stone staircase, stopping in the rod room at the bottom to kick on a pair of rubber boots and shoulder the bag of Spanish leather which the Fly Fisher's Club had years earlier presented to my father. And then there was a tramp round the castle walls to the rod box, its lid had to be propped back, the joints of the rod pushed firmly together, and the line reeled up that had been laid out in snakey coils to allow it to dry. And whereas a trout reel goes "tick", a salmon reel goes "tock." The noise of the furious cities was forgotten. We were standing beside the wall of a castle in a valley among the mountains and in the silence came the steady sound of the river. The Boat pool at the bottom of the beat was rather a long walk and we used to go by car with the rods sticking out of the window. We got careless in the end and the point of my father's greenheart was smashed.

When we first went to the castle we would walk, carrying our rods, to the Boat pool. But as time went on we found we could not bear the delay. We were so keen to get there, and it was a long walk back, particularly if you happened to be carrying a brace of salmon. A special element in fishing that pool was having to fish in front of an audience. Some of us are indifferent to this and others hate it. We got used to it. A creak of brakes behind us would mean that a car had stopped and that we had a gallery of spectators, but the absorption of playing a salmon would deafen you to advice, applause, or encouragement.

Our first spring fishing was in 1949. I was walking back along the road carrying a fish, bright as a bar of silver and caught among the snow showers, when a bus coming up the valley stopped beside me with a jerk. From it leapt a man with a vast camera such as may sometimes be seen in a photographers' studios. He took my photograph with the castle in the background while I stood hunched in the cold with the wind wrapping a sodden mackintosh round me, and the salmon swinging like a pendulum from the piece of hairy string knotted around the small of its tail. To hold up a fish by the gills is to turn a beautiful creature into a hideous corpse. A week or so later my friends were astonished to see the picture as the frontispiece of what is known as a society paper. The castle was said to be Balmoral and I was said to be the author of a treatise on the St. Kilda wren, a modest achievement of mine of a good many years earlier.

But upstream from the boat pool there is a long stretch before reaching the next pool that will fish at all times and seasons. But that one was a delightfully short walk round the green slopes of the castle mound, and through a wicket gate in the fence, and across the rough pasture of the field in which the English garrison had once been drilled. And as you walked towards it with the long rod nodding, you smelt the sound of the river come out to meet you. Once a year a sheep drover, who used the busy roads regardless of twentieth-century traffic, would rent this field to rest his flock, for a day or so, on their long journey from Dinnet to the Devil's Elbow and beyond. He would open the gate from the road and the sheep, like a woolly torrent, would overflow down the bank and through the gate and spread like a tide across the pasture. Once, walking down from the castle, I met a stoat who refused to get out of the way. It stood and stared back, spiteful and utterly fearless, and only moved when I kicked at it with my wading brogues. In 1950 the snow was with us until the end of May, and because of it we did not catch our first salmon until June 9th. The deer died in great numbers on the hills in that lean time. By the wicket gate to the bottom of the knoll we found a beautiful stag one day lying dead just inside the fence of the farmer's field, that marched with the castle knoll and the pasture. It had not been there when we had returned the previous evening. Sometime in the night it had come famished into that field, gorged itself on the farmer's crops and now lay dead and distended. It seemed such a sadly trivial end for something so beautiful. It was a longer walk to the pool above, where the boat was moored by the stalker's cottage. It fished well in April where an icy wind blew fleecy white clouds across a clear blue sky, the classic North Atlantic weather at that time of the year. It was a broad still pool, away from the rapids at the top and a gentle current brought a fly round in slow even motion. The top two pools had to be reached by car for they were the other side of the village. The river had to be waded to the far bank, for we only had rights on that bank at that point, which put it out of reach in high water. As for the rest, both banks were ours.

In the Fly Fishers' Club in London we have two rods that we sent to the great International Exhibition in 1851. The salmon rod was 24 feet long and the grilse rod 7 feet shorter.

54 One Man's Happiness

My father had fished with a 16-foot greenheart because that was the normal size of salmon rod when he had started to fish for salmon. Playing a heavy salmon in the Leardal in Norway in 1912 he had been forced to follow it for over a mile of rocky sloping shore, from which he had fallen in twice over the head. He was a slightly built man and it must have called for no mean effort to climb out of that roaring cascade, with this great wand with a leaping 25-pounder thirty yards away on the end of the line.

Rods since then have been getting steadily smaller. Le Branche fished for salmon with a 13-foot rod weighing 15 ounces which was made in 1916. Wood of Cairnton fished a single-handed 12-foot rod on the Dee. He must have had a wrist of steel. Lee Wulff today fishes for salmon with a one-piece 6-foot rod weighing only $1\frac{1}{2}$ ounces.

After two heart-rending battles in Loch Areanas, as a boy, in which I lost a salmon and a big sea trout, my father gave me a greenheart sea-trout rod. It was broken long ago, and has been replaced by Priscilla's "Grant vibration" rod. We keep all rods in the family in common user. Just to have a big rod handy, I acquired a twenty-year-old 16-foot split cane for next to nothing, and use it if I am asked to fish a big river.

The complicated and inefficient spinning reels of earlier days had been replaced by the thread line and fixed spool reel and the short rod, almost a rapier, of metal or fibreglass. This made it possible for a bait to be cast a tremendous distance with considerable accuracy, and the fish have found a very formidable new weapon arrayed against them. There is one thing to be said for this way of fishing, putting aside all other arguments for and against. It makes it possible for a child to fish for salmon in waters where he could not hope to hook one by any other means.

We had the autumn fishing of 1948 and the successful spring and early summer season of 1949. When Jo and Anne came back to us soon after the advent of our daughter Susie, they were madly keen to catch a salmon. There are some beats where small girls can cover the water and catch salmon with a fly rod, but this was not easy water for a small beginner in that art. Not least of all because a rise or fall of the level changes the set of the currents, and may call for a very long cast. And so the weeds, in the little deserted square of garden below the castle knoll, were dug up in a search for worms, and Ella the housekeeper was persuaded to part with a tin to put them in.

I have had abundant opportunities for sport and a time has come when one of my greatest sporting pleasures is in the sharing of a child's excitement, at the catching of its first trout or salmon. Most of us can enjoy steady excitement in sport over the longest lifetime, but only children feel that explosion of excitement that comes from first achievements. They can share with you. Within a week each had caught her first salmon and by the end of the year, Jo had caught four and Anne had caught one less than that, but by far the largest. This was a fish over ten pounds which she caught on an overcast afternooon at the last moment, when it was possible to fish, seeing that she had to go back, change, pack her school trunk and be taken by car to Ballater to catch the afternoon train to Aberdeen for a new school term.

Later on, we collectively came to the conclusion that a gaff was a hateful thing, and something that you only carried against an emergency of a very big fish or one that was very lightly hooked. Outside those two categories we have always tailed fish ever since. Jo and Anne were taught to look after their own tackle, and were then allowed to go fishing on their own. As the years passed they got quite good at "tailing", although once the fish was ashore they would throw themselves on the top of it for greater security. If you have a large grown-up male hand it will go easily round the small of the tail of all but the very largest salmon. But there were inevitable tragedies of salmon lost when very small hands lacked the span to grasp the tail, and lift the fish out of the water. They became tremendously enthusiastic.

Jo's second salmon very nearly cost us dear. It was in the first week of that cold wet August of 1949. The valley smoked with rain and the mountains had been lost in the mist since mid-morning. By evening the mist was down to the flat of the valley. From our living-room it did not look as if the river had started to rise. We tore ourselves away from the fire in the big stone fireplace which was already starting to weave shadows on the walls, as dusk came early. Outside the rain fell steadily and unhurried, and when we got to the top of the boat pool we could see the water still running clear and shallow over the yellow sand and gravel, and the shape of the grey smooth stones at the top of the pool. It seemed to us that we would have a better chance if we fished on the far side where a herd of Highland cattle stood and stared at

us in the rain, sullen and still. I had carried both the girls over the
the shallows at the top of the rapids several times before. I took
Jo over first, with the rod that they were going to share, and
started her fishing before I returned and collected Anne. It is
rightly regarded as ungentlemanly to mention a lady's age, but
perhaps permissible to observe that their ages added up to
twenty-six, and so carrying them over was a fairly strenuous haul.
I had landed Anne on the shingle beside her sister to await her
turn with the rod. At that moment the pebbles and the shingle
began to wink and vanish, as the river began to rise. Thinking of
it afterwards, we could, of course, have gone round by the bridge
below at the cost of a three mile walk in the rain, but it never even
occurred to us. At that precise moment Jo hooked a salmon.
There was nothing to do but to leave her to grapple with it, and
the current was running stronger and stronger as I carried Anne
back to the far bank and re-crossed. Every inch of rise brings a
tremendous extra force of current. The force of the stream was
becoming greater every minute. There was a nasty feeling of the
sand and shingle washing away beneath my boots. Once back
beside Jo on the shingle her 7¼-pound salmon was subdued by
main force. We set out to wade the river as a strange, unsteady
three-tier figure. The base of it was my waders with the water
boiling round them, and then Jo cradled in my arms and her
precious salmon clasped to her bosom, while the little rod stuck
upwards like a wireless aerial. We just made it and no more.
Falling forward against the far bank Jo and her salmon were
spilled ashore and I crawled on to it after her, wet and worn out,
and utterly breathless as much from fear as from fatigue.

Beyond all other sports salmon fishing opens a path to theory
which is one of its pleasures. And few other sports are followed in
places as pleasant.

It is possible to get complete agreement on the ways of birds
and beasts, but not those of fish. Nobody should hazard more
than a conjecture as to how they feel and why they act. But all of
us do. Regard them for a moment. They breathe water through
their nostrils. Light comes to them bent by a myriad refractions.
They look out on the light and darkness of their distorted world
of varying pressure, depth and discolouration with lidless eyes.
No-one should claim for his theory more than a percentage of
truth, because no-one can escape from the fact that if he does
exactly the opposite from what he proposes, he may very well

catch fish. He can theorise to his heart's content as to what they can see, and whether they can hear, or have a sense of smell. And as the point of all sport is enjoyment, a little theorising is part of it.

Fishermen are highly scientific amateurs. This is not a contradiction in terms as witness the amateur genesis of so many scientific discoveries. In some way, fishing is the expression of man himself. For man is the great amateur of creation. If you are not inclined to accept that, witness the unfortunate and narrow professionalism of so many other living things. Pity the poor ant-eater whose career is limited to marrying another ant-eater and eating ants.

My father always used to say that he never wanted fishing to be made any easier. To him there was the right balance between hunter and hunted that the sport demands. That did not stop him from plunging enthusiastically into fishing for salmon with a greased line or a dry fly, when those methods were devised. They did not, of course, make fishing easy. They were new and effective, and very complicated, methods of fascinating interest which made it possible to take fish in warm water and at shrunken levels.

For three-quarters of a century before that men were catching just as many salmon with their huge shaggy flies, jigged ferociously through the water, and not all in high water or late in the season as some suggest. They had far fewer theories, and argued only about types of fly and how you should strike. If the salmon knew of all the theories built round and about them, if they have a sense of humour, and it is pure conjecture to conclude they have not, they must be extremely amused. In fact, many of these theories are devised to give a scientific twist to acts and decisions that are largely instinctive. Your instinct sharpens with your experience of fishing and you learn to fish in certain ways, without being able to give a reason for what you do. No possible analysing would explain why it was that when I went fishing with my father from early youth to the doorstep of middle age, I always got the largest number of fish and he always caught the bigger ones.

A great friend of mine was blinded in the 1914 war. He had never allowed his infliction to interfere with a busy life dedicated to public duty. He is a very keen fisherman and every year has a competition with a younger friend, also a man of outstanding public spirit, who was blinded in the 1939 war. The competition is won by whoever has caught the larger number of salmon on a fly during that season, and they generally catch about twenty each. Neither of them had ever fished before he was blinded. My friend goes down to the river bank with a ghillie, and wades in with short waders till he feels that he is deep enough. He throws his wading staff over his shoulder on to the bank behind, and proceeds to cast. The ghillie will tell him to cast a little higher or lower or farther out. He probably catches as many salmon as any man who is blessed with eyesight and an equal opportunity to fish. The reason being that salmon fishing is to a great extent instinct, and is most certainly so in the matter of hooking the salmon. He and his younger friend seem to fare much less well when fishing for trout, because that is not instinctive to the same degree, and trout are very hard to hook if you cannot see them rise. In fact it is one of the sports which calls for keenness of sight, as most of us who are over fifty realise when we try to fish dry fly in very fast water.

The salmon will tempt you to make rules about his behaviour. And the day will come when he will tear up your carefully compiled book of rules and throw the pieces at you.

The best instance of that, that I ever came across, was when an acquaintance of mine was fishing the Spey. It was a cold day and conditions were challenging. He had decided to go right through the book until he found the size of fly that would catch a salmon. He started, as one would expect, with the biggest. He fished his water carefully with each one before he changed to a smaller size. He had done this a good few times, and had been fishing for several hours, when he hooked a salmon on a very small fly. As he did so he felt that this was a triumph, a mastering of the salmon psychology. He had found, by his own persistence, the only fly that would rise a fish on that water on that day. He felt as a scientist must feel when, after months of laboratory experiments, he has succeeded in isolating some new element at the end of seven places of decimals. The salmon was a big one and, to cut a long story short, my friend got one foot caught between the boulders and in the course of his floundering the salmon ran the line down to the reel and it snapped at the drum. While he was splashing and squelching his way to the bank the ghillie shouted that the salmon was going up-stream, trailing the whole reel-full of line after him. The ghillie grasped the spare fly-rod lying on the bank, which happened to have an enormous fly on it, to cast over the line to secure it. No sooner did this large fly hit the water than another salmon straightway seized it, and the whole elaborate formula which had led the fisherman to arrive at the small fly added up to nothing.

One of the curses of the present day is a tendency to over-simplify issues and doing this to misunderstand them, and to under-value the aims and objects of those concerned with them. Those who think that fishermen are merely fugitives from the present day, who gain oblivion and some pleasure from catching fresh-water fish by the easiest possible means, their pleasure being measured entirely by their catch, know nothing at all. Only a fisherman knows that in spite of the apparent tranquillity of his art he is the sport of the most violent emotions, from the heights of triumph to the depths of disaster. No philosopher was ever so accomplished that he could summon up, at will, a formula that could smooth away the disaster of losing a big fish. And fishermen, although they need many cardinal qualities, do not need patience. Those who say they have not the patience for fishing mean that they could be happy in the act of catching fish, but not in the fishing for them. A fisherman absorbs a great deal of his sur-roundings, and acquires an instinctive understanding of the science of ecology, which should be raised to a far greater position of eminence among the sciences than it now enjoys. What is needed is far deeper study of this science of the interplay of the natural species and the way that they adapt themselves to their environment, the science of keeping the world in balance. Pollution, indiscriminate chemical spraying, the wholesale cutting of forests and the lowering of water tables, disorganise the fisherman's world. His world is among the earliest casualties from the brutal disruption of the chemist going it alone, indifferent to what happens to the rest of creation so long as he launch his ideas on the world. But this balance is something that a fisherman understands.

When the Dee reaches Braemar it has little suffered from man. You fish it where it comes murmuring out of its mountain wilderness and first meets the haunts of men. It is an acid river. For this reason sea trout like it, though they do not come up very far, and there is little weed and few brown trout. The Don, which runs into the sea only a mile away, is alkaline and, in warm weather, becomes very weedy. The Scottish Loire, my father used to call it from the castles along its course. It is the best brown trout river in Britain, when you consider its fishable length, the very high average size, and the fact that they are all wild fish and behave like them.

Braemar is a long way up the Dee, probably eighty miles as a salmon would swim, though it is said that they have been caught up there with the sealice on them, which means that they left the sea only a matter of hours before. Salmon enter the Dee in December and the season opens in February.

On the Upper Dee we longed for warm rain-water floods to bring the fish up to the head-waters. But a spell of hard frost would stop them running. So will bright sunlight, it is said. And so we would catch only one or two in March and the river would not get into its stride until mid-April, when it was a matter of casting a very big fly on a long rod in the snow showers. It is surprising how long a line you may have to cast in a narrow river to get the angle that you want. The shadow of Arthur Wood of Cairnton hung heavy over the Dee at that time, and everybody fished with greased line whether or not the water was suitable. For salmon fishers tend to follow absolute creeds. The salmon do not. It generally became warm enough for that particular art in May and from then on, until the middle of June, we could have wonderful sport. July was a stale month. But when a chill came to the valley, with nights of August, the fish started to take keenly once again. Our fishing was limited by weekends and parliamentary recesses. Easter and Whitsun recesses came at splendidly convenient times for the salmon. So did the summer recess of August and September. The salmon had lost their silver by then, and catching them presented its own special problems. Any experienced salmon fisherman will tell you that you may well get a real fight from a red salmon. For some of them are fresh from the sea and have entered the river in their red spawning dress. Such a one was a red 16-pounder that I caught in the Deveron, a year or so back, which put up a great battle, and proved to be absolutely fresh run, when we came to eat it.

But as the salmon loses his silver so he loses his prestige. You have only to listen to any Scottish countryman watching Autumn salmon on the move. Scowling he murmurs, "Dirty brutes"; silence, then, "Filthy brutes", and so on. As if the tarnishing of their silver scales was due to some backsliding, some self-indulgence, something that would have been clearly avoided if the salmon had shown the minimum of discrimination or self-discipline. As there was only too much of the fishing season that was neither weekend nor Parliamentary recess, we often sub-let our beat to tenants. In the medical profession, and particularly among surgeons, you will find many a keen and adept salmon fisher. It is perhaps not surprising that the men of medicine seem to have the largest incidence of really fine fishermen, as a clear eye and a precise sense of touch is essential to success in their calling. Several of them used to fish our water, and we enjoyed their coming. If you have salmon fishing tenants, you must never allow yourself to be put into a position of apologising for the salmon. Salmon already have several potent means of making a fool of you, and, to put yourself forward as their apologist is to give a valuable hostage to fortune.

Among our tenants we had only one who was of the peremptory kind. He came to fish during a week when an icy wind was driving the snow showers down the valley, in a Cairngorm April. There were quite a few fish about, and we told him what he might hope to catch. Perhaps we overdid it a little. We gave him instructions about types of fly. We showed him where the salmon lies were, as far as you can do in the spring when they tend to lie in different places to the rest of the year. We even marked the lies by stones on the bank opposite them. We left him fishing in mid-morning and returned tacking against the snow showers, in the late afternoon. He seemed to be fishing mechanically and competently, but without zest. He anticipated our question and told us that he had neither caught anything nor had he even seen anything. We ventured to ask whether he had tried a particular lie that we had marked for him. He replied briefly, and tersely, that he had tried that lie, and all the other lies, where we had said there would almost certainly be a fish. We ventured to ask meekly what flies he had used, and he told us that he had used all those flies that we had said were most effective in that kind of weather, and at that time of year. We then found ourselves trying to explain away the salmon's intransigent behaviour, and eventually gave up and slunk away muttering something about his luck changing.

Trout fishing is a different matter. It is fairly clearly your fault if you cannot catch a trout if they are rising, and nobody's fault if you cannot catch one when they are not.

The big salmon river, grown narrow in its upper waters, is a special study. There seems to be far less chance in that narrow stream of finding that occasional eccentric salmon who will take, when all the rest of his kind will have none of you. The reason is that when the river narrows the conditions become much more nearly uniform in the pools, whereas in a very big river you can get a wide degree of variation. Up at the head waters, whatever excites or depresses one seems to excite or depress them all. In the few years of our tenure there were memorable moments when the river suddenly and briefly boiled with salmon on the take. By the time that the salmon that we had hooked was ashore, several feet up the high bank and several yards back from the water, the river so often seemed to have gone completely dead again. Perhaps that enthusiasm would return, in a matter of minutes or hours. But when it came it was always without warning. But the impression grew that those salmon, who had swum so many miles up this big river and now found their surroundings constricted and themselves packed closely with their kind, were affected by the building up and the breakdown of tensions. It seemed, as one watched the swirls for those many hours winding clear over the smooth stones or darkened with the peat flood, that steady rain, or the steady pressure of the wind at the same speed and from the same direction, could leave the river lifeless. But let that rain stop or that wind abate, or change direction, or the sun come out, and you might well find yourself fast in a fish. Both trout and salmon are put down by the feeling of impending rain. Almost all created things have their own reaction to the imminence of rain. Richard Blome in *The Gentleman's Recreation* (1710) in the part dealing with agriculture, tells us that when rain is coming, cranes fly very high, frogs croak, and water fowl wash themselves, "and make much noise", the crow "walks alone and makes a cawing". Further, that oxen and cows toss their horns and bellow, and asses shake themselves and roll. Supplementary evidence of widely differing kinds is furnished by the behaviour of cocks and hens, pigeons, ants, toads, worms and swallows. But the fisherman, unless he sees swallows playing ducks and drakes on the surface of a pool, has few visible portents to guide him. Our sure guide was the ravens croaking in the crags above the castle. If you heard them with unusual clarity, it nearly always meant rain. But it is because an angler becomes very closely in tune with his quarry he feels the oppression that the fish feel. When the rain comes he feels the same relief. Fishing the pools at Braemar the rain would march down the valley. Each splashing raindrop added its own tiny mite of oxygen that stirred up the fish that had been breathing stale water for days. There would be a head and tail rise, and then another. It is then that the fisherman loses himself in the absorption of casting. Only when he stops is he aware of the raindrops gathering in a row along the peak of his cap, that and the smell of wet mackintosh and wet tweed have added themselves to the smell of wet moorland and mountain and dripping forest.

It sometimes seems to take a great deal of rain to make a river rise. But the fisherman forgets that the rain that soaks him has nothing to do with raising the level of the stretch of river in which he is fishing. The salmon will often move and show their relief that the rain has come but without taking a fly until the waters actually begin to rise and the real stimulus reaches them. And that may be a matter of hours later. For it can take a long time for the mosses to fill to overflowing after a dry spell. It was in that first inch of the rise of water that our salmon would take almost anything. But, by the time we had landed that salmon, the odds were that the river would be too high, and not another salmon would look at us until it began to fall. Or that is the way that it seemed to be at Braemar. Salmon may behave themselves quite differently in different rivers, or even in different parts of the same river. Few generalisations hold good everywhere.

A clear example of this is that Arthur Wood, lower down the Dee at Cairnton, used to prefer an east wind to any other. This shows how unusual was the beat on which he experimented, as on most of the Dee an east wind is fatal. Those of us who have lived among the Eskimos, and spoken their language, always find ourselves in some dilemma here because an Eskimo calls a wind by the direction whither it is blowing and not whence it comes. It is a habit that is hard to forget. Wood also was said to have liked sun shining down a pool, which is generally regarded as fatal to one's prospects. But the baneful effect of downstream sunlight is mitigated, and often neutralised, by very fast-moving water. It is possible in a river in the valley which runs east and west between high mountains, to mistake the direction of the wind. It may be only a few degrees east of south but be channelled by the valley into blowing upstream and apparently straight from the Ural Mountains. Another striking difference between Braemar and many other beats was the attitude of the salmon to the prawn, which we would use with other forms of bait at times when the salmon flatly refused to take a fly. Most writers say that if the salmon do not rush to seize the prawn they rush headlong away from it, and that a prawn may empty a whole pool in a wild rush. You can always tell when a fish is frightened by a prawn as it does a kind of back somersault. I very seldom saw this happen at Braemar and never any indication that salmon were frightened out of the pool or seriously disturbed by a prawn. It was the view of Arthur Wood that salmon could be disturbed but were probably never frightened in the sense that we understand that word. Perhaps Dee salmon have stronger nerves. Trout, on the other hand, seem to flee in terror. Probably the difference is that the trout has somewhere where he can go and hide, and when he is disturbed he goes there like a dart.

Many fishermen will have nothing to do with bait fishing for salmon. We all respect them, even those of us who use bait, from time to time, when the salmon will not take a fly. Some can only discuss the matter with a great deal of heat. But there are certain basic truths to which almost all fishermen would subscribe. First of all, to play a salmon on a fly rod is a whole world more exciting than playing one on a shortish, stiffish, spinning rod, with the kind of reel which neither runs nor sings as a fly reel does. And secondly that, although some forms of spinning call for a great deal of skill, it is possible with spinning tackle to throw a line a great distance with a good deal of accuracy after only brief experience, and furthermore, to govern the depth at which your lure swims. And for the benefit of those who have never tried their hands at spinning, the casting is extremely exciting and enjoyable. To have the same facility with a fly rod calls for years of experience. While the habits of salmon can vary from river to river and even from beat to beat in the same river, it is generally easier to catch salmon by spinning, but is nothing like as satisfying as using a fly. One of the natural advantages of a spinning bait is that it appears to be alive for the whole of its swim. A fly has only to have the line slacken for a moment, in an eddy, to be shown up as the most egregious sham. There is one sporting imperative in spinning. That is to use the strongest possible tackle. For if a salmon breaks he will never rid himself of the big treble hook. His victory is only too likely to bring him a lingering death. For those of us who can pick their own time of year to go fishing the choice is a simple one. But the most of us get rather short holidays, and at times that we cannot dictate. Consequently most of our salmon fishing is for fish that have passed their best, from early August onwards.

At Braemar we did very well with a greased line in early summer and, in the early spring and autumn, with a big old-fashioned fly fished close to the bottom. We were eternally experimenting and took up the challenge of those times of the year when the salmon make it quite clear that they were bored with flies, and wanted certain kinds of bait, to the exclusion of all else. By turns they would want a large leather spinner, known on the Dee as a "leather eel," or they would want a prawn, or they would want a Blue Devon minnow. They were quite clear about what they wanted and under almost no circumstances would they be prepared to take more than one of this trio on the same day. A fly purist would have refused to give them what they wanted, and a regular bait fisher would have denied them nothing. We sought for flies that would be like enough to the bait to attract them. We found that if the water was dark with spate salmon would go for the black and gold of a big Ackroyd in the Waddington dressing. By the same token they would take this same fly, conventionally dressed, in early Spring instead of a golden sprat. When salmon want the prawn they are attracted by anything that is the right shade of red, and because of this they will often take a Thunder and Lightning. A well-known fisherman and friend, Esmond Drury, tied a fly like enough to a prawn to attract them and, curiously enough, it always seemed to attract the larger fish. The remaining problem, which should have seemed the easiest, of finding a fly equivalent to the Blue Devon minnow, completely defeated us. Our experiments never ceased.

My father had been in at the beginnings of fishing dry fly for salmon, which is now a well established method in North America. He brings it into one of his novels, *John McNab*. We could bring the Braemar salmon up to look at a dry fly but they would sink down again without touching it. My father used to say that you needed a water temperature of 68 degrees Fahrenheit, and absolutely fresh-run salmon, to make this method succeed. At Braemar we sometimes had that water temperature in late summer, but the salmon were far from fresh in the upper reach at that time of the year. But this is far from being the last word on the subject.

The General Election of 1950 was happily just before our fishing season opened, and the election the following year was just after it had finished. But politics and business seem to be at their most demanding in the May and June when the greased-line fishing was at its best. I did, however, have a fortnight's fishing in March, after the 1960 General Election. An enlightened doctor, himself a fisherman, had told me that I needed a rest and some fishing. There were quite a lot of fish up as early as March in that year, but the river ran cold and low, and shafts of bright spring sunlight lit up the bottom of the pools. The salmon had no use for the big flies that were generally used at that time of the year, and none for the low water dressing in that very cold water. One day I saw a fish come to the surface in broad sunlight and take down something that was floating. I saw this repeated several times, on different occasions. Salmon will often swallow large objects. The Fishmongers' Company have a sizeable length of bramble that was taken out of a salmon's throat. But these objects seemed to be very tiny and to be taken just for curiosity. I bombarded the tackle makers to make me a hook that would float as my Canadian dry flies, which looked like feather bonnets, were far too big. I wanted a small floating hook, ornamented with only the skinniest of low water dressing. The tackle-makers could not produce the hook I wanted. I had come separately to a conclusion that feathers were by no means the best medium for making salmon flies, and I had a number of them dressed on nylon, of about the consistency of toothbrush bristles, or on wool. They were of no use, but at about this time, the Canadians discovered the virtues of moose hair, which is just wiry enough to make the fly look alive throughout its course. And now an even more effective medium has been discovered in the hair of a polar bear. When I was a Hudson's Bay Company fur trader in Baffin Land, in the thirties, we were paid very little for a polar-bear skin. They were shipped south to be hearthrugs. The polar bear is almost as much at home in water as on land, which means that his fur has a special texture and lustre. It has the right consistency for a salmon fly and a gleam that seems to be attractive. Now, to their acute embarrassment, the bears find themselves only too much in demand and have great difficulty in holding on to their jackets.

Four, almost five, happy fishing seasons went by. Except for 1950 when the late lying snow cost us our April and May fishing, we caught all the salmon that we needed to enjoy ourselves thoroughly, and for quite a number of others to enjoy themselves. Jo and Anne grew up into serious fishers and would set out alone with rods in their hands and bags on their backs, often enough returning hauling a salmon behind them through the grass. The biggest fish that we ever hooked at Braemar, which must have been getting on for 30 pounds, was hooked by a French girl of about fourteen, who was staying with us to learn English. She was broken after a couple of minutes which showed her and us the real strength of the fish. She took this disaster with amazing fortitude. She was not the great-granddaughter of Marshal Foch for nothing.

The seasons came and went starting with silver fish in cold snow water and ending with gaunt hook-jawed dark shapes in the autumn when the leaves came down the current like gold and copper coins. My last day's fishing was September 30th, the last day of the season of 1952. Fishing that day through, I landed three salmon, the biggest being $11\frac{1}{2}$ pounds. It was dusk when I reeled in and started to make my way slowly back from the pool, and, as somebody had taken my fish home for me, I walked beside the river. It was getting dark as I rounded the bend which brings the castle in sight and stopped to stare at the lights in the barred windows in the tower, and the slits in the turrets. On the hillside, close above me on my left, a stag roared and then roared again and then fell silent. It was a still evening as I walked back and could hear the murmuring of the river gliding over the stones, even as far as the castle knoll. There was no creak of the lid of the rod box. The rod was destined to join the other rods in their canvas cases in the gun room, and then to be bundled up for removal.

Since then I have thought of so many experiments that I wish that I had tried. Polar bear flies for one. Fishing with two flies on the cast, for another. And a blow line fished with a downstream wind could be made to steer a fly slowly through the fast water. Fishing a fly upstream in low water, with a trout rod and a really fine cast. It would be a dull world if we stopped wanting to experiment.

We felt that we had learned quite a lot in those four years, but even so, knew very little. And hope that we will get the chance to go on learning.

The seven streams of Belhelvie Parish are of modest size. They are tiny burns, and it is only when they approach the sea that there is any difficulty in jumping them. Several of them contain trout. The Potterton burn yields quite a lot of them when we have children to stay, who fish it with a worm, never catching anything bigger than a few ounces, occasionally varying their bag with an eel. How those trout survive when the mosses are frozen hard, as they are in the winter, with water dead low and the herons quartering the bed of the burn with their long spindly legs.

There are very few trout lochs in this part of Scotland, but only a few miles away we have in the Don the finest trout stream in the Island.

It was in very small burns that most of us learned to fish. And most of us will admit that we have by no means finished learning. If you have had the luck of being a fisherman all your life, you can turn, and rod in hand go back along the corridors of time to the day when with a great heave of a wildly kicking rod, a small trout lay flapping in the grass, to be seized in small hands with an excitement and a pounding heart that only extreme youth knows. That is why in riper years many of us find greater and greater pleasure in taking a child fishing and sharing its triumph. But most of us grow cautious in passing on the dogmas that were handed down to us in our own childhood.

Most of them call for careful examination. The first was that fish can see you unless you are downstream of them. That they have a highly developed sense of taste and that is why they will spit out an artificial fly whose imposture they can tell by the taste of its materials. Further, that fish can hear you if you talk or make even a moderate amount of noise, last of all, if you remove any slime from a fish when returning it to the water, it will die.

Man will always tend to believe that the animal kingdom reason and react as we do. A lot has been written about "the fish's window" and not much of it is convincing. About the refraction of light in water we know a lot and, when a fish darts away, which you were sure could not have seen you, if you have not made the bank vibrate, it is probable that it has seen you through a trick of refraction. But what makes fish utterly different from any other quarry of man is his absence of eyelids. Fishermen accept that when a low evening sun shines down a pool you will be very lucky if you catch anything. In such times it is only too likely that the fish are blinded, although they have some mechanism of the eye to make up for its lack of protection. The ability of the fish to see must vary from hour to hour as the sun follows its course. There was a pool at Braemar where you could almost always raise a salmon on a sunlit evening, just after the bank had started to stretch a bar of shadow across the lie. Perhaps at that moment clear sight was returning to the salmon for the first time for hours. And then, a creature that has eyes on opposite sides of its head cannot have the same stereoscopic vision that we have with our binocular sight, and it is difficult to see how their sight can have the stereoscopic depth needed to judge distance accurately.

Men have long held views on these points. Ronalds* conducted various experiments from his hut on the Blythe, more than a hundred years ago, to establish whether or not fish could hear. He and his friend, the Reverend Mr Brown of Gratwich, fired guns over the trout and shouted at them from a distance as close as 6 feet. They were careful to point the gun where the fish did not see the flash, and the fish remained completely unmoved. But, plainly, they have something that corresponds to taste and smell in human beings. But it must be different from those creatures which, like ourselves, breath air.

Ronalds has a chapter on the sense of taste and smell in fish. He could see no way of testing a fish's sense of smell which did not involve depriving the fish of its sight and concludes "the cruelty of which operation deterred me from prosecuting the enquiry."

But he carried out extensive experiments on the trout's sense of taste. From the concealment of his hut, beside the waters of the Blythe, he blew ten dead house-flies towards a trout who took them all. This was followed by a further thirty flies, plastered with cayenne pepper and mustard all of which the trout duly took, twenty when they touched the water and the rest after they had floated down for a second or two. The next day an exactly similar repast was offered to the same trout who received it with the same enthusiasm. "From these and similar experiments," he tells us, "such as getting trout to take flies dipped in honey, oil, vinegar etc. I concluded that if the animal has taste, his palate is not peculiarly sensitive."

A fish breathes water through its nostrils and separates the air from it. It is clear that he has some sense of taste or smell as he will avoid certain forms of pollution which he could not know about unless he had such a sense.

Generations of young fishermen have been reproved, and continue to be reproved, for frightening the fish by talking in

* Alfred Ronalds, *The Fly-fisher's Entymology,* 5th edition, 1856.

their vicinity. An effort was made to teach John Betjeman to fish when he was very young. He very much minded being forbidden to talk, although he says that he minded taking the fish off the hooks—other people's fish, one presumes—even more. But, certainly, noise amounts to vibration and will frighten fish. They can feel vibration that is not necessarily accompanied by noise, such as a silent footfall on a bank that has been tunnelled by water rats or rabbits, and conveys vibration very directly. Last of all, on the subject of returning fish to the water. Hewitt recalls that he once returned 760 trout in one season to the water and only two of them died. He concludes that it does not matter removing the slime if the fish neither bleed nor receive an internal bruise.*

Most people become keen fishermen when they are very young, and thus it is that fishing memories are taut with an awareness that most of us lose after our early youth. For it is when your world is young that its sights and sounds and feelings strike you with the force of a revelation. And you can begin as a small child. For you can wield a rod before you have the strength to fire a gun, or hold a rebellious pony. But, whenever you start, it is very unlikely that fishing will never lose its magic for you, if that magic ever had the chance to splash you.

A fondness for fishing, unites a larger number of people of these islands, than any other cause. You may forget almost everything, even your own name, before you will forget the catching of your first fish. My father's dictum that fishing is not a pastime but a way of life, must be widely agreed or it would not be so widely quoted. Fishing has attracted some of the best pens, of poetry and prose, back to ancient times. It differs radically from all other sports, in that you can stop short of the last step if you so wish, and release your quarry alive. Many of us, as we get older, tend to do this more and more.

But youth gives little quarter, its triumphs and disasters are acute. My father, at nine years old, had hooked an old red salmon which had come up Lyne Water in a spate and had lost it, just as it was turning on its side, almost within his grasp. He had thrown himself face down on the shingle mingling his tears with the pebbles, and a look of sadness came over his face when he was telling the story half a century later. In a reasoned order of things,

---

* Hewitt, *A Trout and Salmon Fisherman for Seventy-Five Years*. Scribners, New York.

your knowledge and experience should increase and the number and size of your catch should increase correspondingly. But as your opportunities are unequal and fishing is so inexact a science, that seldom happens. I caught my first trout when I was eight and the two largest trout that I was ever to catch, 6 pounds and $5\frac{1}{2}$ pounds, one year later. Opportunity, as well as blind luck, helps to upset arithmetical probability.

Perhaps the wildest raptures of excitement are beginning to leave you when you reach 16 and are starting to look towards manhood. Life is not quite so breathlessly new as it once was. But you still have those vivid sensitivities of youth and not the least of them is the sense of smell. So many of one's out-of-door pursuits have that particular smell. When you smell it today it brings them back. Whether it be the smell of gun-oil or cricket-bat oil or the varnish on an oar—perhaps most exciting—the smell of a fish fresh taken from the water. The most distinctive and a not very attractive smell, belongs to the grayling. Linnaeus thought it suggestive of Thyme and gave it its Latin name of *Salmo Thymella*

As a fisherman's experience expands, so his tackle and gear evolve, though he will nearly always keep some of the older with the new, and the same with his theories. When I caught my first fish I was given the gear that had belonged to my grandfather. It was a beautiful 9 foot greenheart fly rod, the best of its kind that I have ever used. With it came a large wicker creel too heavy for me to carry up the glens but containing a brass coffee-grinder reel and a fly book that had belonged to my grandfather's father and was made in the 1840s. With this armament I was also issued with a set of theories, each stated as an incontestable fact.

There are four elements in fishing, and two are constant. One is the nature and physical makeup of the fish, and the second is the food on which it lives.* The two variable factors are the gear which man uses to catch them and the artificial impersonation of their food which he uses. Perfect models of the natural fly have been made in feathers for well over a century. But there has, in my lifetime, been beside a revolution in the rods that we use, a corresponding revolution in reels and lines. My grandfather's tackle took me back two generations. But the practice of my father's generation is almost equally remote from the present day.

---

* Such recent happenings as the disappearance of the March brown from the Tweed, which gave the trout their basic weight, can invalidate this assertion.

He had his enormous greenheart salmon rod. He bought himself a split cane trout rod when they were a novelty in the 1920s. In addition to this he had one or two rather small greenheart trout rods with permanent bends. He passed over to me the little dry fly greenheart rod that belonged to his father. Much later in life he acquired a built-cane grilse rod excellent for fishing greased line for salmon. These rods sufficed him down the twenty years that we fished together. As his rods became more up-to-date so his fly-books, and boxes and cases for casts, did so too. When he went to Canada he acquired a vast fly book which he filled up with such Canadian as the Parmechenee Belle and the dark Montreal flies, dressed with the hair of moose and polar bear and strange things called streamers and bucktails and skaters, which have no exact equivalent in the British fly book.

Why is a fly book called a fly book? Instead of a fly case, which it is. You would know immediately if you saw the one that belonged to my grandfather and came to me with his wicker creel. When you open it you are looking at the title page of a book. "Merryweather's Companion to the Fly Fisher's Entomology, by Alfred Ronalds." This is followed by a brief acknowledgement to the publishers and a short note tells you that "this work is simply entitled for the convenience of the Angler, to enable him to keep his flies in neat and regular order so much attended to by all good Anglers", . . . adding that most of the flies used by anglers in Britain are described here. On the left-hand page inside the cover and secured by a loop of leather, there is a tapered piece of polished bone. The thin end is forked, and clearly intended to be used as a disgorger. The larger end has a herring-bone pattern of cuts in it for the plaiting of horsehair casts. With the exception of a pocket at the back and two pages of flannel in which flies could be stuck, you have all forty-seven flies described in Alfred Ronalds' classic. Four are described on each page and there are as many parchment pockets on the page opposite to hold the flies described and the curl of gut on which they are dressed. It starts with "Flies for March." "No. 1 Red fly (four-winged dun). In a forward spring this fly comes out about the middle of February; it is in season 'till the end of March and may be used on fine but rather windy days.' The last fly is under 'Flies for September'. No. 47 Black Palmer. This Palmer is used at the same time as the Brown Palmer, viz. on windy days, and after a flood, throughout the fishing season, and equally well when the fish are glutted with a Green Drake, especially towards evening." There follows a paragraph entitled Critiques. "No angler, either literate or scientific, and the best anglers are both, should be without Ronalds." *Blackwood's Magazine, June, 1838.* See also *New Monthly Magazine,* August 18th, 1836, as well as the *New Sporting Magazine* and the *Literary Gazette* for the same year.

If that is not a book, then there is no such thing. The flies described are those for Derbyshire streams, the Dove in particular. But they were also excellent for the Tweed and its tributaries.

Turning the pages of the old fly book today, there are still a few of my grandfather's flies tied to the gut. They look well tied but would, of course, have no longer life than the gut on which they were dressed. The present day fly has no gut to wear out and how long it lasts is a matter of dressing. Once, fishing in the Faeroe Islands, I rose about two hundred trout in the space of about an hour. Their sharp teeth completely disintegrated six wet flies. Nylon has succeeded gut and there can be few, even among the fishers of the Upper Clyde, who still use horsehair. It was tremendously exciting to go to the grocer's shop in Broughton, when we were children on holiday, to buy flies. In fact, we always bought made-up casts which were sold in crackly packets from which one drew them beautifully knotted and neat.

The revolution in rods continues steadily. In Best's *Art of Angling* (11th Edition, 1822) he says that a fly rod, meaning a trout fly rod, should be 14 feet to 17 feet in length. That the butt length of 7 feet should be cut from an ash plank and tapered on a lathe. The next joint should be a 7-feet length hazel tapering in proportion to the ash. But if you could not get a suitable stem of hazel it was wise to use a 5-feet length of it and add a 2 feet joint of yew, rounding off with a 6-inch taper of whalebone. This combination he describes as "long enough for anyone who understands fly fishing to throw 12 yards of line with one hand and seventeen with both."

Alfred Ronalds, in his classic, says that a tall, strong man could manage a 14 to 15 foot trout fly rod but anyone with lesser stature should try a 12 footer. He recommends "the best materials are ash for the stock, lancewood* for the middle, and bamboo for the top; the butt should have a hole drilled down it containing a spare top and a spike is made to screw into the end, which is found useful to stick into the ground and keep the rod upright

* A light, straight-grained wood growing in the West Indies and Guyana.

when landing a good fish." You needed both hands in those days for your landing net.

Our gun room is not just the dusty museum it appears to be. Nor is it a room, but a passage with a window at the end. It has its own strange smells of leather and varnish and waves of citronella to keep off the Canadian black flies and gun oil. From the jumble of lures and flies and hooks and casts for reels in the different bags, mostly army issue of the last war, which hang from the hooks and on the shelves of the cupboard, we assemble what we need to fish far beyond the borders of Belhelvie parish.

Potterton

WE WERE due to leave Braemar Castle in the autumn of
1952. Much of that summer was spent in looking for
a home. If you ever have to leave a house it is a very rare
and happy accident if you find another house that suits you. But
in the late summer we heard of one. The agent, who told us about
it, said in the same breath that it would not suit us. There were
too many doors, he said. But it did suit us and has been our home
ever since. It is called Potterton.

Houses are big or small according to the size of your family,
your purse, or your tastes, rather than by their size. The Valuation
Authorities described Potterton impersonally, and some years
later, as "... a good detached, two storey, small mansion-house."
But we knew from the moment that we first saw it, that we wanted
it. And, as negotiations with the outgoing owner did not last very

long, pantechnicons were soon rolling down the Deeside road from Braemar, with our mixture of belongings.

The house stands where a slope levels out briefly before shelving down again to a burn. And it is approached by two drives. One is short, beginning opposite the gardener's cottage, and is perhaps three hundred yards long. It slopes downwards until you reach and follow a right fork uphill, through a line of rhododendrons and shrubs, and find yourself at the front door. The other drive is tortuous and was made with ideas of Victorian grandeur. We do not use it now, and have allowed it to become a mossy ride, just trimming back the rhododendrons beside it. Our daughter, Susie, used to canter up and down it and rabbits lollop across it.

When we go down the short drive we catch a sight of the house through the only stand of really tall timber that the great gale left to us. The house is above us. It seems to be waiting for us, with a welcome. The land rises gently above it through the plantation, to the ridge above the road. On the uphill side of the house a few yards of sloping lawn separate you from the wall of the walled garden, a big rectangle of old grey stone, with here and there some brick or red granite for contrast. A white gate opens through it to a path that runs the length of it to a little garden, that we call the berry garden, where there is a small and mossy lawn. We are proud of the iron gate at this end. It was designed and fitted for us by a Pole who had been captured by the Russians at the beginning of the last War. He escaped and reached France to fight with the French Resistance. His design of the gate is much admired. He is a master in the art of decorative ironwork, learned one would imagine, in pre-war Poland.

We removed as much as we added. When we arrived there was a small greenhouse just in front of the house. We had it removed to the berry garden.

On the other side of the house the ground falls away down a sloping lawn to a little tiny rill of a stream. Then you come to the drive and, right at the bottom of the valley, is the Potterton burn. It is a fair-sized water with a few little trout in it, and it forms our boundary. Beside it is a rushy field which belongs to us, and which we have converted into a wood. At the far end of it is one of the few working water-mills still left in Scotland, driven by the burn. It suffers from having lived on into an era where oatmeal is no longer paid as wages, but the wheel still turns as it has for three hundred years. The miller who is getting on in years finds lifting heavy sacks of meal more difficult. But he is still in business, seeming to blend two of Chaucer's characters, the miller and the gentle pardoner.

If you stand on the front doorstep you look across the little carriage sweep, across a strip of lawn and through a belt of rhododendrons, to a field, and on to another little field beyond it which is caught up between two woods. These fields are grandly called, in the taxation returns, "the grass parks of Potterton." They are some four acres in extent, and the larger one has three lime trees spaced to make them look like a proper park. If you go to the back door you look out, in the opposite direction, over our big field, surrounded by a rim of little hills. At the far side of it is the ravine, where the burn runs out. This field has all the freedom of fourteen acres. It is undulating ground, although it looks nearly flat at first sight, and falls steeply down to the burn. There has been a Potterton for a long time. It was, to be sure, Potterton in the Register of the Great Seal in 1597. Gordon of Straloch's map of 1654 called it Pottertown and you still find that spelling on some of the maps of the early 1800s. We entered into written record only once or twice. We are recorded to have transgressed in the records of the Kirk Session. That was on June 20th, 1703, when it was recorded that "Bletchers in Potterton rebuked for keeping out their clothes on Sundays."

Looking from the front door in winter, at a blazing northern sunset, you can see through the leafless trees the little church tower of the South Church of Belhelvie. In the summer a barrier of green leaf enfolds you. From the back door you can see where the burn cuts through the ravine between an old Pictish camp on the left, covered with gorse, and a heather hump to which a few ragged trees still cling to the right. It is known to geo-morphologists by the resounding title of the Potterton gorge. The top of the *V*, that these slopes make, is the most level line in the world, the sea horizon. We stop to stare, from time to time, at a distant and toy-like ship framed in it. That the house was once the abode of potters is questioned by as great an authority as Alexander, who says that: "There is no tradition of any pottery being here; on the other hand brick clay is not very far away."* He did not know that there is a kiln down in our cellar and another one beside the garage, and, when we were changing the drainage

* William Alexander, *Place Names of Aberdeenshire:* printed for the Third Spalding Club, 1952.

arrangements, we found an old well, such as potters use. The house has grown from the butt-and-ben, as we call a two-roomed granite cottage, which probably housed the potters and their wares, to a small laird's house. Our predecessor had a large rock removed, from just outside the entrance to the garage and found a quantity of pottery there which unfortunately was broken before it could be examined.

The short scrutiny that we had been able to make before we bought the house, had given us a great many ideas about the changes that we wanted to make. The water supply came from a well, by way of an old leaden pipe that was always breaking. The supply was shared with the former home farm across the burn. In summer if a hundred and fifty cows had a drink we could not have a bath. The water was heated in two small tanks on either side of the fireplace in the pantry. This meant that we had to have a coal fire going all the time, even in high summer, in order to heat even one bath. The electric light was made by an archaic motor which was always wheezing to a halt. When we eventually received from the public supply water and electric light, an impressive row of batteries was removed. They were accumulators of big, square glass construction. We gave a few away to people who wanted to make an aquarium, and sold the rest. Unfortunately some of the acid got tipped out on the lawn, and made an ugly scar which took years to eradicate. We inherited a saw which was driven by an equally ancient and uncertain engine which we eventually replaced with an electric one, which purrs along smoothly. Inside the house we removed two mantelpieces of a particularly unattractive varnished brick, and replaced them with rough granite. The wall between the little hall and the study did not reach the ceiling. It was in fact merely a partition, and we raised it accordingly.

It took a number of years to make all these improvements. In those days we still owned my old home at Elsfield, and my Uncle Walter was still alive at Peebles. It became impossible to keep Elsfield, and when Uncle Walter died in 1954 the contents of his home at Peebles came to fill the house almost to bursting point. The big library carpet from Elsfield is now covering our bedroom floor and makes the room twice as warm. Many people had walked on that carpet in its days at Elsfield, more than one Prime Minister and Lawrence of Arabia among them.

We put up our few big game heads. A twelve-pointer that my

father had shot in the West Highlands in 1912 and another that Priscilla had shot at Braemar. And one or two African heads, such as a kob that I had shot in Uganda, and an impala that my father had shot in his South African days. Also a chital that my father-in-law had shot in the Mysore forest. Priscilla added a most noble caribou head that she shot on the slopes of Tweedsmuir peak in the Quanchus Mountains in British Columbia, when we were hunting grizzlies there in 1955, and the pelt of a Rocky Mountain goat that she shot in the same expedition. They are reminders of the extent of our wanderings, mostly on duties concerned with Britain's old responsibilities of Empire. The hide of a Canadian bison that an Indian chief had once given to my father was our drawing-room carpet, until its rough brown fleece was worn bare. We replaced it by a carpet that we brought back from Persia, woven by the nomads of Kash'nai. My father's library from Elsfield was presented to Queen's University in Canada, but my Uncle Walter was a great bibliophile and his books, together with what we already had, filled our bookcases almost to bursting. And life was easier now. We still did our thousand-mile weekend. We got *The Times* the day after it reached New York, unless we went to collect our second post. But we were only eight miles from the station, or about four from the airport, instead of sixty. We were installed by Hogmanay of 1952, and there was great rejoicing. A month later came that tempest which was to change the whole face of the countryside. If it had to come, that was the time for it to come. We have had many happy years there since to grow a new forest. Time enough to see our young trees grow taller than ourselves.

There was a wonderful strangeness about this Potterton. In the night there are nearly always owls hooting, and, if there is any wind, the noise of the sea. If one hears the sea from a certain direction it is normal, but if one hears it from a sharply contrasting direction it is a sure gale warning. Although the road lies between us and the sea, we mercifully hear more of the sea than the traffic. That road was a narrow and winding one when we came, but bit by bit they cut off the bends (for it was like the coils of a snake), and widened it. But we still hardly hear the traffic. Just the other side of the near wall of the walled garden we were delighted to find a splendid beech, a great perch for the owls after dark. When the spring came, to our delight it turned out to be a copper beech. That first spring brought many other revelations. We discovered clump after clump of snowdrops, and the edges of the lawns were lined with daffodils. In a near corner of the garden was our decaying greenhouse. It was no longer weather-proof and, on a rainy day, the drops would find you out. From the greenhouse a door led into a tiny potting-shed, which was very rickety, smelt of mould, and let in practically no light. Both have been replaced and we idle happily in them for hours. It is surprising how few people use greenhouses as places in which to sit, and even work. You can sit there in winter and summer. There is always something to look at and a delightful smell, and it is always possible to keep warm.

Beyond the back door is a lawn, with a large bump in it where our predecessor had built himself an air-raid shelter in the last war. As he roofed it over with green turf it is not uncomely. Beyond that was a very ugly henhouse, standing on the edge of a quarter of an acre of nettles and thistles. I cut the nettles and thistles and had it fenced round, and have made myself a tree garden there. We have put in a seat from which you can just see the sea, in the gap between the Pictish camp and the hillock opposite it. With the help of six men we carted the henhouse away and put it against the outside of the wall of the walled garden, out of sight. The greenhouse flooded one wet winter, and we tried to make a drain. In the course of digging this drain we ran into the outer edge of a concrete rim, which when we investigated turned out to be a duck pond perhaps twenty feet long and half as wide. We dug it out, had it reconcreted, and it is now a great place for children to paddle and for the birds to drink. On top of it, with one corner overlapping its rim, was a rather pleasant little apple house. We had that moved up against the outside wall of the walled garden. In the course of moving it, with the great sweating and panting of several men, we bumped against the stump of an old alder tree. Out flew an outraged robin who had been sitting on a nest there, entirely unsuspected up till that moment.

A Canadian acquisition was a present from the President of the Canadian National Railways. When the Canadian railways turned over from steam to diesel they removed the famous engine bells which were so much a part of so many peoples' memories of Canada. Those are bells that you can hear ten miles away if the wind is right. This one was a wonderful old-timer that clanged for many decades over the road crossings and scattered the echoes through the Crow's Nest Pass. The only other one in Britain is in a church steeple in Hampstead, where it calls the faithful to worship. Ours is proudly set up outside our back door, and if anybody is wanted on the telephone we sound that great bell and its "dong-dong-dong" goes out across the countryside. The old engine bells were succeeded by hooters on the diesel trains, which were neither as impressive or effective.

When we first arrived we had found that the two grass parks had been ploughed and grown a crop of weeds. We had them ploughed and seeded and took a crop of hay off them. Year by year we added shrubs and blossom trees. And bit by bit we have changed the face of this little property, in the wake of the great gale. We go on changing it and get the most exquisite pleasure from it.

Susie does not remember Braemar. She came to Potterton as a rather thoughtful three-year-old, dressed in the red ski suit that the regimental sergeant-major of my Canadian battalion had given her. We brought Ella, our wonderful housekeeper, from Braemar with us, and our splendid nanny. The latter stayed until Susie left the village school, where she received the most excellent education, and went on to her first boarding school, which was in Aberdeen. Ella left us after a time and was succeeded by Mrs. Grant. Mrs. Grant was another in a series of helpful friends. Her husband was the bosun of a ship which used to ply from London to Aberdeen every week throughout the year. He eventually retired after about forty-seven years' service and was rewarded with the B.E.M. Mrs. Grant did everything well, paticularly the cooking. She belonged to a far-wandering family. Her uncle had gone off in the Klondike Gold Rush as a carpenter, and prospered reasonably. Her brother lived in Sydney, Australia. We rang him up when we were there on one occasion. He was a good deal surprised to hear distant news from so close.

But now we look after ourselves. A lady from the village comes and helps us with the cleaning. Our first gardener, George Farquhar, was the mainstay of the whole establishment. He is now retired. Although over seventy he was still exceedingly strong and a tremendous worker. He was many other things as well, which included being an excellent shot. He was in the Gordon Highlanders in the 1914 war, one of the original "Ladies from Hell." There were two sons in his family. His brother died from eating snowberries at the age of six. But he survived every

F

possible hazard, including three of the bayonet charges of the Highland Division at Loos, and the taking, losing, and retaking of Thiepval. Of his four sons all wanted to join the Gordons, but one was held back and reserved for agriculture to his patent annoyance. Another of them succeeded his father as gardener and died tragically young after only a few months. They were all as sturdy and handsome as himself. Apart from being a great gardener he was a splendid companion. And his red face shone far oftener and more warmly than the sun. He was succeeded by James Robertson, a veteran of Tobruk where he was taken prisoner. A keen sportsman, he is not only a remarkable shot but a fisherman who makes both his own flies and his own rods.

Visitors started to arrive, very varied visitors. Ella came and called me one evening from the walled garden, with the cryptic message that "the cruelty" had come for his money. I peeped round the corner of the house to see what this monster could be, and discovered a very respectable and friendly uniformed official of the Aberdeen Association for the Prevention of Cruelty to Animals. Occasionally a truck would drive up and we would be offered old fishing nets to protect our strawberry beds. The first ones we bought we carefully rolled up and hung in the potting-shed, against the time we should need to use them. Through a crack in the planking a tree-creeper entered, and made a nest in the middle of them, so we lost the use of those nets for the whole summer and had to buy some more. A Pakistani, with a turban, came to peddle his wares. We then made the acquaintance of a fascinating man who was a water diviner, known as Old Willie. He was one of the most remarkable water diviners I have ever seen, and in dry summers, was greatly in demand all over the county, and even beyond. He could divine metal as well as water and could find a coin in the long grass. This gift appeared to be hereditary in his family, for his mother had been a water diviner, and his sister was, surprisingly, a water diviner in Toronto.

This countryside was magnificently farmed, but although we saw the latest of modern agricultural machinery, we also saw splendid plough horses that were needed on the steeper slopes, and explained the presence of two blacksmiths. One of them, who occasionally comes to shoot with us, is one of the strongest men that I have ever known in my life. The other blacksmith, from further afield, was summoned in aid when Susie entered her riding era, to shoe and unshoe her pony. He once told me that the highlight of his career was in the Salonika Campaign, when he shoed an ox in Macedonia.

Potterton has so pleasant a feeling about it, as a house, that we started to get more and more interested in finding out about those who had owned it in its short history. After the 1715 Rising, the Panmure family, who owned the most of the land in this part of the world, were attainted. And if you do not know what that means, we most certainly do in Scotland. The story of the forfeiture of the lands of the parish is told in another chapter. It was some seventy years later that Potterton became a little estate with four or five farms. It was built by a family called Harvey, who came from Forgue in Aberdeenshire, where Priscilla's forebears are buried. It then passed through various hands including the family of Clapperton who had it for several generations. Two rather remarkable coincidences were that the Harveys had owned the place at Forgue, in which Priscilla's eighteenth-century ancestor had worked. The Clappertons had a far-out cousin, in the person of the famous sculptor of that name, who had sculpted the bust of my father that stands in the National Portrait Gallery. All these families had added something to the house. Our immediate predecessor bought the estate and sold off all the farms, keeping just the house and the policies and some forty acres of land, which I have mentioned.

He lived there for perhaps a dozen years, and we are grateful to him for the shrubs and the bulbs that he planted. He was very keen on birds, and the last talk that I had with him was on that subject. He told me that we should see a certain selection of unusual birds, the tree-creeper was one. He was right. We have since seen every single one of them. In the little drawing-room there is a french window which is wide open in the summer time, and the sound of the birds comes in, and big blunt-faced bumblebees wander about, buzz round, and buzz out again. And with the smell of the garden, and the sound of the birds, and the sound of the bees, we feel part of the outdoor world. The birds do not seem to regard the house as being alien. The sparrows, and some others, nest in scores in the clematis outside the french window of the drawing-room. Birds and beasts are always coming into the house. A goldcrest came into our bedroom the first spring that we were there. We once found a bat crawling along the carpet. And one of the few green lizards that I have ever seen in Scotland, appeared on the doorstep when we were having tea outside one hot day.

The lawns are in bits and pieces, one in front of the house, one behind it, one above it and one below it. For the amount of grass they take a very long time to mow. They used to be haunted by rabbits. That is why we called the sloping lawn below the house the "Quartier Lapin". As this is the only place where you find an enclave of trees and shrubs on this particular part of a barren coast, we are very attractive to small birds. That makes the spring weekends so exciting, because there are always half a dozen new nests. There are a good many different mammals, including several varieties of mice. Our most extraordinary visitor one winter was a stoat, white with his winter coat, who managed to climb up the porch and get into a hole under the gutter where the starlings nest. We put a ladder up there, and Priscilla carried up our Scottie terrier, Rory. By the actual rate of his wags and the sound of his sniffs we decided that the weasel had been there recently, but was not still there. Rory descended looking like a black hairy geiger-counter. In January 1968, a white stoat appeared on the dining-room window-sill eating the food put out for the birds. Rory nearly had apoplexy, seeing it a foot away through a pane of glass.

We dammed up the little rill of a burn with the idea of making a fish nursery. At great expense we bought some tiny rainbow trout. They did fairly well, until quite suddenly, silage from a farm above got into the burn and they all died. But we did not dismantle our dam because one or two mallard come and nest beside it. Then we realised that some of the surrounding trees were standing in water, and dismantled it in haste.

There is so much to do at Potterton, you are always occupied. It has all the thrill of exploring. And one never explores the last place. There is always some unknown aspect of the smallest piece of country and something to which to look forward. Village life is now more self-contained. When we first went there we had to go to Aberdeen to buy almost all our groceries, but now the village shops, within fairly easy reach, are now so fully stocked that we can shop without going any further afield. When we are asked where we are going for our holidays, we generally surprise the questioner by saying that we are going to our home. We shall never see enough of it. When we get tired at hearing the sea pounding against the dunes, we shall be tired of life. Because we always know that next year is going to be even more exciting than this one.

6   *The Parish*

OVER the last two or three years the demand for cement, for the building of houses, has resulted in the raiding of a great many of the little coastal hills along our shores. The sand in them was piled there by the Ice Age and some of it is of a consistency which the makers of cement need. From the farm road that crosses our little bridge over the Potterton burn, on its way up to the home farm, we could always make out a rim of sea horizon between the slopes of the ravine. Now a sizeable hillock has been removed beyond it and, behold, there is a great swathe of sea to the eastwards, which is Mediterranean blue when the sun shines. This is the first time we have been able to see so much of the ocean from that particular position for about eight thousand years, which was when the glaciers pushed the sand in front of them to make that line of rounded hillocks. But it has not been dull in this parish for the last few thousand years. Far from it. Not for as long as men have lived in it, which is for about half that time.

In the wake of the glaciers and after a long period of years, came the first of the Men of the Mists. They were called the Strandloopers and they came, it is believed, from the Rhineland. They seemed to have lived mostly on shell-fish, sometimes leaving caches of shells, or chippings of the flints that they had brought, for us to stare at today.

A long time afterwards came what we call the Beaker Folk, from whom most of us on this coast are descended. We find their burial places from time to time. They were little people and were buried with their knees drawn up to their chins, under a single slab of stone, and always in their grave is a little beaker of earthenware. They knew how to grow food as well as to hunt for it.

Looking up from the bottom of the little bowl which forms our property, we can see on the hill above us to the north, and not half a mile away, what are called in this part of the country, the Temple Stones. The recumbent stone, and the stones that were its two attendant pillars and which are now on their sides, make a little island of rock and weeds in the middle of an otherwise faultlessly tilled field. Some call them the Druid Stones. That is not to mean the Druids of the ivy and mistletoe. Rather the word Druid is used to mean a very ancient people who have gone and whose Gods have gone with them. The position of the Temple Stones is such that you get a view as far up and down the coast and inland as it is possible to get anywhere in this part of the world, which was something that the old Gods seem to have demanded for their altars. Perhaps a mile further up the coast to the north a pointed burial barrow crowned by a fringe of trees goes back to the people that followed the Beaker Folk—the people of the Bronze Age. A heavy bronze armlet was found, as well as several torques of pure gold, in the parish. That bronze armlet is a marriage between the tin of Cornwall and the copper of Ireland and had had a long journey before it reached our northeastern seaboard. These men had found the key to skills and crafts that must have given them, for the first time, some feeling of mastery over their surroundings.

Belhelvie is meant to mean "the place of seven streams". There are seven streams. But that is not what the word means. The experts say that it means "Siolbhan's Stead". They further say that Balmedie, one of our three villages, and up until modern times called Eggie, means "the place of the fox or the dog." Who Siolbhan was, or why Balmedie was so named, was lost long ago in the mists and the march of a million tides against the sand dunes.

Then came the Tapestry Men. You see them on tapestries with their angular horses, their steel head-pieces and their long swords. They passed us in a procession of kings and popes and knights on horseback and we felt the strength of their hands, and the law that they brought us. There were the de Berkeleys, de Gildfordes, de Fodringhays and de Bonevilles and others as well. They cast long shadows back to Normandy but they had become part of the bone of Britain. They rode horses. And leather creaked and metal clinked as they moved. Their tall hunting dogs followed their stirrups, when they rode abroad after game with a falcon on the gauntlet of their left hands.

Do not think when you drive through Belhelvie parish that you are discovering us. Nicholas Breakspear, the only Englishman who has ever occupied the Throne of St Peter, under the title of Pope Adrian IV, knew all about us. He took his quill in the year 1157 and wrote a Papal Bull to the Bishop of Aberdeen referring to "Ecclesiam de Balhelvy". A century later our minister was raised to a prebend of the Cathedral Church of Aberdeen. It must have provided a pleasant change of thought for Pope Nicholas who, in that year 1157, was mightily at odds with Frederik Barbarossa, the Holy Roman Emperor. Emperor Frederik and his grandson, who became Frederik II, are much confused with each other in history. The latter was a great falconer and wrote one of the early but standard works on the art and practice of it. It was that reason that led me and others to make a visit to the ruins of his great octagonal castle at Andria in Italy, when we were at the wars in that peninsula. It is curious that the Church has never allowed him to die. Some hold that he sits in a cavern in the Thuringian mountains with a forest of a beard, grown deep into the cracks of the rock, waiting for his country to call him back to protect her. His enemies will not have it that he died, but rather that he was snatched living down to hell. As these two versions are wholly incompatible, the former has since been attached to his grandfather Barbarossa.

King Eric of Norway knew all about us. Indeed, he married Princess Margaret, daughter of our good king Alexander III, in

1281 and the rents of Belhelvie and several other parishes were assigned to him as security for the payment of his dowry. Alas, she died two years later leaving him a daughter whom we called the Maid of Norway. For that period, to all intents and purposes, we were part of Norway. It is no idle form of words when today we describe ourselves as the Norwegian Scots. But it is strange that, with so much Scandinavian in our Aberdeenshire county speech and in Aberdeenshire surnames, that there is said to be only one proven Scandinavian place name.

St. Ternan, a gentle fifth-century Scottish saint, who spent his life converting the Picts, had a chapel hereabouts. It is mentioned in a letter to that powerful Prince, King Edward I in 1305. It said in the letter that "Balhelvie possessed in King Alexander's time a piece of land called St. Ternan's land, lying between St. Ternan's chapel and the sea on the north, which was leased to the Thane of Balhelvie by the parson of Lony, after whose decease the land was . . . taken by force from the Church in the time of the war." Edward I in the midst of his many pre-occupations, had time to order an enquiry into this, but we do not know the result of it. That was the year that he signed the order that committed William Wallace to a barbarous death.

And then came the King's Men who bore names that we know well today. There were two Lords Glamis in succession followed by two more of the Lyon family, in the style of Earls of Kinghorn. The first Lord Glamis was charged with killing Patrick Johnstone at the kirk at Belhelvie and arraigned before the presbytery in Aberdeen, and the record peters out in pot hooks and faded parchments. And then came two Earls of Panmure. The second of them, James, with his brother Harry Maule, rode into the battle at Sheriffmuir on that cold November day in 1715, when the Stuart cause foundered and from then onwards was an exile in France who never looked upon our parish again. But it must often have been in his thoughts, when he would sit and muse and think of home and finger the massive scar on his head from that wound that had nearly cost him his life at Sheriffmuir. The Stuart cause closed with an entry in the records of our kirk service, February 12th, 1716 when Mr. William Dyer was sent by the presbytery of Aberdeen to preach to us, as a probationer. The record says, "Mr. James Keith Intruder, during the unhappy and the unnatural rebellion having absconded himself."

And from then the parish was in pawn to the York Buildings

Company who speculated in forfeited Jacobite estates. But Scotland was entering her second renaissance and a new race was arising—the professionals.

The professionals came to the parish with the first of the Lumsden family whose years of dedicated service, to what is now India and Pakistan, as well as Britain have left there a memorial. They came when Provost John Fordyce came to bring up his vast family at Eggie, and had a tack of the old Panmure lands in the parish from the York Buildings Company. His family left a deep mark on that century in the reading of scholarship and philosophy, religion and medicine, and—let it be said—banking, although that was a mark of a different colour. The Reverend Alexander John Forsyth succeeded his father as minister of the Gospel at Belhelvie in 1791. His invention of the percussion powder was almost as revolutionary as the original invention of gunpowder had been. Of all these I have written separately. But there are several others such as General Sir George Turner of Menie who would have shone brightly in a less glittering constellation. It is the contribution of one Scottish parish to Scotland's greatest century.

Its centre was that ruined kirk standing on the seaward side of the road between Balmedie and Menie. From its steeple, until two years ago, hung its original bell which bore the legend: "Henrik Ter Horst made me at Deventer in 1633". Two years ago the bell was stolen and I trust that the thief got no good of his cloddish crime. Looking at that ruin it is hard to believe that at its zenith (in the 1840s) 550 people a year communicated there. It must have been a most fearsome squash, with the people sitting on tiny stools called "creepies" on the earth floor and, if the minister was late, often becomong obstreperous. Many had walked five miles to get there, in north-eastern weather. Then in would come the minister with his hat on and bow to the various heritors and the congregation would remove their bonnets to replace them during the sermon. We carried politeness too, almost too far. In June 1709 we were "recommended" to "forbear bowing and other expansion of civil respect and entertaining one another with discourses" during the service. There were almost always one or two unfortunates doing penance either on the stool of repentance or standing in the stocks.

The Kirk was fighting for its life at that time. Witchcraft was widespread. They sought to combat religious apathy by heavy penalties for those who did not attend the kirk. At the back of their minds there was always the dread that some lurch of power might bring back a Catholic monarch. Very little latitude of expression was allowed to any parishioner. On April 4th, 1624 George Adamson was accused of blasphemy because he said: "that if the storme continued he could not be able to pay his farme (rent), seeing it is in the Lord's custome to cause cornes to grow bot (without) labouring." The Session found he was not guilty of "hainous blasphemie yet his wordes has a perillous meaning, so was ordained to mak his humble repentance quhilk he did."

Where there was suspicion of witchcraft they were merciless. On September 29th, 1676 poor Isobell Davidsone was summoned; the charge, amongst others, that when she set out to cure different diseases she asked her patients of the month in which they had been born. Asked whether she did so she replied that: "Knowing the months in which they war born she could tell what had befallen them or might befall them afterwards. . . ." That admission was her undoing. She was ordered to appear before the Presbytery for further examination and on the 15th of the following month our minister came to the pulpit and informed the congregation that before the Presbytery had the chance to examine her she had drowned herself. It was a great deal easier death than the one which she would have been called upon to face.

In 1727 Scotland smelled the reek of a burning witch for the last time. A woman was found "guilty of riding upon her daughter, who had been transformed into a pony and shod by the devil." The daughter was spared the burning but "her mother was burned in a pitch barrel at Dornoch, tradition telling how, in the cold day, the poor creature warmed her feet at the fire that was to kindle her barrel-coffin." Thirty-four years earlier the last witch was put to death in the U.S.A. at Salem. Within four months in that year of 1693 twenty supposed witches were put to death there.*

From the pulpit we learned news of the nation and heard the rumble of distant drums. In the troubled 1640s they were only made too well aware of the strife for power. In November 1643 the Solemn League and Covenant was read and the congregation were warned to subscribe it the following week. The minister in

* Henry Grey Graham, *Social Life in Scotland in the eighteenth century*. Adam and Charles Black, 1909.

warmly recommending it to them "did preche behoovefullie for that purpose shewing the laughfulness (lawfulness), expediencie and utilitie of the said League and Covenant." In the following May he thundered out the excommunication of the Marquess of Huntly, Sir John Gordon of Haddo, Alexander Irving of Drum and his brother Robert and others. In September Montrose sacked Aberdeen and the kirk session dared not meet. On March 9th next the minister was forced to flee and did not return until April 4th. In August 1646 our minister sonorously intoned a list of Scottish lairds declared excommunicated, the Earls of Seaforth and Airlie among them. But in spite of all this, there was still thought given to generous actions to relieve the unfortunate. Supplies were sent by the congregation in 1647 to Aberdeen to relieve the suffering from the plague that raged there; just as twelve years before we had collected 53 merks for the distressed people of Orkney and Caithness, and a month or two earlier £3 12s. for the relief of prisoners taken by the Turks. For a more specific purpose in 1679, a collection was "intimated for relief of John Aitchison, skipper Pittenweem and his maryners captured by the Turks". How the sum of a few pounds subscribed in heavy copper coinage ever reached the Turks is an interesting question. Our Scots coinage then was very complicated being worth one twelfth of the corresponding sterling denomination. Starting at the bottom with a dyot, it had bodles, placks, groats, farthings, bawbees, shillings and merks before we reached a pound.

The word bawbee, that is still sometimes used in the corruption of "bas billon" or base bullion. All administrative acts, of parish-wide dimension, were intimated from the pulpit. We prayed gratefully for the Restoration of the Stuarts in 1660 in the person of Charles II. Four years later we prayed against the Pentland Rising of the Covenanters. In 1683 we thanked God for Charles II's escape from the Rye House plotters and two years later we disowned Monmouth and his rebellion. Three years afterwards we thanked God that King James had been sent packing. In our century and half of the lordship of the Lyon family there was an interval when the barony was sold to John Udny of Udny and Newburgh. Of the ancient family of Udny Castle, he and his brother had made a considerable fortune as merchants in Amsterdam. He also acquired Knockhall Castle which dominates Newburgh and the windings of the Ythan. He was a strong anti-Covenanter but was forced eventually to subscribe it. At that time the countryside swarmed with beggars who were a menace to the whole community. The Kirk Session licensed a certain number who were allowed to beg in a certain parish and wore a badge to show their authorisation. In December 1635 we appointed "two men to be sergeants for the repelling of strange beggars" and the Laird of Udny undertook to pay the wages of one of them. But there must have been some confusion about their duties because a few weeks later it was announced from the pulpit that no one was allowed to call them "by the disgraceful name of sodgers". The laird had to produce 12s. weekly as wages and four pairs of shoes and a suit of grey apparel for him every year.

In 1690 Thomas Ruddiman, afterwards to be famous as a grammarian and a man of letters, set off from Boyndlie in Banff to Aberdeen. He was 16 years old and, without telling his parents, was come to compete for the annual prize at King's College for classical learning. He arrived penniless having been seized and robbed by beggars on the way. Scotland and the world nearly lost a great economist thirty-six years later, when the three-year-old Adam Smith was stolen by them from the doorway of his kinsman's house near Kirkcaldy, and was only rescued by the speedy pursuit and resolution of his relatives.

William and Mary came and went, and when Queen Anne was truly dead, the Jacobites challenged the Georges of Hanover in vain and we came to the nineteenth century.

In the eighteenth century the parish produced men whose names were known far beyond the borders of their country, but in the hands of the York Buildings Company the lot of those of the land was hard. Through its period of coming to life one man was minister, the Reverend Alexander John Forsyth. A few houses of that century stand today, some like Orrok to intrigue you as to what their inmates were like.

If you drive northwards along the coast road from Balmedie you will come to the Blairton Inn on your left, a quarter of a mile before you come to our old ruined kirk and the manse on your right. On the skyline above the Blairton Inn you will see the house of Orrok, comely if forbidding, staring seawards from the crest of a grassy ridge. The estate is a good deal older than that house, which dates from the late eighteenth-century. Once called Over-Blairton it became known as North and South Colpnay, up to the time of its being acquired by a representative of the Fifeshire family, the Orroks of Orrok, who renamed it accordingly. John Orrok, who built the house and changed the name, is said to have been a captain in the Merchant Service. He and his family enjoyed it for a century or so, and then disappeared as their forbears have disappeared from Fife. Set on that ridge the house has a curious air of purpose, as it stares seawards. Many who have owned that land have found themselves embroiled in the troubles of their times.

The Wood family had it for perhaps 200 years. At the beginning of the seventeenth-century Alexander Wood is mentioned in a Proceeding against Gordon of Gicht, a family who sturdily stuck to the Papacy. This same Alexander is mentioned in the Proceeding against Lord Glamis, who was tried and eventually acquitted for the slaughter of Patrick Johnstone of Mosstown at Belhelvie Kirk.

In 1630 there occurred, what Scottish history will always remember, the Fire of Frendraught. Sir James Crighton of Frendraught, who was quarelling with the Gordons, had slain Gordon of Rothiemay and paid the blood money adjudged against him by the Marquess of Huntly. He took under his roof as guests at the Castle of Frendraught Lord Melgum, Huntly's son, and the young Lord of Rothiemay and others. The evening was spent in good cheer and the guests betook themselves to bed in the old tower. About midnight the old tower burst into a blaze of fearful fury. Their escape was cut off and they were burned to death wrenching in their torment at the iron bars on the windows. A Commission of six members, among whom were the Earl Marischal and the Bishops of Aberdeen and Moray found that the fire was no accident, but laying no specific charge against person. Sir James Crighton, in his own defence, had three persons brought to trial on suspicion of causing it. And one of them was Margaret Wood of this same Belhelvie family, who was suspected of being "airt and pairt" in this matter. Margaret was brought to the Tollbooth at Edinburgh where she was tortured until it became pointless and only too plain that she had no knowledge of the matter.

In 1708 the Reverend Alexander Mitchell, the minister at Belhelvie acquired from James, Earl of Panmure, a tenure of North Colpnay. His son, Alexander, succeeded and married the daughter of the minister of Fintray. It was in the 1740s that there was an "excessive and long-continued drought" which brought hard times to Aberdeen. We fasted on July 13th of that year as a prayerful gesture for the relief of it. For some years past a hideous traffic had been carried on between Aberdeen and the North American colonies. Boys were kidnapped in the streets and confined in a building, with a piper outside to drown their cries. There they were hidden until a vessel arrived and they were shipped across to the American plantations. Sometimes parents were driven, from grinding poverty, to sell their own sons to those who ran this cruel commerce. It would not be surprising if some did so in the hungry years of the 1740s. But one of those who was kidnapped in May 1743*, at the age of ten, lived to make history. By 1747 he had earned his freedom in North America and set himself up in a farm there. He was captured by Indians and escaped, and then joined the British forces, from which he was invalided out with a wound in the hand in 1757. He was discharged at Portsmouth and furnished with a gratuity of 6s. to take him to Aberdeen. He published a book the year after called *Curious Adventures of Peter Williamson*. It was strictly factual, and left nothing to the imagination, and implicated certain magistrates of Aberdeen by name. They ordered the book to be burned by the common hangman and banished him. He took the case to the High Court in Edinburgh and the guilty parties were dragged out into the limelight, although they were never adequately punished. One of them was Alexander Mitchell of Colpnay, son of our minister and son-in-law of another.

The Mitchells went their way and the Orrocks came. John, the first one died in 1799, and his son Walter succeeded him. Thirteen years later Walter was succeeded by his own brother John, a captain in the 17th Regiment of the Honourable East India Company's Service, who had been invalided back from India on half pay. His memorial tablet in the old Kirk states that he died suddenly on October 16th, 1823 in his fortieth year, from a burst blood vessel. But belief is strong in the parish to this day, that his wife pushed him out from one of that line of third floor windows of Orrok that stares down at you as you pass. That rumour has endured strongly for a hundred and thirty years. They were all gone from the home which alone perpetuates the name.

The "Resurrectionists" as some called the Body-snatchers, came to us at that time, in search for bodies to sell to the medical profession. They came in the dark of night. Our famous minister,

* He was shipped off on the slave-ship *Planter*, Captain Robert Ragg which was wrecked on a sandbank off Cape Ray at the mouth of the Delaware River.

Alexander Forsyth, found a body that they had lifted and then discarded as being too far gone in decomposition. He had a parish vault built to be proof against them.

Knockhall Castle looks down on the Ythan estuary and the country round, roofless and eyeless since the fire that gutted its sixteenth-century elegance two hundred years back. It was then the property of Udny of Udny, whose family had held the Barony of Belhelvie for the span of a life in the days of the King's men. The records of this ancient family were saved from the fire by the strength and presence of mind of the celebrated Jamie Fleeman, the laird's fool. Dashing into the charter room, whose door the flames had reached, he picked up the iron charter chest, which was said to take three ordinary men to lift, and flung it through the window, oak framework, glass and all. Jamie was a famous character in this part of the world, and one of the last of his kind. His master got from him a great deal of amusement and a dog-like devotion, which he returned with a good deal of affection and no little regard. In the Middle Ages the position of a fool in a household must have been a well-paid one and the law required you to be genuinely daft before you could qualify for the position. A Scottish Act of Parliament of January 19th, 1449, is entitled "An Act for the away-putting of Feynet Fools". If a feigned fool was detected, or as the Act says, "only that makes them foolis that are nocht" they were to receive punishment for the first offence by having their ears cut off, and the second offence by being hanged.

Jamie's lack of mental balance showed in his irrational likes and dislikes, but he had powers of repartee that would have made the fortune of any T.V. virtuoso of today. An arrogant laird once asked him haughtily "Whose fool are you?" and got back the answer "I'm Udny's fool, whose fool are ye?". His powers of invention were astonishing. Occasionally the unwise would try to lead him on and test his credibility to turn the laugh on him. Such a one asked him if he had heard the news that seven miles of the sea at Newburgh had been burned up that morning. It drew the immediate and unruffled reply from Jamie that the same morning he had seen "a flock of skate about breakfast time flying past Waterton to the woods of Tolquhon maybe to big (nest) there." On one occasion he found himself in action against another fool who claimed that he had the previous day, seen red cabbage stalks near Ellon so high that you could not reach the top of them without taking a harrow and using it as a ladder. Jamie replied, without emotion, that he had gone to get a creel of cockles and dived to the seabed, when he was terrified to encounter a skate so big that it would cover seven parishes. Jamie sleeps in the churchyard at Longside, and his grave is marked by a pillar of granite, in answer to his dying wish—"I am a Christian, dinna bury me like a beast."

The Reverend Mr Forsyth has left us a very complete picture of the parish as it was in the early nineteenth century, as one would expect from a minister of the Gospel who was also an accomplished scholar, scientist and sportsman. He lived through a period that felt an earthquake of change. In the forty-five years from 1791 he tells us that a third more land was brought into farming use in the parish, and the population rose by 322 from 1318 to 1640. There were then fifteen landowners with rentals varying from £80 to £900 a year. Trees were now being planted, most of them in hedgerows, few of which remain today. Sheep were few and were black-faced, the cattle of the "improved Aberdeenshire breed" were being bred in quite large numbers for the London market. Grain seems to have been staple and the average yield is given as three and a half quarters to an acre. There were about ten thousand acres, so he says, under turnips, potatoes, hay, pasture, grass, etc. But he found that writing round asking questions of his parishioners drew so many different answers that he does not claim for his figures more than an approximate accuracy. And he does not go far into detail. In his own words ". . . though considerable pains have been bestowed to ascertain the quantity and value of the whole of the agricultural produce of the parish, the reports given by different persons are so various and so discordant that it is thought best to say nothing on the subject."

The population rose steadily until 1881, when agriculture fell into that decline from which it was rescued by the needs in the second World War, more than half a century later. In the ten years until 1891 the population of the parish fell by 237, most of whom it was said emigrated to the Dominions. The tide of emigration never ceases but it ebbs as well as flows. In 1873 one hundred and twenty people from Kintore, with some others from Buchan, emigrated in a body to New Brunswick to form the townships of Stonehaven and Kincardine in that beautiful forest Province. Crossing the ocean took a fortnight, and in the course of it a child was born and baptised Castalia Butler Ferguson Brown Morison—rather a mouthful of names for a girl. She was christened Castalia after the name of the ship, Butler after her captain, Ferguson after the ship's doctor, and Brown from a captain of the Anchor Line who had planned the whole Odyssey. This lady lived on into the 1960s, having crossed and re-crossed the ocean between New Brunswick and Aberdeenshire several times in the ensuing ninety years.

The minister was plainly proud of his parishioners. They ". . . may be said to be intellectual, spiritual, moral and religious". Plainly also, the state of grace of the parishioners must be in part, due to their spiritual leader. He mentions the Savings Bank in the parish which held £600 of their savings, but does not mention that he founded it. Of the 1,640 parishioners thirty were in receipt of parochial aid in the sum not exceeding £2 a year. They were a proud people and did not like taking the parish charity. "The poor in general," he comments, "are unwilling at first to put upon the poor's roll." There were few who were deeply afflicted. Two were blind, four were "fatuous" and one was insane. This last was lodged in a lunatic asylum at Aberdeen at an annual cost to the parish of £15.

Today we have three schools in the parish, to one of which our daughter Susan went as a very small child. She not only got a first-class education there, but was extremely happy into the bargain. Children now tend to be taken to the schools at Aberdeen. It is part of that drawing power that cities exert on the countryside around them. But in 1840 there were four schools with 120 scholars, and the many subjects they studied included Greek, Latin, geography and navigation. Very few were, we are told, between the age of six and fifteen were not able to read and "many of them can write." Our old gamekeeper at our childhood home in England used to make a great distinction between these two arts. He always said that he could read reading but that he couldn't read writing. Many of the children would have walked a long way to school and got there red-faced and cheerful, as they do today. It must have been much more exciting watching the coaches, of which three made the return journey each day— than motor cars of the present. Though probably the ships of today are just as exciting as the full-rigged ships that their forbears watched in the old days. Their up-bringing was conditioned by a blend of oatmeal and peat smoke, as only the more opulent bought coals from Aberdeen or the little seaport of Newburgh. Oatmeal was a great element in all men's lives in those days. The minister's stipend was £53 11s. 2d. and 106 bolls of oatmeal (with nearly 10 stones to a boll) and 42 2/5 quarters of bear, which was a variety of barley. His kirk, which now looks so tiny as a ruin, contained space for 519 worshippers, each one renting his "sitting room" for 1s. to 2s. a year, but they commonly assembled between 600 and 700 strong and packed the little building. Again a matter of pride for Mr. Forsyth. Five hundred and fifty commonly took Communion and the congregation was some 1,400 in all. It was a long walk for some when the weather was wild. On our two Communion Sundays today you will see more than sixty motorcars outside the church. In the old days the collection was about £57 a year, and there is a famous picture by a Scottish Academician, of the taking of it in that tiny church by a very old man in a tartan plaid, thrusting a box with a handle like a broom into the lap of one of the parishioners.

The only other kirk in those days was a very small one which catered for 200 Dissenters. Their minister received £70 a year, which came from pew rents and subscribers, but no oatmeal.

A century passed, wars shook Britain and the world. We looked out no longer across the German Ocean but the North Sea. The population fell to some 300 below the high peak of 1881. A tiny industry in the form of the Seaton Brick and Tile Works was set up on the south border of the parish for the purpose which its name implies. It flourished for a good many years and was responsible for the first brick houses to invade these granite dwelling latitudes. A granite quarry grew up in Belhelvie village in 1919 with its workers housed in neat stone cottages. It employs nearly fifty men and produces road metal and cement fence posts. Twice a day they fire explosive charges, at mid-day and evening, as beautifully spaced as the salute of guns. In damp weather the fumes of the explosives are slow to disperse and make men sick who smell them. The need for sand for cement brought men searching for sand in the parish back in the 1930s, and from then onwards there have always been working sandpits. In 1920 the first tractor came to the parish, but many of the fields are too weep for a tractor, and you will still see fine plough horses at stork, with an entourage of seagulls. The distant crackle of military small arms comes from Black Dog Range in the links where our local regiment, the Gordon Highlanders train. Once a year a Wappenshaw is held at which anyone can try his skill for a prize. Now cars hurry along the old coach roads looking like an irregular string of lighted beads, as you watch them distantly in the dusk while you wait for the wildfowl. The noise of them is lost in the sound of the sea, unless it is a very calm evening. Huge lorries thunder along them on errands which are mostly with the rich farmlands further north. And buses, lit at night like liners at sea, bear the names of the various northern destinations. And so all this hurry, to and from Aberdeen and the farmlands and sea-ports of Buchan, passes us by. We have our own world in Bel-helvie parish.

It is not that we do not travel. We go to the ends of the earth and return to the parish. We come from the ends of the earth and settle down and look as if we had come from no further afield than Aberdeen. It has always been so. In centuries past so many sons of the small lairds and the larger farmers took service in European armies and later in the forces of the East India Company. Others joined the Hudson Bay Company's as arctic fur traders, as I did myself, and they still continue to do so. We have left deep footprints in India, Pakistan and the Far East as well. The world is still our parish. My friend who keeps one of the shops in the parish got that limp at Alamein for six bullets in one machine-gun burst. His nearby competitor in business, was cook to, and one of the few survivors of, a doomed prospecting expedition at Chester-field Inlet in sub-Arctic Canada. It is very unwise in North-east Scotland to boast in a public place of distant travel or of the speaking of strange tongues. Still less to believe that you are the only one who can speak Cree Indian, Malay or Chinyanja. Taking the road north past Balmedie House built by the Lumsden who came from Bombay, you come to one more park wall before you sight the Smithy at Menie which tells you that you have reached our northern border. Menie House, which has associations with Robert the Bruce, was owned when we came here first by a retired merchant from Java. The Far East is, after Canada, our overseas parish. The Potterton Home Farm, just across our little burn was acquired a few years ago by one who had planted rubber in Indonesia for thirty years. The only other two buildings equally near to our house are the old water mill and the retired roadman's cottage. The mill used to be run by two brothers in partnership until some years ago one left for Alberta to take a job in Medicine Hat.

The retired roadman is something of an exception. Some fifty years ago he went to Canada to a town in Eastern Ontario, close by the county whose local regiment I commanded in the last war. He did not like it and returned. That is almost unique. In Belhelvie most regard the sister nations of the Commonwealth as being no further away, and at least as familiar as the next county. But Canada we do not regard as being in any way distant. And that is not merely the case with the old and middle-aged. A young district nurse, who served us well a few years back, had spent three very happy years nursing in St. Katherines, Ontario.

That wide world is our opportunity, but Scotland is our home. We live near the city. We see its spire and chimneys from our ridges and our rounded hills. But we live close to the land in Belhelvie. Few of us would exchange it for anywhere else.

7   *Familiars*

SOME of the greatest figures in Britain's history, as well as
so many of the rest of us, have felt the need for the close
companionship of an animal. Modern analysts of human
behaviour tell us that we like the feeling of something depending
on us. That can only be part of the truth as anyone knows who
loves hawks or horses, dogs or cats, because we realise that we
equally depend on them. Prince Rupert, the great cavalry leader,
founder of the Hudson's Bay Company, and an examplar of so
many of the arts and sciences, is said to have been almost incon-
solable when his white dog Boy was killed in action at Marston
Moor, "more prized by his master than creatures of much more
worth."* This was the "divil dog pudle" of the Puritan pam-
pheteers who attributed Rupert's apparently charmed life to

* John Vicars, *God's Ark.*

protection from a devil who followed him about, for greater convenience, in the guise of a dog. Animal lovers make no bones about their dogs and cats and horses and birds being familiar spirits, but spirits having a loyalty, a fondness and an understanding often sufficient to shame humanity. Between a man and his beast there is a sympathy unlike in its quality to anything that is shared between man and man.

Sir Walter Scott kept a whole pack of dogs but to Camp, his bull-terrier, he used to talk as if he was a man, and a man of his own age.

Probably the only living thing in the proximity of Sir Winston Churchill, which did not hold him in awe, was his poodle Rufus, and between them was a bond of deep affection.

We had brought to Potterton the dogs with which Ella our Braemar housekeeper had surrounded herself, and for all practical purposes owned, and which migrated with her a few weeks later.

In the great gale of 1953 much of our little world blew down, after only a month of its enjoyment. We started in to rebuild it, feeling as Noah and his wife may have felt when the ark grounded after the Flood. We set about planting a new forest and in furbishing it with all sorts of new birds. We started the year after the gale and, rather defiantly, bought two pairs of Lady Amherst pheasants. They were the most beautiful of birds with their white and black mantled necks and long tails flecked with crimson. We also bought a large striding silver pheasant cock with two of the longest and wickedest spurs imaginable. He had a mate, who soon departed. We bought him another mate, and she departed too. We found the second one living peacefully with a farmer's hens down by the sea, until she too disappeared. The idea behind all this was that we might breed up a stock of coloured pheasants. No poulterer would buy them to hang up in his shop, since they would be so instantly recognisable, we thought that they might enjoy comparative safety from 'marauders. The Lady Amherst's stayed all through the following winter. But we never saw them after that. A countryman is supposed to have put up one of the cocks beside the road. It is said that the sight of this superb apparition gave him such a shattering surprise that he never touched another drop. The silver pheasant, on the contrary, stayed with us for several years. He had a bullying nature, frequently going off to the farms and savaging the hens. His long sharp spurs made him far more than a match for any rooster.

He was dull-looking in appearance until he grew his full plumage in October, and then he was superb and would strut about showing off his long silver fountain of a tail. People who had hardly heard of us had heard of him. He died eventually in a silver shower of feathers, run over on the stretch of road by our gate where he used to show himself off.

At about the same time we acquired some jungle fowl. These, common from Indochina to Malaysia, are birds of the thick jungle. The jungle fowl is handsomely marked and rather like a bantam, only bigger. Like the bantam, the hens make wonderful mothers, and we once put four mallards' eggs under one of these very small birds, and she hatched them out and brought them up. They stubbornly refused to recognise that the spring does not come at the same time in Aberdeenshire as it does in Malaysia, and used to start laying their eggs in December, and the cold spells would often freeze them. But they succeeded in hatching several broods each year and, like true birds of the jungle, would lead them off into the long grass and the dark shade. These little troupes became smaller and smaller as the months wore on, and the crows and the weasels took their toll, although the jungle foul were doughty fighters. We once found a dying rook, close beside one of our jungle fowl's nests, with marks on its neck that were plainly from the jungle cock's spurs. When they took to the air, as they sometimes did, they wavered between the trees like woodcock. As splendid eating birds, and fast flyers, they have been domesticated as game birds in places where they can breed well.

But the real drawback of the jungle fowl was that the cocks were liable to crow at any time during the night, piercingly and from close at hand. Wan, sleepless guests took to eyeing them malevolently. They died out in the end, for the cocks wandered away, and after about three or four generations our diminishing flock perished through one mischance or another. We never bought any more, and called a halt for a time to these exotic activities.

Nearly four years later, in August, we tried again, but this time with bob white quails which are at home in Georgia and the Southern States of the U.S.A. They have a pleasant, whirring form of conversation, which is supposed to sound like "Bob White, Bob White . . .". One could make out just as good a case for translating their chatter as the repeating of the words "Board of

Trade," or "National Gallery". We had a dozen of them and knocked stakes into the ground in an enclosure of young trees and made a tent of strawberry netting over them. The first night Susie tiptoed down to see them at last light and hurried back to summon us to look at them. It was a sight worth seeing. For the quails had formed a tight defensive circle, with all twelve beaks and twelve pairs of boot-button eyes facing outwards. On the day before we planned to lift a corner of the netting, and let them find their feet in freedom, a cat broke in and killed several of them, while others killed themselves trying to escape. Two only survived and happily they were a pair. We bought another pair and let them live wild. They were devoted couples and were full of charm, and pretty with their white cheeks and their crests. They had a way of standing that made them look like pairs of Easter eggs on legs. Then, in the course of the winter, one pair disappeared. In the following May the remaining cock went. But he had not reckoned with the power of the press. *The Ellon and District Advertiser* (May 21st, 1965) had a headline on page two, "An escapee bob white quail on Donside." It carried a report received from Fintray (about seven miles away) of the sighting of a quail, clearly a bob-white, which was suspected of belonging to us. James Robertson had now succeeded George Farquhar as our gardener, caretaker and everything else and he set off to try to catch it, but failed to find it. On May 28th, *The Inverurie and District Advertiser,* on the first page announced in heavy type, "Bob-white quail re-captured at Blairdaff." It described how it had been seen by a locomotive driver just off Constitution Street in Inverurie (about thirteen miles away) and was caught in a strawberry net by a powerful posse, formed to deal with this emergency, about six miles further on.

But they all disappeared in the end and we reckoned them lost until our neighbour across the burn, who having spent thirty years in Indonesia knows a quail when he sees one, came on a thriving family of them a year later, perhaps a mile from Potterton. That was the end of our bird breeding experiments until in 1966, when we were given thirty pheasant eggs. Whatever economists may say to the contrary, nothing is more expensive in the long run, than the free gift of a living creature. In due course, and after much spending and the making of things like wire pens for which no possible further use could be found, we converted thirty free pheasant eggs into thirteen unbelievably expensive grown-up pheasants, ten of which were cocks. For a short confiding period they walked about our policies and along the garden paths, and we took as much pleasure in them as Disraeli did from his peacocks on the lawns at Hughenden. Then they quietly disappeared, occasionally returning to depart again.

Perhaps the taming of wild things is part of the particular spell of this parish. At Belhelvie Lodge old Sir Henry Lumsden, the founder of the old Indian Army's Corps of Guides and a keen shot, domesticated a complete covey of partridges who would sit on the steps of the house with him. His present-day successor, also of Indian Army fame, was adopted (it was that way round) by a hen pheasant that became completely tame to the extent of being on good terms with all his cats, and nesting beside the house.

We acquired stray and occasional pets for, when Susie was a small child, she was forever finding damaged seagulls and crows and pigeons, and bringing them back, or making us bring them back, and trying to cure them. We never succeeded. Of these, seagulls, who seem easily to injure themselves, were by far the most numerous. We collected several hedgehogs, for these are common in August in this part of the country. Twice we put one in the walled garden, but this ended in tragedy. They tried to get out and failed, and eventually pined away and died, so we did not do this again. On two other occasions we put them inside rabbit wire enclosure. They climbed out with consummate ease and that was the last that we ever saw of them. Although none stayed with us, of their own free will, yet they would eat bread and milk beside us as the tamest of pets.

Susie was a very small girl when horses started to take a greater and greater hold on her imagination. An era had begun. It was started by her looking at pictures of horses, and then it came to cutting them out, then to drawing them. And then to leaning over fences and looking at them. Finally there was steady and insistent propaganda about learning to ride, followed by the idea of having a pony. When she was about six years old we yielded. We were able to borrow a charming little brown pony called Petronella from a kindly neighbour for the summer holidays. Petronella behaved beautifully unless she saw another horse set off at a gallop, in which case she did the same. As we had no other horses she was a model of calm and decorum, but very difficult to budge into a trot or more than a trot. Our surroundings should be a wonderful riding country, with its rolling downs of green pastures within the lines of stone dykes. The gates in these dykes are formidable obstacles as they are often bound up at both ends with wire, so that one has to get off one's horse and secure him, wrestle with the wire and lift the gate—steer the horse through—and then go through the whole process in reverse. But I used to have a lot of pleasant exercise wandering round the countryside of a summer evening, opening and shutting gates, with the clop of Petronella's hooves just behind me and the encouragement from Susie, "Trot, Daddy, trot" which would often spur Petronella into following me at the same pace. Petronella served her purpose admirably, as Susie's first steed, and then departed to have a foal.

Our next step was far more daring. We bought her a pony of her own. It was called Coronation, was half Arab, and stood fourteen hands. It had acquired its name through being born on the night of the last Coronation. Susie was taught to ride at Belhelvie Lodge, a square Georgian house three quarters of a mile up the burn. It would be impossible to imagine two better neighbours than its owners the late Tom Duguid and his wife. He had spent most of his life soldiering in India and Burma, and, even then was one of the best show jumpers in this country. And it was riding at Belhelvie Lodge that he came by his end and he could not have wished to have gone in a better way. Susie had a splendid introduction to riding. Coronation usually behaved well when Tom rode beside him on his big horse. But there were mutinous moments when Coronation was bored, or decided to go home, or was bothered by the flies, and it became clear that a very small girl could not hold him against his will, and could have no real mastery until she had grown up to him. The gap of growing up was bridged by a splendid little shaggy Shetland pony, whose real name we never knew, but whom we called Bumble. That was short for Bumblebee. She was expecting a foal but was in no way embarrassed by that and used to gallop flat out, up and down hills, mane and tail flying, with Susie holding on wild with excitement, and Priscilla following on Coronation. Priscilla had been taught to ride properly and in the English way. I had never been taught but have done quite a lot of riding with the cowboys, and was used to the deep cowboy saddle, and riding for the purpose of getting from one place to another. But I wanted to join in. So we acquired the best, and most comfortable, and easiest of all saddles, the Australian stock saddle. Australian saddles seem to be made of a much softer leather and the Australian stock saddle is far more comfortable than its Western counterpart. You sink into it and you have the reassurance of the bucking flaps under which you can put your knees if you run into trouble.

Bumble was eventually returned to its owner and that meant, for Susie, that it was Coronation or nothing. About that time we managed to buy a piebald pony that we christened Pinto. She settled down well enough. But it soon became clear that she was going to have a foal. Pinto was just the right size for Susie. She had the most comical piebald appearance which made her very conspicuous at pony club rallies. But she had one terrible habit which was of jumping out of her field, and more than once she jumped into the enclosures of my young trees. As she was as conspicuous as a zebra she was seen before she had an opportunity to do too much damage. We were all away during the week and could not leave her alone with her foal arriving. So we sent her to a farmer who took in foaling ponies, and had a farm on the hilltop just above Potterton village.

The foal was born at an unusually convenient time, in Susie's Easter holidays. She and I went up to collect it one Sunday morning. We had two parish churches at that time. Services were held for three Sundays of the month in the north church, and in the south church, close to that farm, on the fourth Sunday. It was the fourth Sunday, and a warm sunny day, when we walked to meet the farmer. He put a halter on Pinto and we set off for home down the farm road, to join the country road which passes the church, the foal following. The church was surrounded by the cars of those who were worshipping inside and we had about three quarters of a mile to cover to the house, in the half an hour before the congregation could be expected to appear. We heard the singing of hymns from within and the sound of larks from above us.

There are some false propositions which are repeated from mouth to mouth from generation to generation. One of them is that a foal will follow its mother, calm and docile, just behind her hooves. That is what we had all been led to expect. Instead of a pleasant trudge in spring sunlight, it was the longest three quarters of a mile that I have ever had to cover. Once past the church all would go well for perhaps twenty yards, and then the foal would stop, and then Pinto would stop, and then the foal would move a few steps back and Pinto would show signs of standing up on her hind legs. We would make a net gain of ground perhaps in three movements out of five. So when half an hour had passed we were hot and distraught and only three quarters of the way upon our journey. And then the little church disgorged its congregation, who got into their cars and the road filled up behind us. They were all dressed in their Sunday best, and we were dressed in clothes suitable for catching ponies. We felt, as we looked, fustian and furtive. Being country people, the congregation had far too much good sense, to say nothing of good manners, to hoot their horns. But the cars became densely packed and moved as we moved, stopping and starting, varied with standing for quite long periods. Then a man came out of the cottage where the water diviner lived, and helped us mightily by shooing the foal from behind, and not many minutes later we reached the top of our drive. At that point the foal firmly refused to take another step and showed every sign of turning round and retracing its steps to the farm from which it had come. Farquhar, the gardener, came to our help from his cottage at the end of the drive, and by vigorous shooing we managed to make it, and its mother, go into the field, and the gate was shut. It was well worth the effort. For to have a pony and its foal close to your house is a source of delight and amusement.

It was not many months since we had decided that we could not afford a pony. We had then gone so far as to say that we might just be able to undertake the immense extravagance of having one. Now, after this surprising sequence of events, we found that we had three. Time went on and we found ourselves less and less capable of dealing with this situation, pleasant as it was. The foal became large and boisterous and needed breaking, and started jumping out like its mother. Then with great regret we had to sell them both. But by that time Susie had grown up to Coronation.

In the long, cold winters of 1962 and 1963 Coronation looked extremely forlorn. In the winter he grew a long coat and looked like a woolly bear. As his winter hair was a white and silvery brindle, he looked drab against the snow. At vast expense we had a stable built for him in his field, but the worse the weather the more determined he seemed to be not to use it. For one summer it had only two tenants, a blackbird nesting in the rafters, and a swarm (or whatever is the collective noun) of wasps, who contrived a nest like a Chinese lantern of grey paper. Coronation got very low when the snow was on the ground, despite the fact that we fed him liberally. He was wont to stand for a long time in one place, and the warmth of his hooves would melt the snow and ice underneath, so that he was always standing in wet. In the worst of the bitter winter of 1962-3 we were so worried about him that we shipped him off to the warmth, and comparative comfort, of a riding school.

When spring came Susie groomed him incessantly, as she did all the year round, and from the brush were combed swathes of white and silver grey hair. He would roll on the ground and leave a patch of hair behind him. Then the birds came and put that hair in their nests. We collected his hair for the birds. Almost all the chaffinches' and the greenfinches' nests had Coronation's hair in them, some being entirely lined with it. As a boy I unravelled an old greenfinch's nest and took all the horse hairs out of it, and found that there were forty feet of them. Birds like greenfinches must be hard pressed in parts of the country from which the horse has practically disappeared.

Susie grew out of Coronation in 1963. We bought from Tom Duguid a horse with an outstanding history, called Galway Bay. He was tall, over sixteen hands, handsome and had performed notably in the Horse of the Year competition at Olympia. He was a very good jumper. In the middle of January 1964, he came to live in the little stable at Potterton, which had been made to hold a pony that pulled a gig, and it was a close fit. His big hooves rang on the road as he went backwards and forwards between Potterton and Belhelvie. Galway Bay and Susie went round the circuit of the Summer Shows. They returned with some ribbons and many placards of Highly Commended, Second, and even a First to show for it. His performance was good and his manners were faultless.

We had been dogless since Ella, our housekeeper, had left us not long after coming to Potterton. We used to tell ourselves that we could not have a dog, as we had to go down to London each week only returning at the weekends. Admittedly at Braemar there was a time when we had four. But they were all familiar spirits of Ella our housekeeper, rather than ours. Susie's first live possessions had been a pair of goldfish. They had thriven well enough in their bowl in the nursery, which was filled up from the bathroom tap, as long as we were on the old archaic water system with the ancient lead pipes. When that system finally fell to pieces, and we were put on the grid, it was replaced by raw new copper piping. The goldfish dwindled and died. We doubled the error by buying her two more which died, in just the same way, before we realised the cause. The idea of giving her a dog for her birthday had been one of those sudden enthusiasms which come upon parents. It came upon us in 1955. It was the only time that I have ever missed Susie's birthday. I was pioneering in Labrador that year, in connection with a now famous hydro-electric scheme, and had to be in a certain area at that particular date in August, So that on her birthday I was slapping flies beside a lake in that high wilderness of dwarfish trees, and muskeg swamp and streams. The night before a black, shaggy little Scottie terrier pup had been smuggled into Potterton, surprise being an important element of the occasion. There had been a great deal of squeaking and barking, and some nipping, but it had not reached Susie's ears. His name was Rory. He was bright-eyed and defiant, with two ears which did not stick up, but curled over in a comical way. He had teeth like thorns, which were employed on anything that he could find. He very soon discovered that he could stampede Susie, and would chase her along the passage until she jumped on her bed to get away from him. Terriers are supposed to be an ancient race. I say race, rather than breed. Their name comes from "terre," and they are literally "earthers". They are supposed to go back to the days of the Roman occupation. A figure of a dog found in the Roman wall, except for a curl in its tail, was very like a Scottie. *Encyclopedia Britannica* says that certain dogs and bears have common ancestry. If Rory's nose had been shorter, his ears round and his tail a mere token, he would have been a very passable imitation of a little black bear. Like a bear, his forepaws were enormous and in the same relation to his hind paws as you will see if you look at a bearskin. He seemed to belong to some category of mini-bear. Like most of his breed he did not seek the company of other dogs, and was hostile, and intensely provocative, when he met them. He hated collies. On one occasion he came back bruised, bleeding and without his collar. Although no one seemed to have been an eye witness, of what had been the fight of the century that had nearly cost him his life, yet the opinion of the countryside was that he had been attacked by two collies. He discovered an atrocious practice by the postman who, driving up to the back door, brought a collie in his van. Having unmasked him in this flagrant Trojan Horse conspiracy he has never felt the same again about postmen. But when those summer holidays came to an end an acute problem arose as to what to do with him when we were in London during the weekdays.

Susie had spent two very happy years at the village school at Potterton. At the tender age of seven we had sent her to a boarding school—or rather the boarding house of an Aberdeen day school. It was a boarding house designed for the daughters of those who were serving abroad. Rubber or tea planting was the commonest vocation of the absent parents. There were also those who, for some other reason, could not provide a day-to-day home to which their children could return in the evening, as it was in our own case. Those who ran it were kindness itself, and they accepted Rory into the school along with Susie. This was a splendid arrangement but it did not last for very long. For at the end of his second term Rory came back with an adverse report, having taken to digging in the flower beds, and we were thrown back on different resources. We had come to believe that if we could have one dog we could have two. The late Stephen Trevor of Auchmacoy, had a splendid golden labrador, who was one of the very few dogs I have ever seen who would go into the water and retrieve a wounded grey-lag goose, on a freezing cold night, with a four-knot tide running. Equally he would go into six or seven-foot-high sedge, with two or three inches of tidal water at the bottom of it, to look for a snipe, and find it. The son of this wonderful dog was not golden like his father but black, and his name was Sooty. We brought him up as a puppy and fell back on our kind neighbour Tom Duguid to look after him and give him most of his training. Sooty and Rory would spend the week there. Two dogs, particularly a big one and a small one, seem to possess some multiple of original sin far greater than the sum of the content that they each possess. There were some very awkward incidents, such as when they went off all night under the moon in lambing time. But they became tremendous friends. Sooty trained up to the point when he was a useful ally on an evening's duck flight and then, as sometimes happens with labradors, his whole training disappeared in a kind of amnesia. He never recovered it, and as he was proving very difficult to keep, being so much larger and more boisterous than Rory, we gave him to a family in Aberdeen as a pet, where he was very happy. In Rory's early days he only made about two visits to London in a year, and that was to have his coat trimmed. He would be converted in a couple of hours from looking like a sturdy little black bear to a trim, and almost sinuous, animal. (It is a mistake to think that dogs necessarily feel the cold more after they have been clipped. It is the last inch and a half of their hair that really keeps them warm.) He and Sooty had been looked after, while we were away in the week, by our neighbours at Belhelvie Lodge. But it became necessary to change that arrangement and Rory travelled with us to London and back every week in the guard's van. He had to spend most of his time with me as Priscilla could not take him into the House of Commons. I used to take him to my businesses and quite often he attended board meetings, there being no prohibition of such a practice in the Companies' Act of 1948.

When George Farquhar retired, around Christmas 1963, he bequeathed to us a bee-hive. James Robertson appeared with his luggage, on a large estate truck from Castle Fraser, which included several hives full of bees mercifully torpid with the cold of the winter. Our single hive was colonised from his supply. It stood on our back lawn, beside the air-raid shelter, with a rabbit enclosure round it to keep Rory from putting his inquisitive black nose into the slit that the bees use as a door. In the astonishing escalation, that seems to happen when one keeps live things, we now keep twenty hives, set well away in a small field beside our tiny park. We hope that one day they will help to keep us. We have now had several summers of them. They are far too mysterious for me to understand—being a mixture between a communist State and a constitutional monarchy. When Priscilla and James Robertson attire themselves in hats and veils and protective clothes I watch, in the most craven fashion, through field glasses. Sometimes the bees mutiny, which the Oxford Dictionary (1929) defines as "open revolt against constituted authority." The bees would deny this. But even to experts the ways of these strange creatures do not seem evenly predictable. They never seem to behave as books on bee-keeping suggest that they should. Keeping them is an endless adventure. Each year they journey to the heather, and the hives are grouped snugly in a quarry beside a moor of luxuriant heather where we visit them from time to time. At home the hives stand in neat lines in a little field and we have planted apple trees between them. Everything grows where there are bees. A year ago I made a big collection of the seeds of that lovely tree the London plane, from various London parks and gardens and filled seed box after seed box with them in Scotland. Only a handful germinated and the reason must be that there are very few bees in London and wind pollenation is a chancy business.

At the moment we have no precise plans for extending our range of familiar spirits. After a great deal of thought we turned down the gift of a West African lion. Having had quite a lot to do with them I felt that this was one of those activities that my old nanny would have warned against, as being likely "to end in tears".

If I ever retire I shall have time to keep hawks and fly them again. I should like to have a cheetah such as I had when I lived in Africa, but it is too cold for them. If you need the companionship of birds and beasts, in the capacity of familiar spirits, you will make sure of satisfying that need in some way. And we shall never again be without a dog and probably several other varied creatures.

We have recently acquired another dog, an Alsatian who grows as you watch him. He does not have the gait of a dog. He prowls, and quickens to a wolfish lope, ending in a gallop more like that of a horse than a dog. Which is not inappropriate for he is named Rupert after that greatest of all cavalry leaders, Prince Rupert. Beside him Rory moves from an amble, to a trundle, and then to a scamper with a powerful movement in reverse when he backs out of rabbit holes. Rupert seems a Don Quixote whose frolic fancy leads him to chase low-flying swallows and bite at the breeze. Beside him Rory is a shaggy Scottish Sancho Panza. You can never tell what you are going to acquire next.

8   *The Great Gale*

OUR first night under our new roof at Potterton was the last night of the year 1952. We spent the day exploring and the evening was, of course, Hogmanay. We had become the possessors of a tiny forest which encircled us on three sides. It followed the road from the old mill past the gates of the two drives, then landward along the top of the ridge facing the sea, where we border with a farmer neighbour, until it reached the burn again. It made a horseshoe of woodland, with its open side to the burn. There was some blown timber in the ravine, but little anywhere else. The trees looked as if they had all been planted about forty to fifty years before, and with very great care, but never have been tended or thinned since that time. One could plunge into this little forest, and have a continuous canopy of spruce and Scots pine and larch over one's head. Looking from the front door across the miniature park, with the three rather stunted lime trees in it, the further edge of the field was marked with a beautiful line of very tall beeches. Beyond it, and up to the road beyond, were two woods. The one on the left of the little paddock field was almost entirely made up of tall Norway spruces, and the one on the right was a mixture of conifers, with some oak and beech, ash and sycamore. In these sheltered pockets there were our few really tall trees. For in this part of the countryside few trees grow tall. When that December darkness came, and we were preparing our Hogmanay evening, I had shot four pigeons and had already made some plans for improving the forest. First there was to be thinning and selective cutting, and then replanting. All according to the book. It was going to take several years.

We settled down beside the fire to enjoy our Hogmanay and drank the health of the New Year several times over, and looked at our familiar possessions from Braemar grouped about these new rooms. As we still had my boyhood home of Elsfield, near Oxford, and my uncle Walter was still alive at Peebles, there was a very great deal of furnishing, and particularly of books and of pictures, for which we had not yet had to find room. But our plans made up for any lack of plenishing.

The University Professor of Forestry and his wife came to have tea with us on a Sunday afternoon, and we showed them our trees. He was a great expert, whose reputation went far beyond this country. He became just as interested as we were. When we got to the ravine he looked at the blown trees and gave his opinion that they must have come down in the storm of the previous January. But he added, reassuringly, that such storms as that were very uncommon and that there would probably not be one as bad again for another thirty years. And so we could lay our plans in our own time.

For the week following New Year, and the next two weekends from London, we explored the forest. Small as it was, it was just possible to lose your way in it briefly. As you made your way up through the closely clustered stems, towards the top of the hill, you nearly always appeared at a different point from that which you had expected. There were pigeons in plenty, but they were hard to shoot; for once they were under that canopy you could not see them, and if you stood outside the canopy they could see you only too easily. This is the eternal enigma of pigeon shooting, and one of the things that makes it so fascinating.

On our fifth weekend Priscilla, having come up a day before, met me at Aberdeen station off the train in the early hours of Friday morning. It was January 31st, 1953. One had only to step out on to the platform to realise it was blowing hard, and realise it even more vividly when one left the station. It seemed a splendid day to go after duck or pigeons (with that very high wind). The last stars were dimming as we reached the end of the long drive at Potterton. It is long only in comparison with the other one, and is perhaps half a mile in length. The trees were bowing and tossing as we went down the drive, and a spindly Scots pine had tipped on its side just allowing the car to go underneath, brushing against the top as we went. It was the first of our trees to fall. Then we sat down to breakfast. Darkness was disappearing and the sleeping pigeons were beginning to take shape in the beech trees across the little park opposite, their silhouettes rising and falling with the swaying branches. We were in country clothes, the log-fire crackled, the smell of wood smoke mingled with the smell of breakfast, and we were enjoying the peace of the country. We had two days of it ahead of us.

Within an hour or so we were to know why January 31st, 1953 was to be so memorable a date. A year later, when all the enquiries were complete and the truth of what happened that day was known, as far as it ever could be known, a number of learned papers were published and one excellent book.* This book dealt with the sagas of some few of the ships at sea that day. To read it was to realise, for the first time, what had happened beyond the confines of our square mile world of bewildered birds and toppling trees. From it I have borrowed from the grim sequence of that day's events to set our own scene in some sort of perspective.

Unknown to us, on the western side of Britain, during the previous evening, a tempest like the scourge of God had come shrieking out of the North Atlantic to reach Cape Wrath by dusk. Driving the Atlantic waters round the North of Scotland it had then headed southwards into the enclosed North Sea, where it had collided with a spring tide running hard to meet it through the English Channel. On the 30th a south-west wind brought about three times the usual volume of water into the North Sea through the Straits of Dover. The congested sea broke down the lands defences, wherever they were lowest, and that

* J. Lennox Kerr, *The Great Storm,* George Harrap & Co, 1954.

gale is remembered more for those that were drowned or driven from their homes on the levels of East Anglia, than for those who died with their ships. Yet three hundred men lost their lives at sea, and some fifty ships called for help. However much we soften our living by our ingenious devisings nothing softens the standards that the sea sets for those that follow it. It is the eternal whetstone of our race which will never allow us to fall below a certain standard of hardihood.

But at Potterton it was still early morning and the world seemed to hold nothing unusual. We went on with our breakfast in peace. Because of my early arrival at the station we had not listened to the B.B.C. news. If we had we would have heard what must have chilled the hearts of the families of those at sea. Warnings of gales are, it announced, "in operation in all sea areas except Sole, Finisterre and Biscay. Northerly gales will be severe in Faroes, Fair Isle, Hebrides, Malin, Rockall and Bailey, Cromarty and Forth." The 7,000-ton motor vessel *Clan Macquarrie* had met the gale off Cape Wrath the previous evening, sought sea room to fight it out, and been cast up on the west coast of the island of Lewis. At that moment waves were breaking over her as the shore rescue party, in driving snow, tried to get a line to her.

At a quarter to eight the *Princess Victoria*, the ferryship that ran between Stranraer and Larne, set off on her daily crossing. At the mouth of Loch Ryan she met mountainous seas and level driving snow. We had finished breakfast at Potterton and stepped outside. It was certainly blowing hard, but one grows used to high winds in the North-east of Scotland. At about that moment the Fleetwood trawler, *Michael Griffith*, with fourteen men on board, from the thunder of the white waste of waters to the west, sent out her last signal, superbly restrained in the face of death, "All ships. *Michael Griffith*, seven to nine miles south of Barra Head, full of water. No steam. Am helpless. Will some ship come and help us?"

Priscilla set off to a morning's work in Aberdeen and the trees were beginning to bend and toss in earnest. The wind had begun to hum in the telephone wires as it hums in a ship's rigging. We assumed that it must have reached zenith. So far this was still an ordinary day. We did not know that the Ferryship *Princess Victoria* in a wild white world of heaving seas and driving snow was signalling at 9.47, "Hove-to off mouth of Loch Ryan. Vessel not under command—urgent assistance of tug required." Then three-quarters of an hour later she sent out her SOS, "Four miles

N.W. of Corsewall. Car deck flooded. Heavy list to starboard. Require immediate assistance. Ship not under command. Ends."

Alone at Potterton I settled down to write an article for a magazine. It was on the Jameson Raid. To that end I had brought up two volumes on Cecil Rhodes, and one other authority, and hoped to get it out of the way in time for a walk in the woods in the afternoon, or at the latest for a duck flight in the dunes that evening. My father had played a considerable part in the early days in South Africa, and had been greatly attached to Dr. Jameson. I was soon fathoms deep in the subject. Although I must have heard the noise of the wind outside, my mind was away to where the dust of the veld was flying from the horses in the mounted columns. It was the smell of smoke rather than the noise that eventually returned me rudely to the present. Smoke from the wet logs was pouring straight out into the room, and spiralling round and darkening it. I looked out of the window, and there what seemed to be a mass of leaves whirled past and a wind that I could see. They always say, hereabouts, that horses and pigs can see the wind. We could all see it that day, as a torrent of rain and sleet and leaves. I went to the kitchen to see the only other inmate of the house. This was Ella our cook, who had come with us from Braemar. From the kitchen window one could see down the sloping lawn, and there was our tall cedar tree sprawled pointing up at the house, with a fine tree flat on either side of it. The world was in torment. The tops of the tall beeches across the field writhed upwards and downwards as if they were giant fishing rods playing leviathans. I opened the front door and forced it shut behind me with difficulty. A torrent of wind was flowing from inland, and pouring down over us and threatening to drown us. There was no shelter from it for it scoured every hollow. The gale was reaching the moment of its greatest violence, which was at about eleven o'clock in the morning, and the trees were falling continuously, singly and in groups. A sturdy willow, several feet in diameter, snapped off a third of the way up and just missed the greenhouse in falling, sliding away sideways off the wall of the garden. To make ground against the wind I had to lean against it, almost, it seemed, at an angle of forty-five degrees. To make headway against it was like breasting the rapids of a river. It tore at me and shrieked in my ears. It fought to keep me back and then throw me down. A tall Scots pine nearby rocked and fell and out of it was shaken about half a dozen pigeons. They faced the wind but were swept backwards. Its speed was nearly thirty miles an hour faster than they could fly. As the trees fell you could see birds, mostly pigeons, struggling backwards against the wind, trying to find some lee out of the roaring race of air. Now a group of trees would fall together like a squad of soldiers fainting on parade. But one would hear their fall only faintly above the roar of the wind. The sound of it had risen to a shriek, an awful wavering shriek that went up and down the octave. Its speed was over a hundred miles an hour. And Priscilla was due back from Aberdeen very soon. And so I set off on foot to meet her.

I made my way up to the rockery giving all the standing trees a wide berth, and just looked round the corner down the long drive. There was nothing to see now but a mass of tangled trees solid and dense from there to the white gate, that was four hundred yards further on. I went back to the big field and climbed the ridge that looks over the sea. Even above the sound of the gale I could hear the sea roaring and pounding away against the dunes, as if it meant to take revenge on the land and break it down. A trawler captain told me that he was about eight miles from Aberdeen when the gale struck. He and all the other vessels made straight for harbour. But it took quite a substantial time to raise a really big swell. What happened was that the water was whipped straight up in blinding spume off an apparently calm sea. By the time they reached Aberdeen harbour and its shelter the sea had risen. And it was on its way to rising to a gigantic height. And it remained there for hours after the wind eventually slackened off.

I made my way down to the road leaning against the wind, sometimes being forced into a run by it, sometimes leaning against it at a steep angle. A pigeon that was flying along near the hill to avoid the gale passed so close that I could have touched it with my stick.

I did not have to wait long for Priscilla. The car made its appearance from the direction of Aberdeen, going very slowly. I jumped in and told her that the long drive was impossible, that we might just get round the road itself, and on beyond past the old mill and up the drive to the farm, before the trees that stood beside the road fell and blocked the way. We did just that, and just in time. The trees fell behind us. We reached the farm and parked the car behind a haystack. About ten minutes later the haystack took off and squandered itself over about a square mile of country, leaving our car rocking at its moorings but still the right way up. Priscilla had had a terrible drive back from Aberdeen. At one place fishboxes were blowing at a perfectly flat trajectory across the road, and just about bonnet height. The car would only drive in first gear against the gale, and had skidded and been thrown all over the road. We made our way thankfully down the track from the home farm across the little bridge, hurrying beneath the big trees which were swinging and tottering in the gale. Back at the house and there we sat in a smoke-filled room wondering what in the world was going to happen next.

The one o'clock news told us of the plight of the *Princess Victoria*. By now we did not need to be told of the ferocity of the gale. Within an hour she was gone; only forty-one out of her ship's company of forty-nine crew and her 125 passengers were saved. Her wireless operator sent out his last signals just before two-o'clock. With that simple, undramatised, and unsurpassable courage of his kind he apologised to his hearers for his morse: "Sorry for morse O.M. (old man); on beam ends". Yet not all the events of that day ended in tragedy. Many lives were saved by splendid seamanship. None was greater than that of Skipper Imlach, of the Aberdeen trawler *Loch Awe*, who sought out, found, and rescued the crew of the 70-foot *Caronia* from Lossiemouth, in desperate straits in the Moray Firth.

We settled down disconsolately beside the only chimney which did not smoke so badly as to threaten to stifle us. It was the dining-room, and it was our living-room for that day and the next. Going up to her bedroom Priscilla looked out from the height of one floor up, and saw the whole hillside above us laid completely waste, with here and there one or a handful of trees that were still fighting to ride the gale out. Then the speed relaxed a little, but it did not fall below some eighty miles an hour for another twenty-four hours. It took four days to blow itself out. In the course of it the Peterhead lifeboat was sunk with all hands.

In the afternoon our morale was raised by the appearance of Andrew Carle, the peat cutter from the Red Moss. He drove up in a red tractor towing a float with our supply of peat. His sunburned face was the very pattern of equability. We unloaded it fast and dexterously, while a tall ash tree swayed like a drunkard above us, while the wind howled its spite. We went out for a walk after that, making headway against the wind as if we were wading a river and took stock of the destruction. A pigeon, flying underneath the branches of a clump of trees that still stood, hit Priscilla a hard blow on the shoulder. This was far too strong a wind for even pigeons to be able to order their going.

At Ellon Castle, on the Ythan, there was a wood of beech trees just above the drive, in front of the house. All the beeches went, and they were old beeches with big root systems. There was a net-work of rabbit holes underneath them, and the rabbits, suddenly finding the sky let into their burrows as the whole covering of their world was reft away, ran shrieking about the drive.

All night long the gale tore at the house. In the early hours of the next morning a flock of geese went over just missing the chimney pots, fighting their way against the wind. The roads were blocked all over our part of the country, but the train managed to reach London along tracks from which they had cleared away a whole forest of blown telegraph posts. The greatest intensity of the gale was in the three river valleys of the Ythan, the Don and the Dee. The destruction of trees was equivalent to ten years of cutting at a normal rate. Few woods under forty feet high were much damaged but, above that height, the well-thinned seemed to suffer with the badly thinned plantations. The bigger trees that were spared in the war years in the interests of continuity were the principal casualties. When these were counted or estimated, it was said that never had so many trees lain on the ground at the same time in Britain, since historical records were kept. Among them were five per cent of all Britain's conifers. It was reckoned to be a million and a half tons of timber which would be between three and a half to four million trees. But it could have been worse. A wind out of the East would have done more damage. Certainly if it had been a wet January and the ground water-logged it would have been far worse. And there was no loss of human life from the fall of trees. For two or three years the timber firms had all the work they could manage, and then, as everybody planted and nobody cut, several of them were forced into bankruptcy.

We were fortunate to make an arrangement with an excellent timber firm. When spring came, and all through the summer, timber carts made their way down the long drive removing this enormous mass of spillikins and leaving piles of slashings on the now open hillside. With the wood suddenly removed we saw the shape of the ground on which it had stood. We came to accept it as a stretch of bare hillside. And with the sunlight being able to reach the ground there came up a cheerful mass of flowers and grass of a varied growth, where once had been dark earth, sterile with pine needles. We talk about that hurricane quite simply as The Gale. By that we mean our gale, and not anybody else's gale, for several parts of Britain have had fearful gales since that time. Our gale made little news because it was almost immediately overtaken by the flood disasters in East Anglia which were attended by a heavy loss of life.

They say that it was the worst gale since 1703 in our part of the world. That one was mentioned by the Reverend Gilbert White in his *Natural History of Selborne* as "The Amazing Tempest of 1703." The Reverend A. Forsyth, the minister of Belhelvie, he who discovered the percussion powder, has a good deal to say about the gale of 1799—

"For on Christmas 1799 when there was perhaps, the most dreadful tempest that any person remembered to have seen on this part of the coast, several cubical blocks of peat moss were cast by the sea upon the sandy beach, some of them containing upwards of seventeen hundred cubic feet." That was about the only thing that did not happen in our gale. For days afterwards the sea pounded and pounded upon the dunes, and made inroads through them and left seaweed and wrack behind. Some of the roads inland were so blocked by trees that they were not cleared for weeks to come. And many an old Aberdeenshire family looked ruefully at ruined forests that they and their ancestors before them had tended so carefully. About ninety per cent of the blown trees were privately owned with a standing value estimated at £4 million.

A year or two later a Mr. Clapperton, a retired veterinary surgeon from Oakham in Rutland, came to call on us. His family had owned the house for two or three generations. He looked at the hillside running up from the long drive. He blinked and rubbed his eyes. He then asked us what had happened to the trees that his father planted, when he was a little boy. The whole hillside had been planted, with the greatest and most meticulous care, so he told us. We explained that it had grown to a forest and that forest had been removed, or eighty-five per cent of it, in round about half an hour. Happily the long line of beeches on the opposite side of the little park stood to a man. They were part of a far earlier planting. The wood on the right-hand side as you looked from the front door also stood, or most of it did, but all the rest went. The wind had come out of the north-west and moved its direction slowly. Thus it went round the trees like a tin-opener, and few had a root system that could stand against that.

Spring came. The birds and beasts soon got accustomed to trees not standing up but lying on their sides, and the pigeons nested in the fallen trees. Even the colony of long-eared owls, that remarkable assembly of normally unclubbable birds that we had inherited, made shift to live in the fallen trees as well. And the weevils came to the trees in their millions. It was no use thinking of replanting a pine tree or spruce until they had had their day and gone. And that was a full five years.

On reflection, if we were to have a gale like that we were delighted that we had it within only a month of setting foot in Potterton. In the intervening years we have had tremendous satisfaction out of replanting the blown spaces and we are far from finished yet. It would have been much more tragic if the gale had come later, when we would have had less time to make good its ravages. The warm summer followed and we were terrified that the whole battlefield of fallen trees, the needles faded to orange, might catch fire. To insure it was prohibitive, so we just hoped and hoped, and happily nothing went wrong. And eventually the last timber cart went down the long drive, and the driver shut the white gate behind him for good. The year following we were hammering posts into the ground and laying out rabbit wire enclosures in large neat, geometrical patterns on the flat beside the long drive, on the side away from the hill, in the place where the big Norway spruces had stood. We foolishly left the survivors standing until they, in their turn, started to wilt and fall. Once the small hairy roots of a tree are broken it will nearly always die. We left our biggest tree, an Abies Grandis, whose roots had made the ground heave round it in the gale. It is just alive, but only just, but very beautiful and tall enough to show off its dark foliage against the background of the sky.

The North Sea emptied and settled down. On February 1st, the south-west moving water through the Straits of Dover was eight times the normal flow. For a week after the fishermen, who cast their nets as soon as the sea had run down, reported that the stomachs of the fish they caught were full of sand. Strangely enough, a splendid fishing season followed. Damaged ships were repaired and new trees planted and the gale became history.

Nearly fifteen years later to the day a tempest called Hurricane Low Q crossing the Atlantic in a north-easterly direction suddenly turned east and made a gash across the waist of Scotland at a previously unrecorded force of wind and costing more than twenty lives on land and not much less damage to trees than occurred in 1953. But, as the Reverend Mr. Forsyth had written of the 1799 gale, so we will remember the gale of 1953—

"It was the most dreadful tempest that any person remembered to have seen on this part of the coast."

9   *Trees*

THE planting of trees is the only thing in the world that
gives you a clear reason for wanting to grow older. You
look at a young plantation and wish that the next ten years
would pass in a flash and your trees become a wood. If you are a
forester you are a farmer, but a farmer with a difference. For if
you plant English oaks you wait three hundred years for your
return. You are faced with the clash between what you want to
plant, and what dreary old commonsense tells you will grow. At
Braemar we planted Canadian trees in our garden with a deer
fence round it. There was a plantation of larches nearly all of
which were dying back that I was allowed to thin, and plant up.
The curious thing about trees is that you get such a family
feeling about them that even if you do not own the land and must
leave it, whenever you see the trees that you have planted you

always regard them as belonging to you. I feel the same about the trees that I planted at my old home at Elsfield after the war. I take just as much pride in their growing as if it was still my home, and it is the same with Braemar.

In the *Statistical Account of Scotland* in January 1840, it is said about our parish that, "The kind of trees that thrive best are the ash, plane, elm, elder and willow". The ash does thrive reasonably well and so does the plane. The elm grows rugged and rather contorted. The alder and the willow grow extremely well. But as far as commercial forestry goes you must be near your market. There is no big furniture-making industry in Aberdeen or, indeed, for many miles in any direction. And if you grow beeches, which seem to love the wind off the North Sea, they will be mostly sold for firewood. About the time that the *Account*, that I have just quoted, was written, trees were beginning to come into fashion in this wind-swept parish. For the *Account* says, "Almost all the growing of timber in the parish has been planted lately, and generally in hedgerows, so the number of acres cannot easily be ascertained." Now each of the little laird's houses and the farms along the coast have a cluster of wind-bitten trees to give them some shelter. They are mostly crooked sycamores leaning away from the wind. There are no great stretches of forest until you get further inland. There the climate for tree planting seems to change quickly, and in no time at all you can find yourself among the finest forests in Britain. But we find in the mosses remains of great oaks and alders. One oak trunk dug up at Aberdeen some years ago measured 15 feet round. They had evidently grown to that size at the time when the world was in a warm spell. Perhaps it was the same one that allowed the Vikings to reach and colonise Greenland, which was then a really green land, with little ice except round its northern extremities. Our present climate could never harden oaks like that.

The great gale of January 31st, 1953, had removed about eighty per cent of our trees in almost a matter of minutes. All summer long in that year, timber wagons had rocked and creaked along our long drive. And by the autumn everything was reasonably clear. We made the mistake of allowing isolated trees that had weathered the storm to stand, as they seemed immortal if they could resist that fury. But their tiny hair roots had been torn and they moped and died. Single lonely trees are, anyhow, a problem. They are not easily pollinated. They are outside the pattern of the forest.

We started our replanting programme in the following year. We are situated in what is supposed to be one of the worst parts of Scotland for weevil. And so there could be no question of planting conifers for about five years. In the spring following the gale we enclosed several acres that had once grown tall Norway spruces. We planted it up with ash. That was all we did that year. Two years later we tackled the hillside. We cut out the remaining trees that had withstood the wind, all of which were beginning to droop by now, and fenced off the rest of the area which had been dense forest when we arrived. It was a long and expensive business. We put up the full extent of the wire fence the first year, but we did not plant it all up at once. In fact it is not all planted up yet. The adventure is unending. We planted a great many beeches on the steep slope which separates us from a view of the sea and Canadian red oaks of which I have always been fond. We allowed ourselves the occasional indulgence of planting what we wanted to plant, rather than what we knew would grow. We planted Spanish chestnut, which is not supposed to grow well north of the banks of the Thames. In addition we planted the face of the hill with English oaks. And thought that by putting in these slow starters and giving them a run of a few years they would get up to a reasonable height, and then we could fill up the gaps with conifers. Surprisingly, some of the Spanish chestnuts did well, those that had to fight with the shoots of birch that were growing up. The shoots of birch and whins pushed some of the fed oaks up to a great height, but their bark is terribly tempting to the mice and we have, as far as I can make out, five different kinds, or anyhow four. Two varieties of little sharp-nosed voles with wickedly keen teeth, a more ordinary-looking mouse and a rather larger ordinary-looking mouse, and I suspect one other. To them a young Canadian maple with its sugar sap, is like a lollipop. In the summer the rosebay willowherb rose in its ranks and we spent sweltering afternoons fighting to prevent the young growth being choked. But we left them very much to their devices, just clearing away as much of the growth as would prevent them being too badly suppressed. And we let time pass. I planted some willows and set about trying to make a little wood of pollard willows, the golden and the crimson ones. I fenced off a little more ground to take in the top of a little paddock field just beyond our little park. And there I could let myself go and plant strange trees from strange countries, that we continue to collect in our wanderings.

A year or two later I got to work on the nettle and bramble patch behind the washing green, which stands about a hundred yards from our back door and has a splendid sight of the sea. I grubbed up all the nettles and wild raspberries and, although I got somebody to help me fence it, prickled and stung I glowed with the achievement of having planted every single tree there with my own hands. We had thus a very unorthodox series of plantations, rather like the elder Mr. Weller's knowledge of London which was described as being "extensive and peculiar."

When the five years had passed, to let the weevils abate, we set to work to plant some conifers. That was the next step. We have always been fascinated by the Serbian Spruce which comes from the Illyrian Alps in Jugoslavia. The Jugoslavs do not sell the timber. They wisely hold on to their existing stands and sell the seed to the world. They are beautiful, but surprisingly frost tender. We planted a great many of these. And, wandering westward through the Rockies, we have always loved the lodgepole pines that cling to the mountainsides that face the Pacific, standing sometimes in great groups, sometimes like lonely sentinels, with their roots reaching into what appears to be no more than a pinch of dust on a rock ledge. We planted quite a lot of these. If they are planted in soil that is in the least good they grow with tremendous speed and then topple over. If you plant them, in the worst soil in the worst exposure, it seems that you have a better chance of growing a straight tree. We were delighted when after three years these trees were as high as our heads, and saddened by their waywardness when they started to topple over, one after the other. For to real tree lovers, trees have human vices and virtues and we felt betrayed. We planted Norway spruces where the old tall stately ones had stood, down on the flat in the wet part beside the long drive. But it is a frost hollow and they have found it slow work to get their heads above that chill miasma. But we planted there some of our Canadian trees, part of our wedding present from Ontario. We planted the black walnut, the black cherries, the canoe birch, and the two kinds of maple. They fared variously, the cherries making slow but fairly steady headway, the walnuts one much taller than my head, few of the others much beyond my waist. The maples made headway generally as leaning, rather spindly trees. The winter of 1961-2 was a very severe one, and for the first time two of them coloured with all of the rich crimson glory of the Canadian fall. It takes a hard winter to do that and a hottish summer as well. I do not think we shall ever be making sugar from our own maple trees. With us they are on wetter soil than in their native Canada. Perhaps that is why they shed their branches so easily. If you bend back a twig it will snap in your hand. But if one leaf on each tree turned to that ripe crimson, these trees would be worth their place.

I plant almost all the trees myself. I enjoy digging. Digging in peat always intrigues me. They say that it takes about one hundred years to produce one inch of peat. So my planting spade, having about a six-inch span, reaches down somewhere towards the era of Bannockburn. Twice only have I ever dug up any tangible history, once an arrowhead, once a completely defaced coin that was worn smooth by age and unidentifiable. If you dig when it's cold then you have to dig with all your might and main to keep warm and the soil is icy to your hands. But you dig at other times sodden with heat and crowned with a buzzing halo of flies. And always it absorbs you and you are blind and deaf to the rest of the world. It is not clear whether in Aberdeenshire it is a convention to plant in the spring. It is believed that if you plant in the autumn you are liable to get frost lift which will lift your plants half out of the ground with fatal results. It obviously depends to a great extent on the winter that follows, and if you get early snow which keeps the roots warm you are probably much better off if you have planted in the autumn. But by and large most people hereabouts plant in the spring, I always do. If you own great areas of land you must catch up in your short season with a vast amount of planting. You must go in for what is called "notching". It is going clean against nature to squash the roots of a plant with the unnatural geometrical pattern of a right angle. I am fortunate enough to have just a small enough extent of ground, although I never get my tasks done in time, to be able to dig a little pit and plant each tree. As a result so large a proportion of those that succeed that those that do not are a reproach. You come back from planting trees with a feeling of absolute satisfaction and tired well-being. It is as exciting to me to set out with a spade as it is later in the year, to set out with a gun and a belt of cartridges. For every one of us hungers for some tiny crumb of immortality and planting trees goes a long way towards satisfying that.

We had got to the point when the slow-growing trees that we planted first had got some distance when there started to be a tremendous eruption of gorse and, what we call in Scotland, whins all over our little bit of land. The whins we removed with great labour and at some cost, and burned them, leaving some for their beautiful yellow blossoms in the spring. They helped some trees to grow, literally forcing them up in competition. Curiously they are the best of all nurses for Serbian spruce. They allowed something else that was really serious to happen. But they set the scene for an invasion of our little world of Potterton.

Not many miles away there stood an old derelict country house which has since been pulled down. Its policies had become covered with jungle. It now carried a population of roebuck who crossed the intervening few miles, in very short time on a clear night, and started to work on our trees. That was another unscripted event in our forestry plans. Roebuck are one of those things that are put into the world to try the patience of those who plant trees. They are excellent for character formation among tree lovers. They are exceedingly beautiful, and people who do not suffer from their depredations always hold up their hands in horror at the thought of anybody destroying one. If you own trees you are quite clear on that point. You cannot keep them out, except at great expense. They will hurdle over a rabbit wire fence. They love Canadian red oak, and take the tops clean out of them. When they come their horns are itchy with velvet and they love a certain thickness of tree, perhaps an inch across, which gives when their horns touch it. Most particularly they like an oak, English or red, that has been growing for about six years, and they rub their horns against it and leave a ragged scar that is often fatal. They are jealous of other roebuck and they mark out their area, which is about the size of our hill plantation, and to show that they are there they bark the corner trees and others outside, as well as a good many trees inside as well to show that the place is already occupied and to warn other roebuck to go further on. So what had started as an even line of trees ended up, through their marauding, as an uneven medley of generations. For we had to replace some trees every year.

After the great gale we had a fearful plague of mice. They ate the little beeches and they ate the little red oaks and they ate the English oaks, and they even ate the Spanish chestnuts, and they were there in enormous numbers. We have never believed in putting down poison, because poison kills and continues to kill through the whole process of nature. They say that strychnine kills seven times, and hideously too.

When we got rid of the gorse and the whins, and we shall have to do it again ever two or three years, the birch came up really strongly. This was different, it was interesting because they were trees. We left the finest and straightest and those that were almost silvery, because they do not often grow very silvery so close to the sea. And we have grown other trees underneath them because their dancing dappled shade is a very good overhead cover. One day we shall have to take several very strong men and cut those tall birches down, and lift them and carry them away without crushing the trees beneath them, but we will deal with that when it happens.

In the old days at Elsfield we were tormented by nettles. The nettle is probably the worst tormentor. In planting trees you must kneel and a nettle in the face is infuriating as well as painful. We do not get nettles at Potterton or not enough to signify, but brambles will and do grow anywhere. If you can take the time to do it and push a crowbar under their root and lift them out completely you can bring yourself peace from them for a year or two to come. If you are planting without rabbit wire you can ensure the safety of a tree by planting it through a bramble bush. But in our short planting season there is so much to do that there is not much opportunity for such a meticulous work. Osgood Mackenzie tells of his father planting out tall hardwoods, before the days of wire fencing, and securing them against the cattle by planting a wild rose bush in the same pit and twining the thorn sprays round its stem.

Not many trees that you see in Scotland were set there by nature. The vast numbers of trees that you see in any part of the countryside of Britain are much later imports.

The lairds of Aberdeenshire have always been noted foresters. The second Scottish renaissance, that which took place in the latter half of the eighteenth century, was the first time that land was drained and dug and indeed planted with trees. The lairds became masters of this particular art and have remained so. When you see the great mountains of cut planking imported from Scandinavia, and elsewhere, along the quay at Aberdeen harbour, you are seeing the amount of timber that we need but that we do not yet grow in this country. But there are very few big Aberdeenshire lairds who are not real experts on this subject. Indeed they have to be. In Aberdeenshire there are a great many old families owning their original land. Agriculture in the past would never have sustained them over a series of really bad years. But the families who held on to their own original acres, are those who have regularly planted a rotation of trees. Therefore the great gale of 1953 probably wrought more damage to those same families than anything political or national has happened for a good many centuries. All things in life are relative. I sometimes think in my dreams of planting thousands of acres or of afforesting the Sahara Desert, and other delightful fancies. But it is difficult to believe that there could be more fun to be had than we get out of the little estate where we know almost every tree by sight. It is like possessing a large family of uneven gifts, some of whom do much better than you expect and many do much worse, while some perish of infant diseases and others by accident. In the minds of some dreary people beauty is something which means little and is not to be encouraged. Forestry without some eye to beauty is not true forestry. A forester feels for his trees as if they were people. In our tree garden we have a silver birch of superb character. Twenty feet away is another silver birch that has no character. You could collide with it, it is so featureless.

It was only fairly recently that we took to planting willows and dogwoods, and their colours begin to glow in that month when the whole land looks as if it has got leprosy and light it up with flames. And then we have our garden. Our little tree garden, behind the washing-green, and our two little woodland plots have special trees either with histories or which came from special and interesting and exciting parts of the world. We have six oaks spaced out in a line, which are off the oak tree at Penshurst, called the Sidney oak, which even in Sir Philip Sidney's day, and that was four hundred years ago, were called the "very ancient tree." It still has live acorns on it and my friend, the present owner, gave me six of them. I have gathered bushels of the seed of the London plane in St. James's Park and Victoria Gardens. Only a pinch of it will grow, as London lacks bees and there is only the wind to carry out that function.

We have oaks whose acorns were collected as far away as New Zealand and Australia. In their new habitat of the South Pacific they are becoming slowly evergreen and the leafless period is marginally shorter. I have seen the same thing in the Argentine. Already the fuschias, that early settlers introduced into Kenya, not so many years ago, have become entirely evergreen.

We have a certain amount of losses. A gum from the Snowy

River grew six foot high before an exceptionally hard frost killed it. A cedar, which a sheik in the Lebanon gave to us was cut down and killed by a misfortune. The trees from the green hills of the Northern Transvaal, which my father first reached on the back of a horse in 1903, and swore that he would return there to die, grew feet in height and then withered away. We had an Oriental plane, the seed of which we picked, rather unsteadily as we had dismounted a breakneck ride in the Elburz mountains in Persia, but it did not survive. But the successes easily outnumber the failures. The effort entailed in collecting these seeds was more than matched by the formalities that had to be undergone to bring them into Britain.

In the Canadian forests in summer, when you pick up your canoe and carry it from one lake to another, secured by a band round your forehead, you are doing what is called a "portage." It may be a mile long, though halfway down the trail you may well say to your companion, when you are being murdered by mosquitoes and black flies and sweltering in the heat, "how long is a mile portage?" The question is rhetorical and is meant to convey that it feels like a hundred miles. At Potterton we have forty-eight acres of land. Coming back in the spring dusk, utterly and happily tired, and knowing that it is going to be impossible to carry out your planting plan before the spring growth gets going, we sometimes ask ourselves, "How big is forty-eight acres?" The answer is, "It is big enough to be a world of its own."

10 *The Shore*

FROM the mouth of the Dee at Aberdeen, to north of the estuary of the Ythan, runs an almost straight beach. It was straight enough to be chosen as the base line for the ordnance survey of Scotland in 1817, as is mentioned elsewhere. If you stand on the rampart of dunes that runs the length of it, the long cold tides come marching in, rank after rank, to break and hiss and bubble beneath you. The upright finger of Girdleness light at Aberdeen is at your right hand. And you can see leftward to where the little cliffs of Collieston form the other horn of what is just a crescent. Somewhere in this broad sweep of sea will be the smoke, or perhaps just the shape, of little ships. They are trawlers or drifters, which will become points of light when darkness falls, and Girdleness begins to wink out its warning.

Sometimes you will see bigger vessels from the northern ports of the world, from the few cities that are further north than we are, and the homely shape of the Shetland packet. And, occasionally, one of the Queen's ships. But in the main it is a sea of small craft. On the seabed beneath them is a weird world. Here are the wrecks of all ages huddled in a petrified forest, whose trunks have been cast ashore in great gales, together with great blocks of peat. Many ships have been wrecked there even in the short twelve years that we have known this shore. One was a Russian vessel which ran aground not very far from the golf club at the Aberdeen end. She had a very large crew, who seemed to our suspicious eyes, to look exceedingly furtive. There is one sad little barnacled hulk on the beach at this moment, whose still readable name has a wistful gaiety—the *Fruitful Bough*. If you had to be wrecked, that stretch of shore would seem vastly preferable to anywhere else. But in part it has a fierce current. If you walk along the shore you will see in places the waves do not come in squarely to the land but at an angle. That is nearly always a sign that there is an undertow which goes out on a corresponding angle in the other direction. After being damaged in Sicily in the war, I was sent to a Canadian convalescent camp in North Africa, where there was a long sandy beach of extremely similar shape. Many people got into difficulties bathing there, and more than one soldier lost his life through being taken out by the undertow. It was there one learned to look for the waves coming shiftily, at an angle, into the shore instead of boldly straight.

In certain emergencies we call for help and expect to receive it —emergencies like fire, burglary or accident. Living beside the coast, the lifeboat is an extra fact of life. In our telephone book the word LIFEBOAT is written out in capital letters and the Directory says—"In emergency ask operator for Lifeboat (with dialling instructions). For other calls see below Aberdeen Coxwain No. 1 boat . . ." and so on, for the lifeboats of Aith, Buckie, Fraserburgh, Lerwick, Peterhead and Whitehills. Up to the month of September 1966 the name of Newburgh was there too.

All manner of ships have been here and all kinds of men have landed from them. In early days you would have seen the Strandloopers, the primitive seafarers from the Rhine who perhaps were the first race to see this coast, land and disappear leaving us only shells and their discarded flint arrowheads. A watcher from the dunes, centuries later, might have seen the slim, rakish galleys of the

Sea-king Eysteinn, son of Harald, converging on the river mouth.

> The Northmen came about our land
> A Christless chivalry:
> Who knew not of the arch or pen,
> Great, beautiful half-witted men
> From the sunrise and the sea.
>
> Misshapen ships stood in the deep
> Full of strange gold and fire,
> And hairy men, as huge as sin
> With horned heads, came wading in
> Through the long, low sea-mire.*

He would not have heard the ring of steel or the cries of the dying, but he would have seen the smoke rising from the burning dwellings.

The Spanish galleon that brought arms to the rebellious Earl of Erroll at Collieston four centuries later and a few years after the defeat of Philip's Armada in 1558, could have been in plain view tossing and tumbling in a beam sea. When she was wrecked at Collieston her crew were kindly received by the villagers, who called them "Philip's men", and the name "Philip" and a Spanish cast of feature is still common among the people there.

In December of 1708 our Kirk Session was informed of the stranding of several Dutch ships on our beach, and further that "there are some idle persons who frequent the seaside, especially after an easterly storm on the sea on a Sabbath day's morning. . . ." The sea shore was then to be out of bounds to the whole parish on Sundays on pain of being . . . "proceeced against as gross prophaners of the Sabbath . . ." but only two months later four of our parishioners were fined accused of "laying hands on, breaking and carrying home of a part of a wreck upon the Lord's Day in the evening between the sun and the sky . . .", and they got into real trouble, being ordered to sit on the stool of repentance the next Sabbath, and be publicly rebuked and "also to pay a pecuniall mulct."

That was the great century of smugglers along that coast, particularly at Collieston. Collieston's most famous son today, after a distinguished career in the South, has retired to live in his native village. He is proud of his free-trading lineage. For what he

* "The Ballad of the White Horse," from *The Collected poems of G. K. Chesterton*, Methuen 1933.

has called one of "his great grandfather's—several generations removed—" was owner and skipper of that famous lugger the *Crooked Meg*, which was lost on the rocks of Collieston by a false light treacherously planted there by the Revenue men. The atrocities inflicted by tax-gatherers in this island, past and present, should be an inspiration to Celtic bards, as masters of melancholy, when they reach for the strings of their harps.

In 1814 the kindly eyes of Sir Walter Scott surveyed the line of dunes from the deck of the lighthouse inspection vessel, under the command of a certain Captain Stevenson, who was Robert Louis Stevenson's grandfather. They stopped at Girdleness, recently the scene of the loss of the whaler *Oscar* with all hands. Work had not begun on building the lighthouse which was still being discussed. With his immense devotion to writing, Sir Walter kept a careful diary, but he must have mixed up the shore line of Belhelvie with that round Newburgh. He wrote of the Earl of Erroll with whom he stayed, and his possessions— "imprudence or ill-fortune as fatal as the sands of Belhelvie has swallowed up the estate of Erroll except this dreary mansion with a farm or two adjoining." A square bracket in parenthesis explains that "the sands of Belhelvie" were "shifting sands that had swallowed up the whole parish." It is in the parish to the north of us that this disaster happened. In 1413 a sandstorm buried a large part of it including the old kirk and the houses of the priest, the laird and the rest of the people. It was a year of disasters with an eruption of Vesuvius, a hurricane in Iceland, and a tornado in Calabria. The gradual creeping of those sands over this once fertile parish was recorded officially in 1678 and again in 1759, the latter occasion called for an announcement by the Sheriff Depute of Aberdeenshire.

When Sir Walter Scott looked at our Belhelvie coast he was enjoying one of the happiest periods of his life. His books were beginning to pay, Abbotsford had become a reality, and almost for the last time in his life he was really fit. Of that we can be sure from the entries in his diary, for when he reached Loch Erriboll he decided on a visit to the Smoo Cave. Before he started he enjoyed "an ample Highland breakfast, an excellent new-taken herring, equal to those of Loch Fyne, fresh haddocks, fresh eggs, and fresh butter, not forgetting the bottle of whisky and bannocks of qarley and oat cakes, and the Lowland luxuries of tea and coffee." So heartened was he by this splendid meal that he then notes in his diary, "take the fowling piece and shoot some sea fowl, and a large hawk of uncommon appearance. Fire four shots and kill three times."

In 1857 the yacht *Fox,* under command of Captain Leopold McLintock, sailed out of Aberdeen and followed our shore line northwards. It was the fifth expedition that had been outfitted and largely paid for by Lady Franklin in a desperate bid to find and rescue her husband Sir John who had gone into the Arctic in command of H.M. ships *Erebus* and *Terrier* to search for the North-west Passage. She could not know that he had perished nine years before, but when McLintock returned three years later the little flame of hope that had so bravely flickered in Jane Franklin's breast was finally extinguished.

In the summer holidays of 1925, my first from Eton, my father took my mother and me to Shetland to stay with a minister who had been at Glasgow University with him and who, among other things, was a very skilful fisherman. We pulled out of Aberdeen harbour in the dusk of early August. Coming up from the heat and light of the saloon to escape the smell of haddock for high tea, and plush, and polish, and tobacco smoke, I walked the deck pulling my school-boy overcoat close, because a wind was ruffling the water under the gathering dark and there was an edge to it. I looked landward at the low shore line at pinpoints of lights appearing in cottage windows. "Dull country" I thought to myself "and not real Scotland." I have eaten my words happily since then. Among the lighted panes would have been those of Millden, the house of our friend and neighbour and namesake, Charles Buchan. Two years earlier he and his sister had, after a night of a tearing, drenching gale been woken by their father to be told that he had a feeling that there was a ship ashore in the night. Lashed by rain and blowing sand his sister and he had quartered the beach. They were blinded if they faced the sea and had to look sideways into a chilling, screeching wrack of storm. Suddenly there was something there. It was the loom of something solid in beyond the breakers where nothing solid should have been. It was the wreck of the *Imperial Prince* and, when they had alerted the village constable who was still abed, the rescue got under way. It was one of the great epics of life-saving at sea, under one of the greatest of all coxswains, John Innes, who is a legend on our coast. It was the last time that lifeboats on that coast used sweeps. The Newburgh lifeboat until 1966 occupied the large and solid shed on the last elbow of the Ythan, where the river turns to run straight to the tumbling waves of its formidable bar half a mile away. The lifeboat house sits on a sandy slope about fifty yards from the water where the eider duck chuckle incessantly the summer long, and the sea trout fishermen stand in rows like herons. Within it the lifeboat sat, spick and span, on its carriage of four broad wheels. It was ready at any moment to be trundled down the fifty yards of sand into the Ythan, if the weather was calm. But if the weather was rough the bar was impassable and the lifeboat had to be pushed for half a mile along the sands, beside the river and then into the open sea itself. It had been out several times since we came to live here and had saved not a few lives; nineteen in one night off a Swedish craft fouled on the Ythan bar.

Back before 1828 there was a primitive lifeboat which sank or wore out and was not replaced until 1877. The boat-house was built at the same time. A rocket was set up at continuous readiness and an up-to-date rescue system was established.

With a boom! up would sail the rocket and every man, woman and child in Newburgh dropped everything. They poured over the bridges of the little burn calling, "Boat ashore—boat ashore—boat ashore". In darkness, when wrecks most often take place they showed as lines of bobbing lanterns converging into a single stream that flowed to the boathouse. It was nearly always too rough to launch in the river with the pounding waves on the bar to face, and so old and young set to pulling and pushing the carriage-born lifeboat along the beach.

When the rocket had boomed and hissed its way skyward the three farmers who overlooked the estuary ran in to put in their horses, and pounded with them down to the beach to tow the carriage. It might be Cruikshank of Ythan Lodge or Moir of Knockhall or Anderson of Little Haddo who got there first. By day the horses could easily be scattered over their broad acres and the people of Newburgh often got the lifeboat to the beach before the horses arrived.

When they changed from sweeps to motor-driven lifeboats the actual form of propulsion produced a problem.

In very rough seas an ordinary propeller would be too often out of the waves, and only too likely to be fouled by the mass of cordage which seems to float loose round every wreck. The compromise was reached with small protected paddles, one on either side of the keel, so far along the boats stem that they can never be out of the water. We felt a great sense of loss when our Newburgh lifeboat left us. Lifeboats may evolve into shapes and forms beyond our guessing, but the calls on the courage of the men who man them will never diminish.

As late as 1907, a description* of the churchyard of the old and ruined Belhelvie Kirk, speaks of a vault divided into compartments abutting on the churchyard "which is still used as a mortuary for the remains of sailors that are cast ashore," and there is in part of that churchyard set aside for their burial and called the "sailors' knowe". A professor of philosophy at Marischal College was drowned while bathing in 1769 and is buried there. Can anyone say that a time will come when there is no need for such provision?

In the last war Charles Buchan was patrolling the shore before his farm at dusk one evening. Above the tide line he found a body, it was a dead German pilot. Dignified and disciplined in death, he lay like a recumbent statue. His flying helmet was adjusted and his dark airman's kit framed his body. Incongruously he wore no boots, but for all that he seemed entirely in control of himself in the face of the Last Enemy. To look into his dead face would leave you with a long memory. Dusk was gathering and our neighbour wasted no time in getting off to get a policeman, and together they returned and made towards him. Even the sea seemed to have gone out of its way to have treated him respectfully. But the sea has a mind and it knows its mind, and it has its wants and it satisfies them. And it meant to have that man. As they went to lift him up the beach there came hissing a long cold comber driving them back far above the tide line. It caught up the body and snatched it back into its own embrace. They watched but it never showed again. Only the sea pounded and pounded and the sea birds slanting against the wind lamented. Like the Strandloopers he had come from the country of the Rhine and like them had disappeared.

The fields that run down towards the sea become little more than ploughed and planted dunes until they come to a wire fence which separates them from the moss and thyme, and rank sea grass that overlays the sand of the links. The word "links" always means golf to those who do not understand our tongue. But, because this kind of shore grassland, which we call links,

* John Henderson, *Aberdeenshire Epitaphs and Inscriptions*.

provides the easiest conditions under which to lay out a golf course, the word has become almost synonymous with golf courses. This meaning has world-wide acceptance. Even to that course that I remember so well, on the shores of Lake Victoria at Jinja, before the Owen Falls dam across the Nile was built to raise the level of this lake by three feet. And it had been a lake the size of Scotland. A vaguely comforting thought to those happy Scottish exiles there. I remember this course, not only for its beauty, but for an unusual by-law. Hippos used to haul themselves out of the lake at night, and tramp about on the golf course. They would leave a footprint into which you could have fitted a top hat. If your ball rolled into one of these footprints you were allowed to remove it, and put it on the edge of the hole, without forfeiting a stroke. The raising of the water has silenced for ever the smoking thunder of the Ripon Falls where the great lake poured over in one smooth dark sheet half a mile long, broken only at the near side where an island to which a tree clung stuck to the lip of the Fall. And the golf course will lie inland above the new water line, and no doubt the hippos wander over it just the same. But that is a golf-course not a golf-links.

These Belhelvie links do not hold much in the way of wild life. Hares and rabbits rise and fall with the myxamatosis cycle. The hares become more numerous when the rabbits die down, as they compete for the same food. There are nesting eider ducks in the late spring and occasionally a few terns will form a colony and lay their eggs on the bare sand, with sometimes a few casual wisps of grass. When Susie was a very small child she and her nanny sat down on a rug on the beach to have a picnic tea. They were dive-bombed and nearly deafened by a screaming tern. When they started to retreat they found that the tern had her two eggs, in a nest in the sand, a few inches from the edge of the rug. On one of the ponds a black-headed gull colony will come and stay for a year or so and then move on. The mallard nest by the pools or by the burn. The teal may go as far east as Czecho-slovakia and the widgeon to Northern Russia. The geese, except for a few greylag, are in Iceland and the gulls go up to Collieston to nest. But from the landward come the sound of larks in abundance, the cry of the whaup and the oyster catcher. The difference between the links and the dunes is that the links have a mossy turf and thyme and soft grasses. The dunes have long grass as sharp as spears growing out of the bare sand.

One spring we went to great lengths to dig up turf from the links to make a grass path at Potterton. Such turf has the great virtue that it stays short like a lawn if it is regularly walked upon. There seemed to be a great deal of work for very little turf. We would dig up a yard at a time, and fold it up like a Swiss roll and put it in the boot of the car. Six such rolls weighed the car down pretty heavily, which was sixteen years old and the same age as Susie; but seemed to make only a small contribution to the path when we got it home. The turf was only about two inches thick with a mat of roots losing themselves in fine sand. When we finished our path it was no time at all, for all our flat-footed walking, before the dominant weeds and grasses of the landward pierced the turf and our labour was in vain.

The road that runs along the coast is a busy one and has become very much of a speedway since it was widened and straightened. It is said that the old road from Aberdeen to North Buchan ran along Belhelvie sands, turning at the mouth of the Ythan to follow the river till it narrows at Kirkton of Logie Buchan, where the travellers would cross on a ferry. It is shown thus on the map of 1776. This ferry was still working at the beginning of this century. As carts only came into use in Scotland in the later eighteenth century, in the place of the primitive sledges which continued to be used on the farms, roads until then did not have to be more than a path for pack horses which showed you were going in the right direction and had solid ground on which to travel. There came to be a big difference between a road and a coach road. But the road along the shore may well have had to make some detours because of the dangerous quicksands. Our neighbour Tom Duguid, out with his drag hounds, which he maintained until the last war, ran into a soft place on the beach from which the horses had to flounder their way out. Beaches are a strip of desert. And deserts, whether hot or cold, are in a perpetual state of transition. But, at the moment we do not have dangerous quicksands as they did on that 24th day of September, 1612. On that day Sir James Lawson of Humby, riding on this very beach, was engulfed by a quicksand, horse and all. His body was found the next day, but that of his horse was no more seen. But this incident became widely known, as it was a rare and hideous happening, and young Sir James was a man of mark, being a Gentleman of the Bedchamber to James I and VI. It is not unreasonable to suppose that Walter Scott took this

K

incident as his inspiration, in describing the death of the Master of Ravenswood, in his *Bride of Lammermoor*.

During the last war such a shore line seemed to offer a clear invitation to the enemy to land his tanks. Big concrete pill boxes were erected at intervals along the dunes and a continuous line of tank obstacles in the form of upended concrete cubes ran the length of the shore line. In a modest attempt to confuse the enemy, by breaking up the symmetry of the cubes, rocks the size of your fist were put into the top of these blocks when the concrete was soft, to distort their outline and make them look slightly less artificial. When we first came to Potterton the obstacles stood shoulder to shoulder as far as the eye could reach, though a few had lurched and some were prostrate. A series of gales over the last few years has entombed them in a great billow of sand and only a few are still visible. The gales and the high tides have eroded the foundation of the pill boxes, and they have slumped drunkenly forward. Gradually they will disappear beneath the sands and archeologists stumble upon them a century or so hence. At Newburgh there is a very large area of dunes which includes a mountain of sands taking the form of a smoothly rounded ridge. Here the sand sings, as it sings in the Sahara, on a windy day. A few years ago a dune blew away revealing a Neolithic circle.

A lifetime of looking at picture postcards, and travel posters, has equated the sea with summer and sunshine for many of us. And there are many parts of Britain's coast where, without sun in summer, the sea has little charm. But this northern sea of ours is different. It has the hard appeal of the Far North. We live here and love it because we are people of the North. And we love it in all its seasons.

The setting up of the salmon nets along the coast would tell you that spring has come, if you had lost your hearing and were not aware of the calling of the plover and the skylark. The nets run out in a single curtain of mesh ending in an arrow head of netting, which imprisons the shore-coasting salmon as he feels his way seawards. Like the lobster in the pot he cannot remember where he entered. The design has probably not changed since the scriptures were written. Nor has the pace of pursuit, except that a tractor float appears at low tide, and square cheerful men in fishermen's jerseys and tall boots wade into the V-shaped dungeons, with long-handled landing nets, to pick out the one or two salmon that each may hold. Caught in the mesh are generally a few small flat fish, which are disregarded. A year or so back we saw three 20-pounders taken from two nets, but that is rare. Often there is not a fish along the whole line of beach. The rising tide obliterates the V-pattern of the tractors' wheels, and at full tide only the highest pole of the net shows above the waves, with a tern sitting on it and looking like the mast of a sunken ship. And summer is ended when one day the nets are gone from the sandy shore, for the fishing season is over. You may know then that summer is ending, even if you had not noticed the first migrant birds down from the Arctic. Birds come that seem unnaturally free from fear of man, partly because they are tired from their long flight, but equally because they come from the frozen rim of the world beyond the ken of humans, from Baffin Island and Ellesmere Land, and other lands in the northern silence.

As you slip into winter you enter that realm of austere beauty, so much more curious and more magical than the colours of summer. A clear cold sky broods over snow-covered dunes, while gunmetal sea rolls the pebbles at their feet. On a clear day you will see snow storms out to sea. Wraiths of white which are outriders of the spirit that presides over the polar world. The sea never grows old, it is never still. It is a million fiends in the times of its fury. It seems shorn of its strength, and lazy and inviting, at others. As a people we would be nothing without it. It is our inspiration.

11 *Aberdeen*

FROM a point of high ground above Aberdeen, the city falls away below you in a leisurely descent to the shore. Sunshine at any season can make that sea look like the Mediterranean. But in winter, smoke rises from the neat slopes of snow-covered roofs, and not much after mid-afternoon sea and sky become one and the first bead of light breaks out on the upright finger of Girdleness lighthouse, and you know that you are looking out over a far Northern Sea.

Aberdeen is one of the farthest northern cities in the world. For it is by latitude well to the north of Moscow and far up the coast of Labrador. It is the capital of northern Scotland. Only the six cities of Oslo, Stockholm, Helsinki, Leningrad, Reykjavik and Archangel, four of them capitals, lie beyond it. As we are nearer to Norway than we are to London we have a feeling of not only being a long way to the north, but being curiously separate from the rest of this island. Aberdeen is still the third largest city in Scotland, just managing to keep ahead of Dundee.

A city was bound to spring up in a place where two river valleys come to the sea so close together, and with the headland of Girdleness giving shelter from the south winds, while most of the rest of that coast is open. It was equally inevitable that it should have a tumultuous history, being a harbour entrance to a rich inland, with communications running north and south along the coastal lowlands, and westwards up the valleys into the mountains. It was always strategically important and almost always, as the times went, prosperous.

To seawards from where we stand you will see, if it is a clear day, a long sweep of sea horizon. One never could tell in the old days what was coming from behind that line. From behind that slope came the galleys of the Viking invaders with their short swords, their shields, and their winged helmets. They were followed eight hundred years later by the German bombers, once more to leave the dead and wounded in our city streets. These are to be added to those armies who marched in on us from the landward over so many years.

Now there are mountain cities and prairie cities and all manner of other cities, but Aberdeen is really a river city, the city of the Dee and the Don. Its name was originally Aberdon, so they say. From the mouth of the Dee ships sail all over the world. Our Lord Provosts, whose office is nearly seven hundred years old, are Vice-Admirals of the coast of Great Britain and Ireland. Between the two breakwaters, where the harbour meets the sea, pass the ships of round about twenty countries, bringing in well over a million tons of cargo a year. Three-quarters of the ships are trawlers bringing a hundred thousand tons of fish from the seas of Iceland, Faroes and nearer at hand. It is a fine harbour but man-made and needing constant watching. It is a tribute to Smeaton, Telford and others who put their skill into it in years gone by. As it is in the middle of the city it is not easily capable of enlargement. Aberdeen has now climbed to the top of the hill, from which I invited you to see it. Before the war, that slope was green fields. After the war prefabs climbed most of the way to the top, like skirmishers, to extend the line of houses. They dug in and awaited reinforcements. These have arrived, the skirmishers are withdrawing and tall blocks of glass and concrete have pushed outward the citadel of the city dwellers.

In a city of contrasts the fish dock contrasts with almost everything, with its own noises and its own particular atmosphere and not least its smell which is an exhilarating one. There is the steady screaming of gulls, the clangour of metal trolley wheels and the grating of wooden fish boxes on a cement floor. A steady pitch of conversation, runs through this staccato accompaniment, just loud enough to be heard above all these noises, which are thrown back by the low roof. And to add to the noise there is the clanking of windlasses of the trawlers packed tight with the bows against the walls of the basin, and so close at times as almost to touch. It was here by custom that Priscilla made one of her first speeches at election time.

This is Britain's third biggest fishing port. Like Dundee it was once a whaling port. Some of the old whalers' men are still alive. Like so many other industries our whaling started in the Scottish commercial upheaval of the second half of the eighteenth-century. At its peak we had fifteen whalers out of Aberdeen in 1820, and three years later they brought back over 1,800 tons of oil in fourteen vessels. But the sands of commerce shifted, as they are always shifting. The Government withdrew its bounty, duty was reduced on foreign oil seeds. You turned a tap in your house and applied a match and became eerily illuminated by hissing gas light. All this ate into the living of those amazingly steadfast men, who developed what was more a way of life than a business. And, on top of all that, they slew so many of those slow-moving and slow-breeding species in the Arctic that the vessels were beginning to return empty. Even so they were whaling in the Arctic up to the 1914 War and the focus is now on the Antarctic.

The deep-sea fishermen never seem to change, but to stay cloth-capped and jerseyed, sea-booted and sturdy and cheerful. Under a canopy of screaming gulls the trawlers will be there on the tide. In the deep-water harbour one can see, at one time or another, the flags of every maritime country in Europe. Big ships come in from Russia with the hammer and sickle on their funnels, and from Poland, with the emblem of the white eagle, and expressionless seamen discharge sawn timber or flax or one of a score of other cargoes, controlled by serious-looking broad-shouldered officers. Smaller vessels run up with potash from Spain. Ships from North America discharge meal and newsprint and, others from North Africa, esparto grass. Very occasionally a ship will be in with phosphates from the Nauru Islands, that little guano-encrusted dot on the map of Micronesia, dreaming in the South Seas. The old coastwise traffic has largely died out, between Aberdeen and London, but a Britain firmly in the Common Market would have a great deal more sea traffic from Europe.

Many of these ships have come from half across the world. Some come from further still. The ships in from Scandinavia with timber pile up their stands of planking on the pier. This represents the amount of timber that we do not grow in this country but which we need. It has been unloaded here from the Baltic for four hundred years. Sometimes one may see a full-rigged foreign ship in there with the naval cadets, which always makes a bold sight. Sometimes there is one of the Queen's ships, shiny and grey and flying the White Ensign. The variety is infinite. There is a graceful line of granite buildings round that dock, as a background to the ships, and the offices of the merchants that serve the ships—compass adjusters and ship's chandlers for example and even a shop where you can have yourself tattooed.

It is another element and another world to drop into Aberdeen airport in the dusk. It is a very cosy airport. Oyster catchers sit on the runway, and you smell the air of the hills as you come down the aircraft's ladder and feel deep country around you. As it is only 6 miles from Potterton it is an almost miraculous way of reaching home on an end-of-week evening. We can do a whole day's work in London and not leave the city until five and be back at Potterton at about ten o'clock. And if it is summer, being so far north, we can still go round the garden and look at the flowers, or go fishing. You could read print, if you felt like it.

Almost everybody who comes to Aberdeen says at some stage, that the place is remarkable. It is remarkable in a lot more ways than the visitor notices. It was built, as Priscilla once said, in moving the reply to the Queen's Speech in the House of Commons, on, "stone, salt-water and skill." At the highest part of the city is Rubislaw Quarry, one of the two largest man-made holes on earth. (The other is the Premier Diamond mine in South Africa.) Out of this quarry the whole of the granite of the city was howked —dug if you like, or rather mined. One does not have to be very old to remember an Aberdeen in which there were no buildings except granite buildings. It is called the "City by the grey North Sea"* by a contemporary historian and "the silver city with the

* Fenton Wyness, *The City by the Grey North Sea*.

golden sands" by those who promote its holiday attractions. Both are right. It is usually a grey city but, when the summer sun blinks at it through strings of summer rain, it can turn to a brief and blinding silver. And its sands are golden. Like Oxford, the finest view of its spires is spoiled by a gasworks in the foreground, and, like Oxford, its main feature is a long and beautiful and historic street. However, the traffic is less chaotic than in Oxford. For although Aberdeen is a university city, it does not have Oxford's myriad bicycles, ten thousand of which cross Magdalen Bridge every day in term time. Aberdeen has now done away with her trams and taken up the cobblestones in King Street, which was the longest cobbled street in Britain, and the traffic is now much as you will find it anywhere else.

France before the French Revolution was governed by its three Estates of the Realm. Anything that affects Aberdeen as a whole is, in effect, referred to the judgement of three communities which collectively make up the mind of this ancient city. These communities are world famous. The university, the city's celebrated commercial class, and its equally celebrated professional class. They are our "three Estates". King's College is one of the most beautiful university buildings in Britain, or in the world for that matter. Now that Britain is becoming encrusted with ugly and formless university buildings, it is worth remembering that it would have been quicker, cheaper and easier, back in the Middle Ages, to have built ugly and formless university buildings. But they attached tremendous importance to youth being taught in beautiful surroundings. We are lucky to have inherited from their hands as many of these buildings as we have, to remind us when we see today's glass and concrete boxes, rising drab and graceless from their foundations, that once men cared as much about growing the rose as they did about growing the cabbage.

The splendid stone crown on the top of the tower of King's College is not the crown of Scotland, nor is it the crown of Britain. It is the crown of the Holy Roman Empire. It was set there when Scotland was beginning to share the sunshine of the European renaissance, when Lorenzo the Magnificent reigned in Florence, and the first and worst of the Borgia popes gave his authority to the founding of that college and university, in the northern part of James IV's kingdom "where the people were rude, ignorant and almost savage." There is no need to explain our commercial community. It is known all over the world.

Since we have never had easily accessible markets we have always had to sell hard and far off. Today we sell flowers to Fiji and heavy granite rollers to Canada. South Africa buys the most of her seed potatoes from us and the Red Chinese buy cattle gallstones and with them make medicine. If you eat a steak in an hotel in Gibraltar it will be fresh because it was probably flown from Aberdeen that day. Our professional community, like our commercial one are, has had to be twice as good to start level with the cities of the South. Those who go into the professions, from our many seats of learning, know that only the highest standards are adequate, unless they are to spend their lives poor and unregarded among our northern mists. So they have absorbed the learning of Europe and sold their skills across the world.

In the early 1830s, when we were entering the first Industrial Revolution (we are now in the second) we had a strange balance of trades and professions. For every twenty thousand of our citizens, who were less than half today's total, we had only one veterinary surgeon, accountant, architect, dentist and optician; two auctioneers, bankers and surveyors; four printers; five insurance and ship brokers as well as physicians; sixteen surgeons; thirty-four teachers and forty-two advocates. We had one hundred and seventeen different trades, and, on the same basis of calculation, there were thirty-four tailors, forty-seven boot and shoe-makers, sixty-five vintners and seventy grocers and spirit dealers.

If one does a city job in a Canadian city like Vancouver, or a New Zealand city, like Wellington, or more than one Australian city, one can have the life of the city and can throw away everything of an evening or weekend and lose oneself in the countryside, fishing or riding, bathing or sailing, enjoying oneself in half a dozen other ways. And this is because there is the right balance of population of the city to the surrounding countryside. There is room for them all there. Aberdeen is very much the same. The life of Aberdeen hums at a furious rate in office hours, but those who sit on office stools can, in their weekends, go up to the Dee valley to walk in the high hills, or try their hand at serious rock climbs. Nearer home they can enjoy the sea beach. In due season they can fish, for the Ythan at Newburgh is one of the few places in Britain where seatrout will take a fly in the salt water. In winter there is wildfowling, and wildfowling is free to any man on the foreshore. One can breathe in Aberdeen, unlike those great clusters of cities in the Midlands, where one is only just clear of the sprawl of one before one is into the next one, and a man may wonder if he is ever going to see green fields and growing trees again.

Aberdeen lives in the world. If you do not have relations who live in Hong Kong or do business in Singapore, or farm in Kenya, or Canada, or do one thing or another in a hundred other parts of the Commonwealth, one will know friends and neighbours who have. The names on the sterns of the ships in the harbour are as familiar to the people of Aberdeen as the villages of our county. Being the largest fishing port in Scotland, and the third biggest fishing port in Britain, our community of deep-sea fishermen is a substantial one. Few people in Britain stop to think of how much responsibility a railway signalman carries until there is an accident. Until a trawler is lost with all hands in the cold northern seas, few ponder what hardship and how much risk these men are taking day in, day out all the year round. They see their wives once, on average, in every seven days in the year. That community of wives, when all the rest of the world may be peaceful, turn on the radio night and morning to listen to the shipping forecasts—to the voice intoning "Iceland, Faroes, Fair Isle, Bailey, Hebrides, Rockall". When you saw them in the street, they look no different from the rest of us. But their world is their own, their hopes and fears are bound up with the sea.

But there are no sturdier folk than the Aberdonians when it comes to that. This strange, far-northern city of stone has sent its sons, regularly and without question, to the farthest corners of the earth, and continues to do so. The Scots are perhaps the most famous small nation since the Ancient Greeks, because they have not all stayed at home. Their historic seats of learning have always produced a far larger number of highly-educated men than for whom highly rewarding jobs could be found in so small a country as Scotland. The rule of primogeniture has meant that a farmer has left the farm to his eldest son, and the rest have had to go out to seek their fortune. We have two natural gifts when it comes to seeking our fortunes which sell high in the right market. One is an ability to live happily anywhere else in the world, and far more happily than anyone else in real isolation. While doing this we stoutly maintain that Scotland is the best country in the world, and somehow the world does not find us unbearable. And we have a genius for survival, which the Poles and the Israelis also have. Survival is not an art, still less is it a science, and least of all is it an accident. And finally that wide range of intonation and brogue, that we loosely call the Scottish accent charms and intrigues the rest of the English-speaking world. Her sons never forget Aberdeen and many come back there to retire. Thus it is most unwise in a public place to boast of your knowledge of a distant part of the world, or that one can speak Eskimo or can navigate the Hooghly River, or use a bolas. There is quite certain to be an old Hudson's Bay trader there who speaks Eskimo far better than you do, or a Hooghly pilot with years of experience, or someone who acquired his sunburn on the South American pampas. There is sure to be somebody about who has not only been to the part of the world you mention, but been there for longer and penetrated far farther. To take one group alone, and that not a large one, consider the taxi-driver of Aberdeen. Over the last few years I have been driven by one driver who at the age of fifteen had been a harpooner's mate, on the old wooden whaler *Active,* out of Peterhead, in the Eastern Arctic Seas. This fact came to light when we got stuck in a snowdrift. Another, in his youth, had met Buffalo Bill in the old West. A third, and this time a young man, speaks excellent Swahili that he learned in the King's African Rifles. Some Scots think that we should never leave Scotland. But you will not change us.

If you sit up on the high dunes on a summer day, as we often do, you will see ships, some of them big ships, coming from distant countries, and heading for the mouth of the harbour. They are drawn to Aberdeen by the skills and energies of its citizens. The city's name is known the world over. It is distant, but it is not remote. It is a metropolis in its own right.

12   *The Journey*

IN OUR time we must have been British Railways' favourite couple. For Priscilla represented South Aberdeen in the House of Commons for some twenty years, and London claimed the most of my working hours. For eighteen of those years we were married and must have covered more than a million railway miles between us, between our home and our work. We each spent, during that time, more than a year and a half in the train until air services improved. Setting off for the north never became any less exciting, but we found that the return journey south depressed us more and more as time went on. This depression began to set in after luncheon on Sundays and spread to our dog Rory. We came to understand how it was that, in the American Civil War, some of the troops suffered so severely from home-sickness that they were listed as campaign casualties under that heading.

In winter we started our railway journey in the dark, and arrived in the chilly murk of a London morning. There was nothing to see as we travelled. It was a period of confinement in a swaying, creaking compartment, in a dark, noisy world. The changing note of the rails, the rattling over the points, and the lights of small stations flashing past, were the only clues that we were travelling. Footsteps shuffled and clattered outside at a halt, and echoed under the wide roofs of the big stations—Dundee, Edinburgh, Newcastle and York—to tell you of an occasional arrival. Then there were sudden noises on and off—the hollow rumble as we went over a bridge—the noise like a tropical thunderstorm as a fast train passed us in the other direction. Going south we now see the red Cyclops eye on each tall upright of the Forth road bridge, and the undulating necklace of lights which hangs from them to join one shore to the other.

There have been changes. Where the old steam trains used to start noisily, in a series of laboured leaps, the diesels now have the silken start of a motor car. We now have to say which Forth bridge or Tay bridge we mean. Each in this last decade has become plural, where before they were majestically singular, like Stonehenge or Cleopatra's Needle. But nothing alters the fact that a cold sooty dawn at King's Cross will be with you only too soon.

But the journey gives us a splendid opportunity to get some work done. Work that we took north to do, but never got around to doing, because there was so much else that was so absorbing. And then there is a great deal of pondering over the events of the weekend, and a poring over diaries of the events of the week to come.

Although Aberdeen station may be bitterly cold when we arrive in the half darkness of a winter morn, we always get a wonderful lift from fresh air, the smell of fish fresh from the fishing vessels and slapped on the fish dock, and the keening of the gulls, which tells that we are back beside the Northern sea. Aberdeen makes sure that its station is as clean as any in Britain. It is a neat building with a neo-Georgian front. Its name of the Joint Station goes back to the days when the railway from the South shared it with the Great North of Scotland Railway, the Deeside, the Donside and the Buchan railway, five companies in all. The train is met by a comely crew of ladies sensibly dressed to clean the train. They carry mops with handles so long that they might be vaulting poles. But by now we can hardly wait to get through the barrier and cover the eight miles to Potterton, to throw open the house and light the fires, wind the clocks and unpack the groceries, and get into our old clothes.

Fellow passengers in winter are all alike, muffled up in over-coats, stepping gingerly down to an icy platform. But February brings a new type of traveller. A man who has a case of salmon rods, and a great deal of luggage. A fortnight later, when we are taking the train south, we sometimes see the same man, almost unrecognisable after his holiday. His face is burned brown with the casting of fly in the cold winds of a Deeside spring. His luggage is probably augmented with two or three floppy bags of straw containing salmon. His face shows that he is just as sorry to be going south as we are.

When we are going south by the night train, with the summer light at its longest, the early part of the journey is beautiful even though we are going the wrong way. We used to take our Scottie terrier with us. Rory had to be weighed in his basket on the station scales, so that he could travel as freight in the guard's van. His weight remained constant at exactly two stone, so that the weighing became merely a ritual formality. We often thought that he felt depressed, immured in his basket, and secretly longed to look like one of those great sporting dogs, who lie like the lions in Trafalgar Square, their paws extending beyond their noses. Those lordly labradors who do not travel in baskets, but are tied up in the guard's van, with a ticket on their collar ad-dressed to the head keeper at some magically named destination— Gannochy or Hunthill, Millden or Invermark. On several occa-sions Rory escaped from his basket. Once or twice in the very cold winter when he found it too cold, he literally ate his way through the wicker work. To our horror we learned that the guard had found him pottering about the platform at Newcastle. Occasionally he was subjected to temptations so terrible that they had not even scriptural precedent. On one journey he found him-self in the guard's van with a box containing cats, and another box containing rabbits. He did not like travelling. But he endured it cheerfully, as part of the price that must be paid if you are possessed by peculiar people.

The train pulls out of Aberdeen and then, gradually gathering speed, crosses the viaduct over the Dee swollen or shrunken according to the tide, and a few minutes later it has shaken off the city and there is the sea upon the left and crawling round the headland on which Girdleness lighthouse stands. Up until a few years ago it crowned a ridge of green fields. But the city now reaches out to challenge its isolation. In the 1951 election, the first two congratulations that Priscilla received were from the keeper of that lighthouse and Sir Alexander Bustamante in Jamaica. The telegrams arrived together. The rail runs beside the coast to Stonehaven. Here and there, are deep gashes in the cliffs that run down to a sea that is heaving and boiling below. In spring and early summer we see the gulls sitting there on their nests in tiers along the steep sides. In the cuttings, many of them built by Peter Thomson, Priscilla's great-great-uncle, you will see in April on the banks covered with primroses, which always seem to thrive at that angle of grassy slope. Newcomers to the Northeast, looking at the fields on the cliff edge, see that the farmers have ploughed to within a foot or so of the abyss, and arm themselves with another story about our Scottish frugality. A mile inland, and above you, the tiny and beautiful Muchalls Castle stands among its trees. The ruins of Dunottar Castle, which held out against Cromwell for nearly six months under Keith, the Earl Marischal, defy the sea from their headland beside Stonehaven. There is a perceptible change in climate here, and in early summer you will see that the white may is far thicker in the hedges than it ever grows with us at Potterton. The soil turns red as you leave the sea and wander down through those rich farm lands to Montrose. The chimneys of Fetteresso Castle, where King James held his first Privy Council after landing in the 1715 Rising, have not smoked for a dozen years now. You catch a brief glimpse of it in its valley on your right, desolate and dispiriting.

It takes about an hour to travel from Aberdeen to Montrose. Nearing Montrose as the train rumbles over the North Esk, there is the flash of a view of a tall black-and-white eighteenth-century house, in a frame of trees on the far bank. If it is a fine evening the trout will be making rings in the big pool below the bridge and beside the island. And soon afterwards you are slowing down for Montrose. The old steam engines used to stand and puff there mightily, as if they were out of breath. That halt is all too brief, for this is one of the world's most beautiful railway stations. On the seaward side is the big church spire rising above the roofs of the most graceful of all the North Eastern boroughs. And inland lies a lagoon, square miles in extent through which runs the South Esk. At low tide it is alive with birds, from tall striding herons to the smallest waders. At high tide it is an inland sea which washes the embankment on which the station stands. One day when it was blowing a gale from off the land, the sea spray lashed the windows of our train. If the Dutch were ever to see it they would yearn to wall it off and drain it, and grow lupins on it, and turn it into green fields. Let us hope that it always survives as it is, to be twice a day an inland sea.

Not very much farther on the train seems to stumble on Arbroath, not realising that it is approaching a town, as it runs down a grassy valley into it. Among the tall red chimneys and red sandstone buildings you get two or three glimpses of the ruins of the ancient abbey. Then the line runs beside the sea again and follows it to the mouth of the Tay, and past the formidable castle at Broughty which John Knox held against Mary Queen of Scots, and holds the north shore of the estuary until it reaches Dundee. As the train rumbles across the Tay bridge you have the view that you have from the bridge of a ship. To the inland the river narrows in perspective and loses itself in a huddle of hills behind which the sun is sinking. If it is very low tide, sand-banks appear, and sometimes you can see seals lying on them, quite close to the bridge, like grey bolsters. As you get somewhere near the middle you see the stubs of the old Tay Bridge, the one that collapsed, on the seaward side. They are now crude mosaics of disintegrating brick and stonework far below you. On almost every one of them, in the spring, you will see a gull or two sitting on their nests, indifferent to the train. The old bridge was blown down in 1879. And the loss of the train that went with it was a story that chilled us in childhood. It was said that my Grandfather, who was at that time a minister at Kirkcaldy, had held up my four-year-old father to look at that "wicked Sunday train." It was at that moment on its way to pay for its wickedness.

And the road bridge which seemed for so long to be stealing stealthily across the estuary below, column by column, now looks as if it had stood there as long as Broughty Castle. The train halts briefly at Leuchars, which serves a modern aerodrome and the ancient university town of St. Andrews. The country settles down to an evening landscape. You feel part of it. The summer dusk may carry the smell of beanfields or of new-mown hay. Quiet comes with it. The train seems to have become invisible. Cattle and sheep in the pastures no longer turn to look at it. It stops twice more in the kingdom of Fife, at Cupar and Kirkcaldy, and then makes its best pace to the crossing of the Forth.

You probably wake up in Hertfordshire in all the beauty of its trees and fields and leaf. Close to the village of Welwyn you pass through a tunnel, and then out over a viaduct beneath which runs the little river Mimram, once a noted trout stream. There are some houses beside it. One of them is lived in by the son of H. G. Wells, the author, who had half a dozen good trout in the pool in his garden, so he has assured me. That was until the water weed died back and the fish went downstream. But they are expected to return to feed on the shrimps and share their old haunts with crayfish. This little collection of houses used to stand completely alone, but now Welwyn Garden City has moved out towards it and runs down the hill almost to the river's edge.

Year after year and, for long periods, week after week, of this journey, has given us a most detailed knowledge of those parts of the landscape that we pass in daylight. We see an annual change in the plantations. Some of them we remember when they were newly-planted and have seen them become substantial timber. We can become so intent on looking out that we forget the time. But when, above the town of Hatfield, rises the great Elizabethan pile of Hatfield House, we start to prepare for London.

The train leaves the countryside at the end of a cutting crowned on either side by a wood of oak trees. London has begun. A line of houses with a straight edge begins just beyond it. From then onwards it is houses all the way. There is a different noise now, as echoes are thrown back from the buildings. Empty stations flash past where the commuters will be gathering in an hour's time. Streets crowd close to hem in the line, and tall factory chimneys rise up beside it. Clanking over a maze of points, and after threading a series of smoky, rumbling tunnels, you slow to a halt at King's Cross platform. There is an opening of doors and a hurrying and scurrying, and a great deal of noise. It was somebody's task to go back to the guard's van to collect Rory. His basket would be lifted down to the platform, with earthquake scufflings inside. Then out would step that furry philosopher shaking himself, sneezing mightily, and ready for anything. A new week's work was starting for each of us.

Few men ever lose their schoolboy love of trains. The little railway that used to run from Symington to Peebles was one of the greater features of our childhood holidays in Peeblesshire. Biggar Water, where my sister and my brothers and I spent most of our time fishing, ran beside it. We never owned watches as children and had to tell the time by the trains. There was a train that went Peebles-ward at about 12.30 which was our reminder to head homewards for luncheon. If we were up among the hills we saw it as a wisp of smoke, seeming to come from a crawling ant, miles away, and far below us. If we turned our footsteps farther afield, out of sight of the valley, as we did when we fished Holm's Water, we would have to borrow a grown-up's watch, which was always a great responsibility. But if we were fishing Biggar Water we heard the train coming from a mile away. The engine-driver used to wave to us and we would hold up our fish to show him as he passed. He mimed applause and encouragement for the sound of his voice was lost in the commotion of his engine. That railway was a great playground. We would sometimes put pennies on the line, when we were feeling very rich, to be flattened to twice their size and paper thin. Cheaper and just as rewarding, was the laying of two crossed pins on the rails which became flattened and welded into crossed swords. On one of our expeditions to Peebles I was allowed to ride on the footplate on the return journey. Nearly stifled in the tunnel I came out blinking into the light to look down giddily as we crossed the tall stone bridge that spans the Tweed, a mile above Niedpath. Along the valley of the Tweed we thundered along at all of forty miles an hour, slowing to where Lyne water ran beneath us to pull up at Lyne Station, which has, now that the railway has gone, been turned into a very agreeable house and garden. We left it behind and watched the rabbits scampering up the banks at our approach. Nothing else seemed to notice us. Stobo Burn ran strong and shallow beneath us. At Stobo Station we looked down in a lordly way, from the height of the cab, on the human race massed below us on the platform. There were at least five of them. And then the Tweed that had run beside on the left, as big as the Amazon in the eyes of childhood, turned away to its cradle in the hills of Tweeds-muir, and we were following the course of Biggar Water. Like thunder we passed through the rock cuttings, from the top of which we sometimes so far forgot ourselves as to throw down on to the trains the great red toad stools which grew under the darkness of the pines. Satan always found us very easy to tempt, when the fish refused to bite. And we were out of the cutting and there was the broad rolling valley of fields beneath the hills that smiled down in the sunlight of an August evening. And all transformed with excitement, as your own street would look if you rode down it on an elephant. There was the familiar old Biggar Water, beside and beneath us, on the right, where we knew most of the fish by sight and some of them by name. There were the dippers that bowed and bobbed, and the one and only kingfisher.

Many who have had the luck to have had a country upbringing will remember country railways, and the little village stations with footsteps crunching on the gravel on a drowsy summer day, and the neat beds of geraniums, and tall hollyhocks like a cottage garden. And they will remember the affection that we had for the almost traditional advertisements for Pear's soap and Virol, Mazawattee tea and somebody's sheep dip. They went with the years of our youth. Those country trains then seemed like domesticated wild animals, because they were big and lumbering and good-natured. It seemed reasonable to suppose that you could tame one. To do so became my ambition. Those country railways posed, to those whose task it was to keep the railways solvent, a deepening nightmare. "Don't come on that train," our elders would say, "it is a horrible train, it is always full. Wait for the next one, it's a splendid train, there's nobody in it." It was not only our elders who said it. We said it ourselves when we grew up. Small wonder that those country railways have become stretches of fox-gloves and willow herb, that run through green cuttings and embankments over which the wild flowers and the weeds have swarmed. The rabbits have other problems, but country trains no longer disturb them. And the steam engines went, and the strong and silent diesel engines replaced them.

The railway revolution was being matched by the less conspicuous, but continuing, improvement in flying. Where we used to have to change planes at Edinburgh, there was now a direct flight to Aberdeen. But ever so often we must needs fly south to London from Edinburgh and that has always been to take a long step back into childhood, particularly on a summer evening. For then you see the countryside marching below. Peebles is easy to recognise, with its big stone bridge across the Tweed, which was built in the 1880s, when my great-uncle was town clerk, and bears his name on a plaque. Neidpath Castle rises from its tall green mound that the river almost encloses. They choose a new Warden of Neidpath each year. Several of our family have served beginning with my father, and in 1967 Priscilla was installed. The Tweed winds upwards along its lovely valley, past Manor Valley and the House of Barnes, and Dawyck in its famous woodlands. Then the hills get higher and steeper and the country sparser when you pass Merlindale where the wizard is said to be buried. But it is confusion of legends for the great Merlin did all his wizardry in Wales. There is a ford in the Tweed, just above where my grandfather, a Presbyterian minister, drove his gig across in a rising spate. Every one of his children was aboard, which helped to ballast it, but the pony lost his footing and began to swim and the gig started to float and be swept downstream. My grandfather lashed the pony to a final effort and it found its feet and the wheels found the bottom. Otherwise it would have been the extinction of the whole of our branch of the family.

This is the foot of the upper reach of the Tweed which is called Tweedsmuir. You can see where the old peel towers stood, each sited to see their neighbours' beacon fire, and pass it on to the next tower in the chain. Some are no more than heaps of stones, with here and there the angle of a medieval wall. The side glens open. There is a Hopecarton on the left, and just visible in its folds is the tiny burn where my father and I once caught fifty trout in a few hours, in the days when nobody fished these burns at all. We had been given a lift from Broughton by the postman in his pony trap, who picked us up on his way back down the valley in the afternoon. Our primitive car (it was the early 1920s), as was not unusual, was out of commission. A blink of sun flashes up at you from the mirror surface of a pool, with its wrinkle of rapids above and below. Two gentle (or as we say in Scotland) "douce" eighteenth-century houses, still possessed by their original families, dream among their trees from up on the hillside on the right of the road into England. You can just see white foam as the Tweed pours under the arch of its bridge at the village of Tweedsmuir, and the little kirk that stands on the left on the mound where the Covenanters were buried. We were sometimes taken in childhood as a variant to the kirk in Broughton. The shepherds at Tweedsmuir used to bring their dogs to the kirk, and they would sit under the pews while their masters wrestled in prayer. There are fewer than two hundred of a population of Tweedsmuir, but the name of this clachan has taken root in far places. A sheep station in Queensland, which Priscilla and I came upon, one very hot day, was named for an earlier son of the village. After my father is called Tweedsmuir Glacier in the Yukon, a provincial park in British Columbia, a township in Saskatchewan and, after both of us, a group of islands that are locked for eleven months of the year in a jigsaw of ice in Canada's Eastern Arctic.

The village is falling astern. You cannot put your head out of an aircraft and look back. There is Talla reservoir below, already in nearly full shade from the westering sun, so deep in its cleft between the steep sides that the sun reaches it for too short a time to its waters to nourish food for its trout, which are lean and rakish. Talla Linn sparkles with its horse tail of foam. We used to picnic there as children and catch those yellow-bellied trout with their black backs. Above, there is the plateau from which Talla and Gameshope burns tumble, and where we once thought that we saw a Golden Eagle. My father was sure that it was one. A century of bare-legged Buchan children have wandered these hills and fished those burns. But the valley of childhood has fallen behind now, and in fifty minutes we shall be in London and in an uncomfortably grown-up world.

But not all our summer memories were of that valley, for several times my father had taken me to the Highlands on a short sporting holiday, with some of his host of friends and twice we took a place in the Island of Mull. The journey to Oban on the Highland Line was particularly exciting. The lines not only ran through some of the noblest scenery in Scotland, but the stations had magic names, which the station-master used to stride up and down his platform intoning. Almost every place name has magic when it is chanted in a Highland voice, and names like Crianlarich became not a word but a line of music.

On one occasion we were travelling slowly across the Highlands. I do not remember when or whither we were going. My nose was to the window panes when with dreamlike suddenness a salmon river passed beneath us. There was a roundish pool in it and on, what was now, the far bank stood a young man. He was dressed in brown tweeds and was standing in an attitude of strained stillness, like a figure on a Grecian vase, a mighty green-heart salmon rod bent and bending in his hands as he played a salmon at the end of a long line. A fold of green bank rose up and hid him for a moment. Then we were beginning to leave the riverside as our train sped slowly down the glen. My father had seen this vision. He followed my anguished glance to the prim plaque on the wall, beside the communication cord "penalty for improper use £5." Too well I knew how great a sum of £5 was in those days. But what a noble cause in which to spend it. You could not turn your back on a man playing a salmon. Not in a civilised country. Any more than you could deny the use of the ship's boat to women and children on a sinking ship. The engine driver must have seen it and be surely about to bring the train to a halt. But no. We did not even have the chance of enjoying the vision in diminishing prospect. A great bank, crowned with a thick and useless wood, rose to blot it out. I was forced to the Jacobin conclusion that the ideal train would be one which was democratically controlled by its passengers. Since then I have come to believe that although trains are large, friendly animals, only given the right circumstances, can you tame them.

About ten years later, having chosen a career in H.M. Colonial Service I landed in Mombasa and took the train whose terminus was then Kampala, having been appointed to a position in Uganda. It was one of the most thrilling railway journeys in the world in those days, when the Athi plains were alive with animals of many species. The engine was reputed to be the biggest and strongest in the British Empire of the 1930s. It was not very long after the days when it was considered quite legitimate to pull the communication cord to stop the train to have a shot at a buck. I had just missed the era of the tamed and controllable train. As it was the railway police would sometimes sit on the front of the engine and shoot at guinea fowl. Trains seem to have degenerated as a species. The modern diesel engines do not draw boyhood, as steam engines once did. And boyhood has exchanged trains for the space-ship.

Nine years later, in the blistering sun of the Sicilian hills I was second-in-command of an Ontario battalion, which I later commanded, and we possessed ourselves of a train. It was a little dumpy engine and a tender and it stood on a spur of line in a country station up in those hot dry hills. On another spur were some carriages. They were small, and open, and rather more like trucks with roofs to them. At last my boyhood ambition was realised. I had miraculously acquired a tame train. We were to set off on a long and strenuously opposed advance, and the map showed us that the railway went the same way as we were supposed to be going, and passed through the same objective. It seemed that if we could appear by passenger train in the midst of the enemy's position we should have achieved a degree of military surprise unequalled since Hannibal brought elephants across the

Alps. In a Canadian battalion there is always somebody who can do anything. So that it was not surprising to find that we had a seasoned engine driver, from a famous Canadian railway, standing ready and waiting to drive it. We filled our water-bottles from a spring, and from them the boiler, which was a very long slow job, got up steam, and prepared to shunt all the little carriages that stood sunbaked in the siding. At that moment the train's regular Sicilian crew emerged from hiding, clad in their railway livery and took up positions on the foot-plate under the critical eye of our Canadian engine driver. We pushed one sturdy truck in front of the engine to explode any mines, hitched up the carriages and set off on a reconnaissance. We seemed to have devised a rare stroke of strategy. We reached the first bridge. It was not there, the lines twisted over into an abyss. We got the brakes on just in time, and sadly reversed whence we had come. There is something about trains, as a species, which defies all prediction.

One summer evening, in 1955, headed north, I asked for and received permission to ride from London to Grantham on the foot-plate. I put on some old clothes and some goggles, showed my pass, climbed up into the engine, getting very dirty in so doing. The engine driver was a short man and a doyen of his profession. In Canada most of the steam engine drivers were young, but in Britain all the crack drivers were men well on into middle life. And this was one of the aristocrats of the foot-plate. They called them the Grantham men. Those who drove on the London-Grantham or Grantham-York runs were supposed to be the pick of the engine-drivers of Britain, for it took years to master that piece of line. When you rode on the foot-plate of a steam engine everything was a novelty. First of all, there were no springs. In spite of its enormous weight, the engine seemed to roll and even pitch. There was something else that you do not associate with a railway train, a forward view.

There was quite a squash on the foot-plate that evening. For an inspector was travelling as well as myself. After the guard had shrilled his whistle we were off into the black portal of the first tunnel, with our own smoke pushed back into the cabin by the tunnel's confines, with nothing but the glow of the fire to see. Occasionally we would meet a train coming the other way, which at first sight always looked as if it was coming headlong to meet us on our own line. We cleared the tunnels. When we passed the line of houses where London stops we sped into the countryside drowsy with evening sunlight. The engine-driver, perfectly placid, leaned out of the left-hand side of the cab looking for signals. The stoker, a young man from the Isle of Skye, stoked expertly with a pointed shovel, hurling the coal right into the farthest part of the fire. Every now and then he would have to rush to the right-hand side of the cab in order to look for signals, while the engine-driver was looking leftward. It became clear that the driver knew every inch of that journey. Occasionally we would have to shift to get out of the way, while they flooded the floor to clean it. And then one fell into a reverie of speed, no longer disturbed by the bumping and lurching.

I remembered the experience of a friend who, in the 1919 strike, had learned to drive an engine and got a certificate to prove it, just as the emergency ended. He produced it proudly in the General Strike of 1926 and was instantly appointed to drive an express from London to a Midland city. A booking clerk was lent to him as a volunteer stoker. They took with them a timetable to be able to tell how nearly they were running to time when they passed stations. They got going after a jerky start, and were just settling down to an even speed, when the booking clerk fainted from the heavy exertion of stoking. My friend made him comfortable as he could and set about stoking as he drove. From the timetable he could see that he was making reasonable time. And just when he was beginning to think that engine driving and stoking were easy, if arduous, he came round a corner and saw, on the long straight in front of him, that the level-crossing gates had been shut across the line. His first reaction, to put on the brakes, was vetoed by the voice of instinct. Had he braked he would almost certainly have derailed the train. As it was he opened the throttle, as wide as it would go and hit the gates at round about ninety miles an hour. With a crash, and he was through, and the train was safe, leaving two vivid memories. One was of the big lamps on the gates soaring skyward from the impact, and the other of long spears of wooden splinters from them executing a graceful arc falling to impale the roof of the guard's van. He was only a few minutes late when he pulled into that Midland city.

Our run to Grantham was nearly at an end. I became used to the motion and could feel the peace of that June evening, beyond the smoke and the smell and the noise. The light was beginning to dim a little, and two hours had passed quickly when we saw, as from a ship at sea, a tall spire. It was the spire of Grantham

Church, one of the tallest in the kingdom. I had earlier asked the engine driver how fast we were going, for there was no speedometer on a steam engine. He unbuttoned his overalls and took out a large gold watch, opened the front, looked at it, looked out at the telegraph posts, thought for a while, snapped his watch shut again, put it back, and said, "Eighty-two-and-a-half miles an hour." One of the fastest runs ever made in the history of railways was made on that line, but that particular year they were governed to a speed of eighty-five. The spire marched towards us, the engine driver put his hand up to touch the button that governed the vacuum brakes. The pointer of the vacuum indicator, above his head, moved upwards from zero. He released it, then made it mount up again and, as if a giant had suddenly laid a restraining hand on the train, we slowed until we drew to a halt and the station loudspeaker began to chant the incantation. "This is Grantham; this is Grantham." We all said farewell, and the backs of engine-driver and his fireman disappeared down the platform, another day's work done. They looked satisfied, as men do who get their satisfaction from a perfect mastery of their jobs.

In October of that same year Priscilla and I had exchanged the nodding gait of pack-ponies in the mountains of British Columbia, where we had been hunting grizzlies, for the C.P.R's crack trans-continental train "The Canadian". It seemed unfinished without a bell and a cow-catcher. But we had the rare good fortune to ride on the foot-plate going up Kicking Horse Pass and crossing the Great Divide. The diesel giant, with its banks of dials and which was driven like a motor car, was utterly novel, and bewilderingly complete. "Got two college graduates back there to work all that stuff" said the driver, whose homely appearance did not suggest deep technological insight. We wound our way up Kicking Horse, whose steepness makes it more of a slope than a gradient, hauling a train that was more than a quarter of a mile of steel up into the cold winds of the high passes. On the Great Divide an elk with a splendid spread of antler turned its head to stare at us from beside the rail, then cantered up a bank and the curtain of the forest closed behind it. We started gathering speed with the slope on the far side and the driver engaged the dynamic brake and the whole train slowed at his bidding. For it is a brake that reacts the more strongly that it is resisted. And this was a train of the present. We had grown up with the trains of the past.

13　*London*

LONDON is probably not quite the same to any two people. Like life itself, everybody has their own London. Very few of those who work, or even live, in it know more than a very small part of it, unless it is their business to do so. And, like life itself, it is always changing. I remember, as a small boy, when there wasn't a shop or an hotel in the whole of Park Lane, and my grandmother's house nestled underneath the shadow of the old Grosvenor House. Gradually, over the years that part of London has become less of a place for living and more a place for trading. Now the new sky-scrapers are starting to take away the old character and give it a new one. There were parts of Hyde Park in summer, when the leaf was on the tree, when one could see nothing but leaf all around you. And then, one by one, tall up-ended cubes of glass and concrete rose up to fore-shorten the sky. London's river reflects the life of the London on its banks. At dead low tide, above the Houses of Parliament, rapids appear, which give it something of the appearance of a salmon river, and some of its shingle beaches can look, from a little distance, as clean as those of the Dee or the Spey.

It was once a wonderful salmon river. As late as 1757 the Water Bailiff of the City of London could assert that, "There is no river in all Europe that is a better nourisher of its fish and a more speedy breeder, particularly of the flounder, than is the Thames." It remained a very good salmon river, until the end of that century, and as many as a hundred and thirty of them were sent to market in a single day in 1766. With the beginning of the next century, the population of the County of London doubled and sewage pollution steadily intensified. In 1818 there were still twelve fresh water and six salt-water species of fish in the estuary, and in 1828, four hundred fishermen earned their living from the river between Deptford and London. As the people increased so did the pollution and, as far as is known, the last salmon were caught in 1833 and all commercial fishing had ended by 1850. By 1858 the river smelt so terrible that "the Houses of Parliament had to be draped with curtains soaked in chloride of lime so that Members could breathe."*

In 1884 a Royal Commission addressed itself to the problem of discharge of sewage, and action was taken which brought back fish to a twenty-mile stretch of deserted water, over a ten-year period. Whitebait feasts had been a feature of old London. There were now whitebait at Gravesend again and three years after, in 1895, they appeared off Greenwich. They came back to the London market, that year, together with the first flounders taken off Chiswick for more than a decade. By 1900 smelts were reaching Teddington again. The fresh-water fish began to move downstream and the Putney reaches filled with bleak and dace and roach, the last two finding their way as far downstream as Westminster. For the preceding forty years repeated attempts, always unsuccessful, had been made to bring back the salmon, by putting salmon fry in both the Thames and the Lea. In 1961, after more than ten years cogitation, the Pippard Committee reported that it would be uneconomic, even if it were technically possible, to raise the condition of the river to the level required for the regular passage of salmon—in other words raise it to the point

* Nicholas Barton, *The Lost Rivers of London*. Phoenix House, 1962.

where there was sufficient dissolved oxygen amid all this impurity.

The two world wars, and their aftermath, had resulted in a steady worsening in the pollution of London's river. There was too much else to think about. And so it became a stinking and lifeless stretch of stained water, rather than a river. It was beyond believing that it contained the waters of the Windrush, the Evenlode and the Kennet as well as a score of other clear streams.

In the mid-1950s foreign shipmasters complained that the pollution was so vicious that it took the paint off their ships. Divers needed the beam of a powerful torch to penetrate a distance of only a few feet of the water that had become the liquid equivalent of smog. Anyone who fell in was rushed to a stomach pump. But now as the result of vast expenditure and a great deal of research the Thames has turned from black to grey. It requires a prodigious effort to keep it so.

Life has come back to the tidal Thames. There are sticklebacks again in the Royal Group of docks. At Bankside Power Station, almost opposite St. Paul's Cathedral, in the space of five days, eleven roach were taken in 1965, as well as stray specimens of other species. The warm, cleaning water spilled out from the power stations is attractive to fish, and shrimps have begun to swarm round them and block the condenser tubes in the sea reach. Small crustacea, timber borers and salt water eels are becoming a nuisance in places where they had not been seen in living memory. In October, 1966, more roach were caught, the largest being about 1¾ pounds, which could well aspire to a glass case, on the upper river. Other fish, believed to be bream, have been caught as well. In November of this same year it is said that up to 20 pounds of fish were caught on every tide in the filter screens of Fulham Power Station; the waters of the tidal river live again. Seals, porpoises and dolphins are occasional visitors, and have been during the darkest days.

A. P. Herbert tells us that—

> During the War, for three days, a small pale seal sat on the eastern side of Chiswick Eyot, watched indignantly by the swans who made way for him, and protectively by a policeman posted on Chiswick Mall. Another was reported romping below Teddington Weir a few years back. In April 1965, a third got as far as Kingston —that is, it must have passed over Teddington Weir at the top of a high spring tide. After two or three weeks it made a dignified departure through the lock.*

* A. P. Herbert, *The Thames,* Weidenfeld & Nicolson, 1966.

The French have an ideal river in the Seine, which hurries through Paris at eight or nine knots, while our Thames is tide-bound. But we do not envy them. Throw in a floating object near London Bridge when the tide is turning to the ebb. It will go eight and a half miles down river, to return eight miles up with the returning tide, and will take six weeks to get to the Estuary. It has been said that London's ideal river would be the Congo. Of course it would be, but, as a people, we are deeply attached to the Thames, just as it is, the "liquid history" of Sir Winston Churchill's famous phrase.*

It is loved all along its length, right up to the well where it rises in the Cotswolds. On Sunday, March 13th, 1966, the last fishing day of the season for many coarse fishers, there were 8,777 rods in action over a distance of a 125 miles, between Inglesham and Teddington. It is a heavily fished river but seemingly as full as ever of big fish and many species. If you visit that Valhalla of great Thames fish, the Swan Inn at Radcot Bridge, you will see a record Thames trout of 9 pounds weight which was taken only a few years back.†

So much in our national life is spent in trying to solve the problem of adjusting the lives of our millions of people, confined to small areas with narrow national resources. The Thames is one of these problems. So is the Tyne to which salmon are returning and the Wear whose sea trout now get past Durham, and even the Tees is showing promise. But the position can be held only by great care and experience and the river must flood at the right time. Meanwhile a hundred miles of fishing bank is lost a year by pollution, over the country as a whole. A quarter of all the electricity in England, Scotland and Wales is generated in the twenty-four power stations on the tidal Thames. Power stations are great demanders of water. Because of the massive abstraction of water for industry, the Thames ends by carrying far less water to the sea than the Tweed. Ships in the London docks, as well as the numerous river craft, add to the problem roughly the same disposal needs as would a town of 9,000 people. In the clean city of Sir Christopher Wren, before it became the "monstrous fog-bound city" of Dickens one would have seen many of the tributaries of the tidal Thames running clear and fast. In those days the city smelt atrocious but the rivers were reasonably fresh.

* The phrase said to have been coined by John Burns.
† With the exception of the record trout mentioned all the other fish were caught in a single stretch of river.

They have charming names. The Mardyke and the Ebbsfleet sound like wild fowling in a windy sunset in East Anglia, and there is Beverley brook and the rivers with gentle names, like the Wandle, the Rodin and the Ravensbourne, and the two river Cranes, the full title of one of which is the Duke of Northumberland's River. To all but a handful of present-day Londoners these names are merely historical, and not even geographical, expressions. For they now run their courses to the sea, almost out of the sight of men. Izaak Walton loved to fish the Wandle where the trout ran big and had marbled markings, such as you see on a tortoise. As late as the 1830s it is described as running clear on its gravel bed at Croydon and holding trout a foot long. Much of that gravel has now been quarried and that stretch has been built over.

When you look at the buildings which once stood among green fields on an open river bank, such as Lambeth Palace, Somerset House, the Tower, a cathedral and an abbey, and a bevy of churches, the old London seems to come out of a fairy book. Take the year 1252 for instance. King Henry II received a polar bear as a present from the King of Norway, and decided to keep it in the Tower. "The Sheriffs of London were commanded to pay 4d. every day for its maintenance; and in the following year, an order was also given to them to provide a muzzle for the said bear, and an iron chain to hold him out of the water, and likewise a long stout cord to hold him when fishing in the River Thames." It must have taken some stout men to control the bear, on the end of his long stout cord, if he decided that he did not want to come ashore. Successive kings of England maintained a menagerie in the Tower. Edward II kept a lion and a leopard there and they had a quarter of mutton a day costing 6d. The keeper's wages were 1½d. a day while certain unfortunate esquires imprisoned there were allowed a daily allowance of only a penny.

In the City itself you can still see many signs of Roman buildings. For many years to come there will be reminders to be seen of Hitler's bombs. Ragged, broken walls of brick or the sides of a building with fireplaces, one above the other. But much of that desolation is now turned into neat and seemly car parks, and buildings are arising to fill the rest. One had become so used to being able to see St. Paul's from about 400 yards' distance, it is rather surprising now to find it hedged in again as it always used to be.

To anyone who has ever been concerned with politics, the Houses of Parliament will always be the centre of London. That great Gothic building takes a powerful hold on its inmates. Priscilla and I met there, and became engaged there, and so it will always mean something particular to us. In spite of being so vast and Victorian, there is nothing oppressive about the Houses of Parliament. One can always walk to the windows or to the parapet of the terrace and watch the tides hurrying past and the duck flighting up and down. Or just opposite the House of Lords a hundred yards away, one can stroll over to the Jewel House and see in its moat large rainbow trout slowly weaving their way round their rectangular pools. And the unexpected never gets tired of happening. During the heated debates of many years ago about what was called the Flapper Vote, the extending of the franchise down to ladies of 21 years old, my father was beckoned from the Chamber by a friend. My father was a keen but not particularly expert naturalist, but as enthusiasts are frequently taken for experts he was generally regarded as one. His friend said that a strange and outlandish bird was seated on a pinnacle of the roof of the Palace of Westminster, and they went out on the terrace to look at it. He had no difficulty in identifying it. It was a cormorant. A large figure appeared at his elbow, and lit a cigar with great care, as he stared upward at the bird. It was Winston Churchill. After a puff or two of his cigar, he shrugged his shoulders, and turned away. "This is the end of parliamentary government", he rumbled, "It is the arrival of the flapper."

If you enter by St. Stephen's entrance you look down Westminster Hall, to which Barry has added his monumental Gothic masterpiece the present Houses of Parliament. Westminster Hall is one of the oldest and most historic and most significant buildings in the whole of Britain. Here, William Wallace, Strafford and Charles I stood their trial. Here kings have lain in state. Here, much of the history of Britain has taken place since William Rufus built it. Look up at those vast hammer beams of oak, as they lose their outlines in the gloom of a late afternoon. They were put up there in the days of King Richard II, getting on for six centuries ago, from the oak that came from an estate in Sussex. Hitler's fire bombs damaged them, and a competitive tender was won by the family living on that estate, and they cut oaks to mend the hammer beams. Those that they cut in the late 1940s were growing at the same time as those that were cut in the days of the second King Richard. Before the Thames Conservancy was formed to control this sluggish giant of a Thames from its tide-end-town (which we have shortened to Teddington) to its source, there was flooding on a very large scale. In 1236 boatmen rowed their wherries into Westminster Hall on the flood waters. After the flood of 1579 they picked up fishes from the floor of the hall when the flood waters had subsided. The Palace of Westminster was almost all of London to me until we got married in 1948. Then it became imperative to earn a larger living.

London started to have a new focus, in that square mile of city whose physical boundaries are little changed since the Norman Conquest and which has built up not only the countries of the Commonwealth but many of the countries of the world as well. It lies a mile down river from Westminster on the same bank. But it is a long mile for the two are worlds apart, too far apart for the nations' good. Halfway between them, and just before you meet the lawns of the Temple on your left, you come on a line of ships moored to the river wall. At the head of them is the *Discovery*, three-masted and single-funnelled, moored as a memorial of Captain Scott of the Antarctic as the Victory was of Nelson of Trafalgar. But before Scott's Expedition she was chartered to the Hudson's Bay Company. On her had sailed my old chief of the Company's fur trade, John Anderson, by name. He had signed on as an apprentice of the Company at the beginning of the century, in his native Aberdeen, and had sailed on the *Discovery* from Peterhead. He had taken twenty-eight days to reach Charlton Island in Hudson's Bay, where he was set to work under Alec Nicholson who had had two furloughs in forty years and spent them in Peterhead. If you are not actually a man of cities your eye will always be straying in search of something of your own world.

The expression "business world" is a generalisation almost too wide to contain any real meaning. Many people have a picture of a successful business man as a stern figure of dynamic driving force, rigidly professional, whose private life is moulded to conform with his work. This Identikit figure, which many publicists present, exists but he is by no means necessarily the most successful business man. I always have reservations about men who are photographed in the attitude of falling forward at you out of a window, or clasping their chins. For all the drive in the world is of no use to you if you lack imagination. Good businessmen come in all kinds of guises, both professional and amateur. And you need both in your business, otherwise you are trying to look through a pair of binoculars perpetually out of focus. The professional knows his business. But the detachment of the amateur is mightily important and he does not fear change. Many people who have come to Britain since the last war have made fortunes, and just about as many have lost them. Strangest of all, several have made fortunes in the City of London this century who spoke only the barest modicum of English. During the last years of his life I was in business with the late Sir Walter Fletcher, who left a great name behind him in places as widely separate as the House of Commons, the Far East and the worlds of art and commerce. He had learned trading in the clove market in Zanzibar, where nobody spoke because they would be over-heard, but you conducted your bargain by putting your hand on the table and a silk handkerchief over it, and your opposite number did the same, and you made your bids by a code of touching the other's knuckles. He had fought against Von Lettow-Vorbeck in East Africa in the first war, nearly died of blackwater fever, been treated, and he believed cured, by a witch-doctor, and had run a sisal plantation out there for some years afterwards. In the last war his great elephantine figure had been carried more than a dozen times over the hump of the Himalayas to Kunming, where he commanded a force behind the Japanese lines, which, as an expert speaker of Mandarin Chinese he was well fitted to do. Years of trading in the Far East had made him a gambler, which was tempered by instinct built up over a lifetime, in the commodity markets of the world. He always managed to guess right three times out of five. Several of his pictures were hung in the Royal Academy. You could never have squeezed Walter into a card index. Good business men cannot be stereotyped.

I was exceedingly fortunate in finding means of earning a living which were really satisfying, and threw me among pleasant and interesting people and took me into businesses whose roots went to the ends of the earth. Our office was just across the road and uphill from Billingsgate Fishmarket, looking at probably the prettiest Wren spire of all, that one which is supported on what looks like four bent fingers of stone. That little churchyard is full of daffodils in spring, and there is a plane tree from which the seed hangs in little balls. One could, at certain seasons, read the time on the clock on the steeple on the far side of this tree, but it became invisible when the leaf was on the tree in spring, and in winter, tree and tower and all else merged into the darkness at about four o'clock. There was nearly always a sooty ring-dove sitting in that tree. Three times I have seen a kestrel perch on that spire. That part of the city has a particular fascination. These small and beautiful old churches are thrust in among all kinds of latter-day buildings, mostly dealing with the farthest parts of the earth. They house firms who deal in metals and rubber and spices, and much else besides. Not far from there, in a brand-new skyscraper, my colleagues and I discuss matters relating to tea estates in Ceylon and Southern India. But just beside the hard geometry of this new building there runs a section of the old Roman Wall, looking little changed from the days when Roman centurions changed the guard there. In another the concern is with cattle running on the green of the South American plains where even in these days we still have many thousand horses. Or again it is a matter of great machines, literally moving mountains and taming rivers, in many parts of the world.

My father once used a phrase, which has since been much quoted, "Let no business man take too narrow view of his calling." It is often said of people that they think about nothing but their business. Of anyone of whom that is true, it must also be true that he must be one of the most unhappy men in the world. I have never known a successful businessman who did not have a score of other interests. The businessman who thinks about nothing but business is very unlikely to be even reasonably successful in it. Business can be one of the most fascinating of all pursuits. In my particular pattern of activities as we are very close to nature we are enormously dependent upon the elements. The worst possible piece of news may be of too much frost in Ceylon, drought in Australia, the sudden rising of the waters of a river with a half-built dam—to say nothing of hurricanes.

If anybody doubts that we are at heart a nation of countrymen, they should wander round the city and look at the crowds who have come out of their offices stopping and looking in the windows of shops where they sell gardening implements, camping equipment, and even mountaineering equipment, or things to do with boats or sailing or anything else concerned with the open air. The makers of fishing tackle and things that go with field sports have opened shops in the city. And the crowds who look into the windows of these shops, having probably done a long day's work in the office, relax immediately as their minds bound away to their chosen pursuits.

We will not have it that we live in London though we work

there four or five days every week, and only go back for a night or two to Potterton. From our flat we see a lot of sky and the shapely skylines of Westminster Abbey and the Houses of Parliament. The big planes to and from London Airport pass close by us along the invisible paths to which they are so rigidly confined that their appearance of freedom is the merest illusion. But although we do not regard our flat as being our home, it is nonetheless an anchorage. Visitors to Moscow always comment on the fact that one never sees a dog there, for Britons feel their absence. If all the birds deserted London it would be a dead city. Strangely enough, whereas the national density is about twenty breeding land birds for every ten acres, the density in Inner London is between forty and fifty. The national density is weighted by the great birdless stretches of certain kinds of bare moorland and forests which are not woodlands but are exercises in conifer geometry. Hitler's bombs left bare spaces and up grew undergrowth and scrub, and with them insects and mice to feed an expanded bird population. The kestrel has become a common bird of Inner London, where it was unknown before the last war. Horses are gone from London streets, and modern living leaves little open garbage. The kites and the ravens are no longer London's scavengers, but the gulls have taken their place, above all on London river, where they make a rich living, principally out of spilled grain. Nearly half of London's families keep cats, and there is a prowling fringe of those gone wild, yet London is rich in birds and Inner London has many varieties.

One night Priscilla was at the Dispatch Box from ten o'clock at night till just after a quarter past three the next morning. We came back to our flat together, and the early May morning was just beginning to show blue-black and the blackbirds in Smith Square were singing. Close by, a mallard flew past quacking vociferously, and it was infinitely soothing after the very long ordeal.

But one only has one real home, and ours is Potterton. We have that old schoolboy feeling of exhilaration going off for the holidays when we go north at the weekends, and the same corresponding feeling of gloom as we go south. If one only sees one's home in tantalising snatches it is an adventure to go there and the idea of retirement seems more and more attractive. It is very difficult for people of my generation to retire, to accumulate enough on which to retire. One just looks forward to a time when one goes on working, but does less work and has more spare time.

Protection of Birds Act, 1954

IN THE autumn of 1953 Priscilla returned to our London flat one evening with the startling news that she had drawn a place in the ballot for a Private Member's Bill. She had entered the ballot with nothing in mind, in the same spirit as one takes a sweepstake ticket. She had half forgotten that she had even done so. Only a short time is ever given to the passage of a private Bill, and so many concessions may have to be made to the Bill's opponents, if it is to pass its various stages in time, that it may lose a great deal of its original purpose and most of its force. The member has to organise a private system of whipping to round up the Bill's supporters in the House and hold them there when the Bill is before it. However, one of the few advantages that the Member enjoys is that of having the assistance of a Parliamentary draughtsman, if the Bill is one that comes from a Government office. Priscilla was very keen to produce a Bill to revise the "McNaghten Rules," on the defence of insanity in criminal cases, but it was not at that time practicable. Having no other cause in mind, she ran through the list of Bills that are always to be found in the pigeon holes of the various Government offices, waiting for the dust to be swept from them, and the upper and lower millstones of our Parliamentary system to grind them into the Law of the land. They were an uninspiring collection in this dovecot, save one. It might have been designed for us. It shone like a bird of paradise among crows. "18th November," Hansard reports the Protection of Birds Bill, "To amend the Law Relating to the Protection of Birds, presented by Lady Tweedsmuir: supported by Mr. Alex Anderson, Major Beamish, Mr. Elliott, Mr. Grimond, Mr. Glenville Hall, Air Commodore Harvey, Lord John Hope, Mr. Noel Baker, Mr. Ormsby Gore and Mr. T. Williams: read the first time; to be read a second time upon Friday, 4th December and to be printed (Bill 19)."

It was probably the largest Private Bill ever introduced, possessing sixteen clauses and six schedules. It replaced all existing twenty-six Wild Bird Protection Acts dating back to the reign of George III, including the one that my father had fought so manfully to pass just twenty years earlier, and over 250 Regulations as well. It was a very large craft. It had been rigged and founded by two powerful advisory committees, one responsible to the Home Office and the other to the Scottish Office, on which were represented ten powerful Bodies comprising all that was knowledgeable in the spheres of ornithology, both protectionist and sporting, and of forestry and agriculture. It embodied the advice of some of the greatest experts in the world. But large craft as it might be, it was just as fragile as all the others.

Up to that time the law on bird protection had been a tangled skein, varying from county to county, and often between a county and its own county borough. For example, whereas 101 species were protected in Carmarthen, only one was protected in Flint. 117 were protected in Inverness and none in Bute; 60 in Aberdeenshire, and only 35 in Aberdeen. The law was unintelligible, almost unenforceable, and the penalties were negligible.

If a dictator should ever be so reasonable as to want to protect wild birds, he would, no doubt, sign a decree, blot it, and hand it to a minion to proclaim, laying particular emphasis on its penalties. It would quite certainly be a very bad instrument for its purpose. Those who do not have the chance to understand the workings of Parliament, may imagine that everybody would not only want to protect birds, but would immediately agree upon how it should be done. The measure would then fly, like a bird itself, through all its stages in both Houses, and become law, its passage marked by nothing more than a series of approving nods. Little do they know. No sooner had the Bill received its first reading in the Commons, than the Home Office found themselves getting 4,000 letters in a week. Priscilla's personal post bag was like Santa Claus' sack. The men of Morecambe attacked the oyster catcher for stealing their livelihood, presumably the shrimps and the mussels. The fruit growers of Kent attacked the bullfinch savagely, as a destroyer of their fruit. The trout farmers entered the lists against the kingfisher, as the underminer of their profession. There was a rogue's gallery in the Bill, of birds that could be destroyed at any time, and another category of these could be destroyed if they were shown to be creating a special or local nuisance. Argument raged, and really raged, about what birds should be included and which reprieved. Above all it became the passionate interest of people of all parties and of none.

The seasons during which wild fowl and woodcock could be shot, became another battlefield, and Members drew their swords in a score of other causes. That is democracy. But that so many had become so passionately involved on the subject of birds was something more. It was the sign of a still civilised country, a country that valued its birds. Thus at the very beginning, the phrase "noxious birds" was struck from the drafting to everyone's satisfaction. For whereas many birds, like men, behave in an obnoxious way, to stigmatise them, by species and names, as "noxious", seemed an affront to creation as a whole. An enormous number of anecdotes and example were put forward in support of argument. Parliament learned that a pair of barn owls would bring three hundred rats to their nest. And that the farmers on the south side of the Humber had become so disgusted by the slaughter of geese, shot by the use of decoys, that no less than 530 of them, farming a huge acreage, had banded themselves together to forbid the use of such decoys on their land. In fact, Parliament acquired a great deal of miscellaneous information. And there were deeply human stories such as how the patience of a clergyman had become exhausted by the persistent attacks of a woodpecker on the wooden shingles of the steeple of his church, that he had sought out the relevant authorities to get permission to shoot it. His application had gone to the police, the County Council and the Home Office. Permission had been so tardily given, that when he was armed with it, and a gun, the woodpecker had gone his way having done £200 worth of damage in the meantime. Figures were produced of a terrible slaughter of Brent geese punt gunners on the Northumberland and other coasts, which were countered by doubts cast on the validity of the figures and the claim that Brent geese were still there in great numbers.

This argument even went beyond the shores of Britain. For it was claimed that, although Brent geese might still be common enough around our coasts, these were all that was left of the once vast Brent population of all Europe, driven from their old haunts by the disappearance of the zostera grass, and we must preserve these as a sacred trust.

The names of Peter Scott, Max Nicholson, James Fisher and many other great experts were called in aid. Amidst all our worries about getting the Bill through on time, without too much alteration, there was something mightily companionable about all these discussions, and the fact that even the most unpopular birds had their defenders as well as their critics. The jay, the magpie and the hooded crow all had their passionate advocates. An eloquent plea was made for a single human being—Brixton's only wild fowler—and that not very large group of mortals, the trout farmers. Controversy raged round the house sparrow. Within the compass of one Honourable Member's speech defending the house sparrow, authorities were quoted as widely ranging as Holy Writ, W. H. Hudson, Victor Hugo, two different encyclopaedias, and a Ministry of Agriculture circular. The speaker spoke of the sparrows' "Perky gaiety, cheek and friendliness to man." But the speaker following consigned them all to perdition as "aggressive little bullies."

And the standard of debate was high. Students of our legal system and the accepted canons of guilt would have heard something to make them ponder from the opponents of the Little Owl who demanded its suppression on the score of it being "an anti-social bird". Whereas a well-known Privy Counsellor defending the moorhen made a fine distinction with the words, "this bird is not a criminal; he is eccentric."

The Bill became a public topic. *Punch* had a good deal of fun with it. Prisclila and I were cartooned in strange hairy clothes with wide frog-like smiles with a halo of birds around us. On April 9th it passed its third reading in the Commons. The French Prime Minister visited Britain. He was reported to have remarked on his return home that the British Parliament spent two days of his visit hotly debating birds, and the other day briefly debating the nuclear bomb. But he added that it was proof that democracy was safe in Britain.

The same evening it had its first reading in the House of Lords.

The late Lord Templewood, much better known as Sir Samuel Hoare and a former Foreign Secretary, had a long East Anglian heritage of sport and the study of birds. He had already introduced this same Bill, with the one material point of difference on the matter of egg collecting, and receiving its second reading in the House of Lords a month or so earlier. Had the Government been able to promise time for its passage through the Commons, Priscilla's Bill would have been unnecessary. But then he very sportingly agreed to withdraw his Bill, if she could pass her Bill through all its stages.

The Bill had been launched in the Commons in the midst of November. It was now high spring. It came to the Lords with most of the rough corners knocked off it. But there remained the two major sources of friction, the length of the shooting seasons, particularly for wild fowl, and the protection, or the withdrawal of it, of certain species. As is often the case, the House of Lords fielded more real experts. It was then claimed, with a good deal of justice, that no-one spoke in the House of Lords unless they had something to contribute. There is a tendency there now to give lectures rather than to speak. Experts anywhere are few. But there seemed to be a formidable number assembled to scrutinise this Bill. I was forced to make a whole series of concessions, notably on the taking of plovers' eggs, the use of repeating shot guns, and the protection of the peregrine. Had I divided the House I would probably have won but there might not have been the necessary total of thirty votes cast to make it a valid division. That would have meant that the clause would have lapsed and would have to have been re-debated, on the next occasion that the Bill came before the House. There simply was not the time to spare, if we were going to get it through within the limited compass allowed. The late Earl Jowitt, who was Leader of the Opposition, was a life-long sportsman and ornithologist. On the second reading he expressed the fear that the provisions on egg collecting would have the effect of turning small boys into criminals. I stupidly let this go without challenge. His words were repeated on the radio that evening and came back to me from the lips of many agitated people. The reverse was, in fact, the case. We were profoundly relieved when we reached third reading on May 13th, and sent back a crop of Lords amendments to the Commons. They swallowed all but two. These two indigestible subjects were the source of much powerful advocacy. They were the little owl and the moor hen. The Commons refused to allow them to be black-listed as rogues, as the Lords desired, and sent them swiftly back to us. With all the signs of a fundamental dispute between the two Houses blowing up, we bowed to the inevitable.

On May 27th I came to the House to move that we "do not insist" on the two amendments. As I reached the Chamber, the Deputy Leader of the House asked me to come to his room. I glanced at the order paper. There were nine orders before my appearance. I talked to him for ten minutes. As I rose to go a frantic official rushed up to me and said that the Bill had been called during my absence. The preceding orders had gone like a morning mist. We had almost been torpedoed coming into harbour, and would have been but for Lord Jowitt. He earned our undying gratitude that day by rising to his feet and doing my job for me. I crept shamefaced into the House which was, by now, discussing something quite different. The Lord Chancellor motioned me to the Woolsack and told me that at an appropriate moment I must apologise. At the end of business I rose to do this and take the chance of thanking all those who had helped me with the Bill, and helped me steer my difficult course between "Priscilla and Charybdis". At that they all laughed and I was forgiven.

The Bill was passed and needed only Royal Assent. It had been before the House on fifteen Parliamentary days, spread over seven months. Nearly 175,000 words had been added to Hansard which was now the fatter by nearly 250 pages. Priscilla and I had made 236 speeches or interventions. And by and large we had got nearly everything that we had wanted. If you want to realise a dream you must let some of it go.

We were profoundly relieved. For there had been so many times when it looked as if this craft of ours must have been sunk. The Royal Assent was given on June 4th. Two days earlier Lester Piggott had brought Never Say Die, first past the post in the Derby. We had used those words often to each other, in the seven months that were past.

Of the eighteen other Bills that had set sail in the previous November, ten reached port with us and the rest had been sunk.

15　*Birds*

THE great advantage of being fond of birds is that one can enjoy them almost anywhere, even in London. From our flat in Westminster we have seen herons, a magpie, two skeins of geese, several kestrels and had our milk bottles opened by a blue tit. In Smith Square, below us, the bushes that have grown up round the blackened shell of Queen Anne's shapely church shelter a number of blackbirds, and an owl often hunts there at night. In St. James's Park the exotic wild fowl, among them old friends of the Arctic summer the blue geese, snow geese, and Canada geese, move among scores of mallard and tufted duck, who are docile as their farm-yard kin, and unrecognisable as the same birds that have hurtled past the wildfowlers on the Essex flats. The re-building of the city has at last expelled the black redstarts, one of the rarer birds of Europe, who moved in when Hitler's bombs turned so much of the city into a rubble of broken stone, which windblown seeds turned into thickets. They were, at one time, so common that the Cockneys called them "Blitz sparrows."

Some people manage to be tiresomely professional about what is called bird-watching, as anybody can be tiresomely professional about anything. Being keen on birds simply means that one is more than just aware of them. It means that one can really enjoy them because one is excited by them. No-one could fail to be stirred by the sight of Lake Nakuru, in Kenya, where you can see at a glance a sizeable part of the flamingo population of the whole world, making the lake look as if it was bordered by a beach of coral pink, or by the migration of the wild geese to the swamps of the Mississippi from their Arctic nesting grounds, hundreds of thousands strong. The late Lord William Percy, one of the great field naturalists of this century, told me that he once rode a horse through these swamps many years ago and put up and on the wing, what was almost certainly, every blue goose in the world, gathered there on their southerly migration. But it can be mightily exciting to see an English sparrow hawk fly at sixty miles an hour through a quick-set hedge or a heron to catch an eel, or gannets diving.

The recognition of birds in Britain owes a great deal to the paintings of the late Archibald Thorburn. As children we grew up mostly in Oxfordshire and partly on the Scottish border and could hope to see about eighty varieties. Having a country childhood and with the Thorburn illustrations for reference, we all grew up enthusiastic and moderately expert. A current reviewer of Thorburn's pictures, and the effect that they have had on so many of us, says—"for me the ideal golden eagle is for ever snatching a mountain hare from the snow-covered hillside, the red-necked grebe rises from the water with bent wings, the sand martin pursues an elusive feather."* He wrote for a host of others besides himself. I would have added the bearded tit, a pensive pater-familias sheltering his serious-looking mate under an outstretched wing†. Though no wit less keen I am far less sure of naming a bird now. More than thirty years, much of it spent beyond the borders of Thorburnland without benefit of the bird

* Bruce Campbell, reviewing *Thorburn's Birds* by James Fisher (Ebury Press and Michael Joseph, 1967) in *British Birds* Vol. 1, No. 12, Nov.-Dec., 1967.
† This is by another artist but is among the illustrations which are predominantly Thorburn's in *The Birds of the British Isles and their Eggs* by T. A. Coward, 1920.

books that now exist, have dulled the edge of recognition. Without a book one ceases to try to put a name to a bird. It is like enjoying the company of strangers at a party without bothering to find out their names, which is what most Britons do anyway. Interesting words cropped up in the Oxfordshire dialect of our childhood, not least the local names for birds, which we learned as children before we learned the real ones. Such a one is "gor", meaning a carrion crow. It is a Saxon word, and is still used. Local names for birds are always intriguing. In Aberdeenshire the Minister of Lumphanan listed the birds of his parish in 1843. He and his fellow ministers were contributing articles on their parishes to the *New Statistical Account of Scotland*, which was published in 1845. His total of eighty-three varieties included the ox-eye titmouse, the red wagtail, and the blue hawk. A fellow minister at Methlick included, in his slightly shorter list of a year or two earlier, the green-headed quaketail, the ringfowl, and the sandy laverock. Both listed the kite. But an Aberdeen minister at the time, wrote sadly that "the beautiful bird, the Bohemian jay, is sometimes seen here but seldom." This is the waxwing whose old name was the Bohemian chatterer, a title which sits strangely upon a silent species. In the previous *Statistical Account,* published in 1793, the minister of Strichen which is five parishes farther north, speaks of the coming of the Californian chatterer in November. He is confusing our wax-wing with the cedar wax-wing of North America, of which he may have seen a picture. It was also called by Gilbert White the German silk-tail, when somebody brought him in a specimen in 1776.* It was not until 1856 that its nest was ever found, by anyone qualified to record it, and that was in remotest Lapland. Today they come to Aberdeen almost annually, sometimes as a handful, sometimes as an invasion, and provide us with a topic of conversation.

Now we live in a place so rich in bird life, that it is rather humiliating not to be able to put a name to all of them. This is particularly so when the autumn migrants come down from the Arctic. It is like forgetting a language that one once spoke fairly fluently and trying to pick it up again. One concentrates mightily on translating single words, without being any nearer to getting

---

* That splendid naturalist was rarely at a loss. He was a close and accurate observer but his broader conclusions were often far off the mark. For instance, he disbelieved in bird migration and thought that swallows were torpid all winter. Others believed that they wintered under water.

the drift of its meaning. Perhaps it is a weakness of middle age, like having to concentrate so hard to read the name of a wayside railway station when you travel through it at speed. In boyhood it seemed so easy to carry the Thorburn pictures in your head. But birds are just as exciting even if you do have to fumble for their names. A Cunard captain told me of the escort of sea-birds that follow him across the Atlantic. Leaving Britain he had several varieties with him until he reached the hundred fathom line, but only a handful followed from there to the edge of the Continental shelf. And one or perhaps two across the Atlantic. He was vague about their names but their presence meant a lot to him.

At Braemar we had plenty of birds in the summer, and very few of them in the winter. Up the Dee Valley came the birds of the river, the duck and the oyster catcher. We could hear the curlew and the cuckoo, the skylark and the peewit at one and the same time on a spring day. Stonechats added their red and black contrast to the white flash of the wheatears, and dippers bobbed on the stones of the river all summer long. But as nights drew in and the river filled with gaunt discoloured salmon, and the sun was early lost behind the hills above the castle, the birds followed the river down the valley and out of our ken. They smelt the onset of winter. It is near arctic winter in the Cairngorms. Those that were left were birds of the mountains, the eagle, the raven, the hoodie-crow and the ptarmigan on the high stony slopes, the grouse in the heather that was stiffened with frost. In the gardens of Braemar small birds lived largely on human charity, and the tawny owl, that kept them in order, had his headquarters in a cypress tree near the Invercauld Arms. A few coveys of partridges kept alive on weed seeds.

The Cairngorms were strongly reminiscent of the Canadian Eastern Arctic, and in so many ways. For in the arctic the great flights of geese clamour their way south when they sniff the first frost, the gulls and the eider-duck and the waders go with them before the sea freezes, and the snow buntings and the horned larks before the snow falls. We were left with only three varieties for companionship in all that silence. They were the great snowy owl and the ptarmigan (both of whose legs are warmly protected by fluffy feathers that reach to their claws) and the raven who exposes two long black bare legs to the arctic winter. The raven and his cousins the rook, the crow and the jackdaw, must be among the hardiest birds in the world. The indifference of our own ravens to cold was clear from their habit of nesting in the Cairngorms in February.

Spring at Braemar was like the spring "break-up" in Canada. Winter's grip loosened with the ice floes grinding and crunching their way down the Dee. But some patches of snow would last all summer through. One has only melted twice in this century. In one summer we could still ski in certain secluded corries in June, and we did not catch our first salmon until that month instead of in March or April. We found few nests at Braemar, except those of the oyster-catchers. The hillside opposite had been stripped of its forest during the war, and sawdust and shavings covered an area, of about an acre, on the other side of the river where they had set up their saw mill. This was always good for an oyster-catcher's nest and, so were the shingle beaches beside the river. Unfortunately our best pools had shingle beaches from which we fished. The oyster-catcher nested at the best part of the fishing season. We had first to find the nest, on each beach, so as to avoid stepping on it. Then we often had to give up fishing as we could not bear to make the oyster-catchers so miserable. They would fly round our heads screaming, or sit down on a rock and look so utterly disconsolate, that we would have to pack up and go to the next pool, where there was another shingle beach and another oyster-catcher and it would happen all over again. Very rarely geese would fly over, a long wavering ribbon of them high up and headed westward. The jackdaws, who for so long had made their homes in the tall square castle chimneys were expelled, and the chimneys were covered with rabbit wire. After a year they saw they had lost the battle and left us. We missed their jangling talk, because they had been there at our coming.

These were the birds of Braemar but they were few compared with the birds amongst which we now live at Potterton, where the dawn chorus wakes light sleepers at four o'clock on a summer's morning. If one goes in for falconry, as I did as a very young man, one comes to know one's birds as individuals, as people, whether they are the short-winged varieties, like the sparrow-hawk, or the long-winged, like the peregrine. Two of the same species will turn out to have entirely opposite characters. You came to realise what intricate mechanisms go to make up birds. The loss of one of the big flight feathers to a bird like a peregrine, is said to be the equivalent of a penalty of 10 pounds extra weight to a race horse. They have higher temperatures than mammals, and a pulse rate which can rise and fall as fast as the revolutions of a powerful motor engine when one presses down and then releases the accelerator. A peregrine can put up no performance if he is fed upon poor thin fare like rabbit, but must have the best beef or freshly killed game. And its food must be chosen with discrimination. Too much of the flesh of the wood pigeon, for example, is heating to a hawk and unhealthy. Birds and beasts must be at their best to survive. Hawks and falcons have to get to know you as well as you know them, if you are going to have a working partnership. I found that you must always wear the same clothes and affect the same mannerisms. You must always seem the same.

Otherwise, except for a caged bird, one rarely has a chance of getting to know one individually. Robins, and such other birds that have defined territories, are an exception. That is one of the exciting things about the nesting season. The thrush that nests in your garden is your thrush, from the moment she starts to build her nest, until all the fledglings have gone and they once more merge into anonymity. People will tell you that they have a bird that nests every year in the same place. They may be right. It is hard to be sure that it is the same bird. But it is their bird to them. There is a feeling of partnership as much as ownership. We have two or three places at Potterton where there is nearly always a woodcock in the winter months. We rarely shoot them now, but regard them as pleasant ornaments. But in the days when we did, if you shot one of them, as like as not there would be another one in the very same place the very next day. It is the wish to involve oneself with birds and to share their world, and know them as individuals, that marks the lover of birds.

When we left Braemar Castle, in the autumn of 1952, we exchanged all that Sir Walter Scott had meant by "Caledonia stern and wild" for the lowlands of the Aberdeenshire coast with the shores of Norway nearer to us than London. We were now on the direct flight lines from the breeding grounds of Iceland and Scandinavia. Because we had become possessors of a wooded enclave, set amongst the bare rolling fields that run down to the sand dunes of the shore, we had the only nesting cover for small birds for some miles in any direction. One of the most thrilling things about settling in a new part of the country is the exploring of it and of the country around it. After a month of owning a property that was fields almost entirely surrounded by thick forest we found, when dusk fell on the shrieking tempest of January 31st, 1953, that our property was fields surrounded by tangled wreckage of fallen timber. The original slopes emerged again, as the wood merchant removed the debris over a period of months, and heather and bent and fern re-established the hold that they had lost for fifty years. To the birds we now presented an entirely new world.

Following the burn to the sea was one of our earliest voyages of discovery. When it reaches the high dunes it forms a good-sized marshy pond, a dense mass of yellow flowering flags in summer, and then slants through a canyon of tall dunes to the sea half a mile beyond. Not far off, a tiny burn sinks into the sands when it meets the barrier of dunes and builds in wet weather, up into a series of ponds. On the sea beyond the dunes the wild duck spend their days and fly when night falls to their feeding grounds inland. Tired migrants from Norway pitch gratefully in among the benty hillocks to get their first rest, and their first beak full of fresh water, since many a weary hour of flight with the stars above and the moonlit sea beneath. There are other marshy ponds dotted about amongst the bents, and in the heather mosses inland, but there is only one loch with a name to it within many miles.

After we had explored the immediate shore we pushed north to the estuary of the river Ythan at Newburgh. There are few places in Britain where, in the nesting season, such a landscape of bird life can be found. For as one walks down the north shore of the estuary, nesting eider-duck lumber out of the heather beside one, while the idle drakes chuckle on the water, newly white and green in their breeding plumgae. The fifteen hundred nesting pairs make it the biggest eider-duck colony in Britain. Before one reaches the big dune (a bald mountain of sand), the screeching of the terns, common, arctic, sandwich, and little terns, starts to merge into a steady rasping chorus. And at last, as one rounds the bend of the estuary, and climbs the tallest dunes and looks down at the sea beyond, one sees what at first sight seems to be a mirage. It is the weaving of thousands of slim white wings. The Nature Conservancy has now taken it in hand, and movement there is much more restricted, which is just as it should be.

North of Newburgh is the little fishing village of Collieston with a tiny harbour enclosed by a breakwater. It was built just before the advent of the steam trawler, which has concentrated most of the fishing vessels here in the big fishing ports. The level sandy beach has given way, to the northward, to low cliffs which run up the coast to Peterhead and Buchanness. Here is one of those strange bird frontiers. For with the cliffs come the gannet and the razor bill, the puffin and the guillemot, who rarely stray even a mile to the sands to the southward. From all this it will be clear that, in weekends from our work in London and such holidays as we have, there is so much to do that it is impossible to do more than a little of it. Once one has lived for a season in a new place one finds out the general pattern of things. And from then onwards one fills it in, in more and more detail. Keeping records becomes the more exciting the longer one keeps them and the more that there is for comparison. We had pintails the first year in the pond in the dunes, but never since. In some years we have a substantial number of shovellers. About every three years we have an invasion of wigeon, some of whom have whistled their way to this coast from the Russian steppes and beyond the Ural Mountains. Perhaps the geese are later in coming from Iceland, the swallows leave earlier for the warm south, or perhaps it is the other way round. Such records are great fun to keep but have little accuracy if one only sees one's home at weekends. One may miss the birds at one weekend, when they are there, and record them at the next one and be wrong by a fortnight.

Then there are the rare birds. I was sitting down in the dunes with our dog Rory, a few years back, waiting for duck. Priscilla was away in New York as delegate to the United Nations for the second session running. I was sitting in a belt of rushes watching the light that was fading from the sky at the end of an October afternoon mirrored in the water beside me, when a harrier came lazily swinging over the tops of the reeds, questing in long, sweeping circles. Occasionally it would alight on firm ground, only to rise to continue its steady weaving as the dusk deepened. The hen harrier is not a great rarity in this part of Scotland, but the marsh harrier is. Although its head was not as pale as the bird in Thorburn's picture, which I studied beside the fire that night, it looked like a marsh harrier. I had seen them in Egypt and thought that I could not be mistaken. But now I am not so sure. But I would not dream of telling you just where I saw it. We found a gold-crest in our bedroom early one morning. Strangest of all we found a tern in an old rusty oil drum on the beach at Newburgh. One end had been prised open an inch or two. It was only because we were sitting beside it, searching for a sandwich which had not got sand in it, that we heard a faint movement inside the drum. We prised the sharp rusty edge open with a bit of driftwood and out walked a tern. After a few flexings of its wings it took to the air and flew off low, but slowly mounted up to become one with a flash of wings above our heads. It must have crept in there when it was smaller, and finding that it could not escape, somehow lived on the tiny living things in the sand which half-filled the drum.

Birds still maintain a mystery about their doings and the way that they go about doing them. Their migrations are a saga. It is only a few years ago since that the theory was advanced that birds on migration steer by the stars, which brought a new slant to a controversy as old as man. The several willow wrens that nest with us, and the spotted fly-catcher that nests in the creeper on the house, take their young to the Congo, and perhaps as far south as Natal. Long before the clamourous battalions of geese plane down upon the Ythan Estuary in October, waders are appearing along the shore of a score of different varieties. They come from the northern rim of the world and they are on a journey that is going to take them many miles farther yet. The Arctic tern goes from the Arctic all the way to the Antarctic. One feels the tundras are not all that far away, when one sees the snow buntings—a flock of little birds weaving and turning against a winter landscape which has been drained of all other colour. At one moment there might be chaffinches, but at the next, as they turn and show their white against the dun background, they are a shower of snowflakes. That is the old country name for them in Aberdeenshire. Many of our blackbirds and some of our robins, as well as our hoodie crows make a long journey to Norway every year.

Even the tiny gold-crest makes the journey, which is a heavy test for any bird, let alone a bird that only weighs 76 grains, much less than half an ounce, and whose wings are only just over two inches long. It is the smallest bird in Europe although not much smaller than some of the warblers. One night when I was after duck, at the tides, the dunes were full of blackbirds, too exhausted to take the trouble to get out of the way. One can see woodcock on the shores of Holkham Bay in Norfolk, so weary that they move six feet from one in the dusk and then flop down dead-tired. The old fowler with whom I used to go out after geese, said that after a nap and a drink of water they would be off again and might be fifty miles inland by first light.

Most of us have grown up to believe that great flocks of pigeons come to Britain from Scandinavia when the weather is hard over there. There is no vestige of proof of this or, indeed, that pigeons came to us from any other country. The exception is the collared dove from Asia Minor, who arrived here a few years ago and is now included in the list of British birds. Its first appearances in Aberdeen, fittingly, was opposite the houses of the Principal of the University and the Regius Professor of Natural History.

On October 12th, 1962, just three days before the geese arrived, and nine days after the larks sang to celebrate the first fine day since June, the wind blew fresh from Norway. It was the night before full moon. The birds knew that they would never get a better night for their crossing and next morning we were surrounded by chattering parties of tired field-fares, and the lawns were covered with blackbirds and a few robins who made little effort to get out of our way. But the strange thing was that there were greater spotted woodpeckers and lots of them. A wild-fowling friend telephoned to me from Newburgh to say that he had just seen six sitting on neighbouring fence posts. Our garden had several in it. The wind had plainly carried them to a landfall a long way north of their destination. They looked round forlornly for oakwoods and, finding none, hammered the bark of the sycamores in a search for insects, leaving pale patches on the trees. Unwilling to go further, lest they double the error, they took the bark off every fence post in their search of food, and then dispersed to the tiny climps of trees that break the wind round the farms and cottages along this coast, where they spent the winter. "How's your woodpecker?" became a conversational gambit as between one farmer and another.

The minister of Strichen, mentioned earlier, writing in 1793 mentions "different kinds of woodpeckers" coming regularly in November to his parish which is forty miles further north. But there were well-grown plantations there then, some 180 years old which compelled the admiration of Dr. Johnson on his Northern tour some twenty years before the minister's account. In the previous 200 miles, said the great doctor, he "had only seen one tree not younger than himself." But both the woods and woodpeckers alike have gone.

Exciting in a different way are the birds, not necessarily migrants who sometimes come to nest. One year it was a heron who planted a great flat nest in one of our few remaining Douglas firs, utterly unmoved by the barracking of the hoodie crows who roost nearby. A kestrel nests regularly with us now, in an old crow's nest, never bothering to build its own. Some blackheaded gulls established a fair-sized colony on one of the ponds near the dunes. On a spring day with the wind off the land we went to fly a large and curious kite that we had bought from a vendor of such things, on the beach at Rio, the previous January. It was pink and brown and shaped like an eagle, and took a lot of putting together. It soared upwards in a fresh off-shore wind as we paid out the string at our best speed. The black-headed gulls no sooner saw it than with wild cries of horror they fled, not to return to us for several years. They wanted nothing to do with a place where there were pink eagles. A goldcrest hung her little mossy ball of nest from the needles of a yew tree. The stoats got it and we have never seen another nest, although we often see gold-crests. Our then gardener, George Farquhar, made some nesting boxes. Perhaps we put them too low down on the trees. Anyway, the birds shunned them for several summers and then a robin moved into one and the sparrows into another two.

The British list of birds contains a widespread community. It includes any bird that has ever been seen in Britain since records were kept. And then there are those that have been brought to Britain, and bred there, and are now sufficiently widespread to be considered as wild, rather than tame birds. The Canada goose is an example. The first of its kind were brought to Britain before 1678 but they were not officially listed as British birds until 1948. The list has grown over the last fifty years due to much closer scrutiny of the spring and autumn migrants by a growing army of knowledgeable bird watchers. As the country becomes steadily more urbanised, an increasing number of city dwellers find this an absorbing way of refreshing themselves, in a peace which contact with the countryside alone can give. But there are some of them whose zeal is greater than their discretion and steps now have to be taken to protect birds against not only their enemies, but their more inquisitive allies as well. We have been driven, over the course of the last century or so to value our rare birds, the more so as many have become extinct in Britain, and many more have come near to the brink of extinction as breeding species.

Charles St. John was an eminent naturalist and sportsman of the last century. His *Tour of Sutherlandshire* which was published in 1849 is not only an absorbing account, but casts an interesting light on the mind of a naturalist of those days, and the pressure, even in the remote Highlands, on rare species. He tells us that in spite of the prices paid by the London collectors, to shepherds and gamekeepers with whom they had established contact, for eggs and skins the white-tailed sea-eagle was still "tolerably common" on the northern coasts and islands "and much commoner than the golden eagle because its nest was much harder to reach." He believed that the golden eagle would soon become extinct at the hands of the game preserver and the sheep farmer, and that the buzzard had been "completely exterminated," except in "the wilder districts." The kites numbers were falling fast, as a game bird and chicken stealer who could be easily trapped. "The goshawk," he notes "seems very rare everywhere in Scotland.

But it is the osprey that fascinates him and about it he seems to have a curiously split mind. Perhaps all those of us who are sportsmen and naturalists have some element of this. He decries the killing of ospreys, saying that "as they in no way interfere with the sportsmen or others, it is a great pity that they should ever be destroyed." He then proceeds to a long description of stalking and shooting one, and he includes a print of it and several pages of description. He is said to have killed the last ospreys in Sutherland at Loch Assynt. Even kindly Sir Walter Scott, on his tour of the Northern islands in 1814, when shown an osprey deplored his luck in not having his "rifle-gun" with him. But let it be remembered that to these two travellers the Sutherland of the 1840s was as remote as the Gobi desert or the Matto Grosso of today, where few of us would feel restraint about collecting any specimens that seemed interesting.

The killing of handsome birds for their plumage was at its height when Victorian and Edwardian fashion decreed it. A heavy toll was also taken by the demand for a wide variety of bright feathers with which to dress salmon flies. St. John tells us being shown a white-tailed eagle shot the day before by a forester.

It was in a mangled state. "I procured, however" he tells us "some feathers for the large salmon fly which we fish with on the Spey river, in making which the eagle's feather is the principal material employed." He wrote of the making of salmon flies "How many birds from every quarter of the globe are laid under contribution, to form this tiny but powerfully attractive bait." The fact that salmon flies are now very sparsely dressed, and that deer's hair and bear's fur are being used as well as feathers, should offset the fact that there are many more people nowadays who fish for salmon, and need flies. The Badminton Library on Fishing (first published in 1885) tells us how to dress the two dozen or so most popular salmon flies of the period. The original Silver Wilkinson is fair example. For the wing of the fly you needed "two strips of Canadian wood duck feather barr'd and a few fibres of red macaw". The cheeks of the fly must be of blue chatterer, its horns of blue and yellow macaw and its head of black ostrich herl. Golden pheasant and jungle cock feathers were added for good measure. Eight different birds contributed to that fly. The Canadian wood duck is now heavily protected. The blue chatterer is probably, so a famous ornithologist tells me, a Central American bird now known as the Lovely Cotinga. Eighteenth-century European naturalists are thought to have given them this name from a fancied resemblance to the wax-wing. But like the wax-wing he never forgets himself so far as to chatter, and is rather notably taciturn.

A contemporary of Charles St. John was that dedicated Hampshire sportsman, Colonel Peter Hawker. His total of just over half a century's shooting takes no account of the number of fieldfares and wheatears that he shot for the table, they being amongst his favourite dishes. A typical entry is (August 1833): "Took a gun to get a few dozen of those delicious birds the wheatears, I knocked down a curious owl." In a total of nearly 18,000 head, there appear, though only a few of each, spotted crakes, whimbrels, ruffs, green sandpipers, sanderlings, bitterns, phalaropes, nightjars, goshawks, an avocet ("June 14th, 1804. Shot an avocet (swimming). This is a bird rarely to be met with but on the Kentish coast")—and a hoopoe, who rates no special mention. Apart from shooting what are, nowadays, birds to be carefully protected, the proportions of his total are interesting, As against over 7,000 partridges there are only 575 pheasants, and 20 wood pigeons. The total of hares and rabbits is under 1,000.

with almost twice as many hares as rabbits. Those were hungry days in the country parishes, and the rabbits would have been heavily snared. But there are two elements there for which full allowance should be made. The first is that scientific knowledge was in its infancy. Sportsmen shot and stuffed every rare bird that they saw for identification and record. By the same token, and at the same time, governesses were teaching their charges to look at pond weed and pond water through primitive microscopes. Although at that time it is said that there was a strong move to close the Patent Office, as it was claimed that there was nothing more to be invented, in the world of nature most people felt that scientists knew relatively little. Here was a sphere where the closer that one was to the countryside the greater was one's opportunity. Furthermore they believed, as Canada has believed until this very moment, that one can cut down forests, poison rivers, fish out the lakes, and destroy bird life, and there will still be enough to go round for everybody. Today's pressing problems of population did not exist. We had only half our present people.

As a child poring over bird books to the detriment of most other reading, I put a tick against any bird that I'd seen. They were a handful compared with the birds the book contained. Since then, after much travelling, there are a great many more ticks. Perhaps the most indelible was from the day my father and I stood mute and still for half an hour watching a kite in Wales, nearly forty years ago. The sun shone warm on the Towy Valley that day and the kite, huge by our standards of judgment, sat hunched upon a rock beside that clear stream. Since then Africa has spoilt many of us for kites. But other occasions added memorable ticks. At the end of the last war I was in Holland with the Canadian Army. With a comrade I had a chance to visit Texel Island and see there in plenty, birds which were once common in Britain. While we watched a colony of spoonbills, Montague harriers perched on the German radar installations, while a hen harrier hunted close by. Only lack of time to explore further, and a minefield or two, prevented us from seeing the Sclavonian grebe, the ruff, and the black-winged stilt. The only year since then, that was comparable to that visit to Texel was in 1958. Priscilla and I began with the lilac-breasted rollers in the hot breeze that blows across the southern part of Masai country in January where the snow peak of Kilimanjaro showed splendidly clear that day against a bright blue sky. We saw bee-eaters in Persia. Later, in Labrador, I saw an osprey carrying a trout that must have weighed a full 7 pounds, where the Hamilton River plunges into Boudoin Canyon and sends up a smoke cloud that can be seen from fifty miles away on a clear day. All the world now knows its new name, the Churchill Falls. We ended in the autumn with the collared pratincole and the cream-coloured courser, where the flat desert of Kuwait meets the waters of the Persian Gulf, on the border of what is known as "the neutral territory". Last of all, was a Persian nightingale, at the top of a bush in Bahrein in the early morning, beside what seemed the clearest pool in the world. Many people never become actively interested in birds. But even if one is only just aware of them one can never tire of them. We often tend, as with animals, to invest them with human attributes. Perhaps this is the highest compliment that we can pay them, although our cousin, the monkey, whose human attributes are only too apparent, repels most of us. Take the robin. He seems to seek out man's company. We are flattered. His relationship with the gardener is the same symbiosis as the rhino and the tick bird, or the shark and the pilot fish; it is a companionship based on mutual benefit. The robin has the worms from the freshly turned earth, the gardener has the pleasant companionship in what is often a lonely job. The wedge of geese flying high seem to us the embodiment of that discipline which we admire in fighting formations. The simile goes further when one sees the geese alight and put out a sentinel who makes another, probably with several sharp pecks, take his place before he lowers his own head to feed. During the Dieppe raid in 1942, in which the Canadian forces suffered heavy casualties, at the height of the battle a small skein of geese flew over and, veering neither to left nor to right, flew straight through that hailstorm of fire. More than one who was there has told me of the profound effect that the sight of their perfect discipline had on the men who were fighting on the beaches. Geese when flying short distances more often than not fly in weaving half circles. It is on the long journeys, when they fly high, that they form the perfect symmetry of the wedge. Each one has the advantage of the "up-vortex" from the wings from the one in front, which makes for easier flying. All, that is to say, except the leader, who has to fly through dead, unbroken air. That is why they rotate leaders so often. We see in the bird that nests for life, such as the swan, a splendid example of human constancy. Then there are the partridge and the mallard mothers, holding pursuit in check while their young ones scuttle away, by feigning a broken wing, usually at some risk of overplaying their hand. This to us seems a noble motherly action. And birds seem human enough to have their wayward moments. There are the outbursts of their temper which you know only too well if you have ever kept and flown hawks. The starling was described by T. A. Coward as an "avian humourist".* Some even seem too to have a developed sense of humour. A few years ago, in May, we were sitting on the garden seat outside the house at Potterton, and we listened to a starling in the copper beech, which imitated faithfully every single one of the noises which you could hear in the countryside at that moment— a curlew calling, and a seagull screaming, a pigeon cooing, one of our Burmese jungle fowl making its characteristic sounds, a thrush and a blackbird. Then Rory began to bark at what he believed to be a distant postman. The starling, tried to imitate but, after one or two tries, gave up. Rory had defeated him. Small birds mobbing an owl as he sits glued to his perch on a tree are mightily suggestive for the rougher kind of election meeting. But we do not know and probably never shall know how birds think. When a mother mallard or mother partridge has put up a splendid fight to save her young and failed, and in the space of a minute or two finds herself alone, her distress is heart-rending. But how long does she pine for, for how long does she remember? An hour? A day? For ever? And that is just one question out of many. Why do they sing? It seemed to Gilbert White "to be the effect of rivalry and emulation". And his guess is as good as anybody's, but it is only a guess.

Birds have many obvious functions. They are the counter-balance to a wide-spread of creation taking in the small fast-breeding animals and the insects. They help mankind in so many ways and within their world apply all kinds of delicate checks and balances upon each other.

If one does not believe that the world was created, but just happened, then birds must just have happened with it. But if one believes that it was deliberately created, then birds were surely created to make life on it more worth living.

* T. A. Coward, *Birds of the British Isles and Their Eggs,* Frederick Warne, 1920

16   *Animals**

FROM our home at Braemar we looked out on a countryside that was much as nature had made it. Once we had left behind the fields, and the village, and the clumps of alien trees, and reached the higher glens we were in a Scotland as it had been for centuries. Once above the tree line we might have been among the tundras of Arctic Canada, treading a wiry carpet of rock plants, mosses and lichens on the slopes, our boots sinking now and then into a green morass round a spring of water. It would seem that to go up another five hundred feet in the air is the equivalent of going several hundred miles further north. In the high Cairngorms in summer, I involuntarily look for an icecap plastered over a mountain saddle such as you see in Northern Baffin Island. The ice-caps alone are missing to make the two

* Considerable use has been made of the chapter on Fauna in *The North-east of Scotland*, Central Press, Aberdeen, 1963.

countries indistinguishable. Thank heaven, the Arctic mosquitoes are also missing.

This is the country of the golden eagle and the raven and the ptarmigan. It is the country of the blue hare who goes white in winter, as does the stoat and the ptarmigan as well. It is the country of the wild cat, which is part way towards being a Canadian lynx.

In the mountains of British Columbia the tree-line is reached at about 4,500 feet. It follows the shoulders of the mountains and the slopes of the valleys in a line as level, and exact, as if it had been cut with a razor. Below is the forest, and above are the slopes where grizzlies shamble among the bare rocks and the wiry tufts of tundra growth. In Scotland the 3,000-foot contour has an almost mystical meaning. Anything that rises above it is entitled to be called a mountain, whereas anything lesser is only a hill. It has no sign by which man can mark it. But there is an invisible division of which other living things are fully conscious. The ptarmigan will not live below it. As company in the nesting season she will have a few wheatears and meadow pipits and see an occasional mountain hare. There are a few varieties of butterflies, moths and beetles, some of which are of Arctic origin for it is an Arctic region in everything except line of latitude, who live above that line. Brown trout have been caught at almost exactly its level, and frogs spawn until they reach it and rarely go higher. The big hill foxes have their dens below it but hunt above it, for the high ground carries a good population of wood mice, shrews and voles which are found right up to the high tops, and the golden eagle in his own sphere does the same. Occasionally, in high summer, the hooves of the red deer ring on the screes and the rocks of a high plateau, but the roe and the rabbit and the brown hare are left far below and so, happily, is the adder. At migrating time birds make their way over the mountains and but for most of the year you will not see much life on the high tops. The time was when almost all of Canada's present fauna lived in this country. There were beaver dams in plenty in Wales and we had wolves, and when you go back to the cave drawings you will find the bear and the bison among other beasts. The Irish elks, whose horns are occasionally dredged from the bogs, were a larger variety of the moose, as the wapiti is of the red deer. The marten, that is the pine marten, is now exceedingly rare, but was once widely spread.

People talk a great deal about the balance of Nature. But surely the balance was laid down when the earth came alive again, and men and beasts spread out over the land in the wake of the Ice Age. If we allow various beasts in the mists of antiquity to have cancelled each other out, like the bison and the sabre-toothed tiger and many others, we get down to a fauna that we can understand and recognise. Man's first assault on this balance was in changing the face of the country to win himself more food, in draining swamps and putting up hedges and fences and stone dykes, and covering the country with roads and a growing concentration of human beings. There were old men at Braemar when we went there who could remember the tales of their grandfathers, and could point to tall woodlands which had been planted without any fencing of any kind. The last wolf in Scotland was killed at the end of the eighteenth-century. They do not seem ever to have been very numerous, but like the lone wolves of Western Canada they probably killed heavily.* It was possible in those old days to plant without fencing because the deer were kept down to the point of being comparative rareties. If you read the works of St. John, that great writer on stalking and highland sport of the early nineteenth century, you realise that going after a stag was then rather like going after a tiger and you might easily have spent a week in getting one, and you slept out every night on the hill. If the wolves kept a check on the deer, it was the pine martens who kept a check on the squirrel, and something else besides merely man must surely have kept a close check on the rabbits and hares. Osgood Mackenzie describes the loving care with which his grandfather imported rabbits from England, and put them down at Conon in Ross-shire, around the beginning of the last century. To ensure their survival and comfort burrows were dug for them. They over-ran the whole of that part of the Highlands. It is frequently claimed now that gamekeepers and others are interfering with the balance of Nature. Man had never done anything else since he came into the world. Sometimes his onslaught is on a large scale. It has recently been announced that there is to be a slaughter of the great grey Atlantic seal, whose depredations on the salmon are only too well proved. The demand is for salmon, rather than for seals, and so the

---

* A massive deer hunt was held in honour of Mary Queen of Scots in 1564, which involved a driving of the deer over an enormous area. The bag was 360 red deer, a few roe and five wolves.

balance is tipped. Certain Canadian national parks, where shooting is not allowed, have suffered from a plethora of wolves, who have got to a point of numbers where they have seriously reduced the deer whom everyone wished to encourage. If you want to encourage the deer you must reduce the wolves. It is just as simple as that. Mervyn Cowie, one of my closest friends since Oxford days, is probably the greatest living expert on African game. He has attempted in his Kenya game parks to keep, by the most complicated means, a real balance of Nature. Where a leopard has been worrying stock, they go to great lengths to trap the leopard and carry him off to a part of the country where he can do less damage. The object is to balance without destroying.

At Potterton we have a very limited amount of animals, as you would imagine, in this open closely-farmed countryside. But Potterton has the feeling of a land that has been trodden since the sun melted the last glacier of the Ice Age. Nothing that happened there would ever surprise us. So we are not at all taken aback when out of the sea mists, a year or so after our arrival, a walrus heaved himself on to skerry beneath the little cliffs of Collieston. He stayed there several days and then slid back into the waves and was no more seen. He must have come from Greenland by way of Iceland and the Faroes, the Shetlands, and probably the Orkneys too. A few mink appeared in our little burn. A Government trapper comes occasionally to set wire netting traps on the lobster pot principle. He is said to have caught one a mile downstream of us. This spring an otter was caught in a rabbit snare on the heathery part of our surrounding horseshoe of land. He must have been on an overland journey, with perhaps the Don as its destination. It was a male and young enough to be a foot shorter than a grown dog otter would have been, and lighter by some 17 pounds. We used to have rabbits in plenty and a few hares and then, when myxamatosis struck, we had no rabbits but a sudden surge of hares. They grow big here do the brown hares and we shot two of 9½ pounds each. One rises at the expense of the other, for each eat the other's food. The myxamatosis virus was brought from South America, from a part of that continent where it grumbles slowly round in a cycle. The rabbits die out, a few survive, the disease moves on, the rabbits build up behind it, and so you inevitably end up, as we shall assuredly end up, with both myxamatosis and the rabbit. But the mere absence of the rabbit for a short time is a blessing. With us the disease can be communicated only in the rabbit burrow, by a flea that can move in that still air for perhaps a foot or two. In Australia it is communicated by a mosquito, which, with a fair wind can probably cover fifty miles in a day. When they brought myxamatosis to Australia it put millions of pounds Sterling on the wool clip that year, so much more grazing was there through the absence of rabbits. In New Zealand there is no universal carrier and they work hard and extremely successfully in eliminating the rabbit by the most old-fashioned but most effective means.

The disease reached us at Potterton in 1955. We saw the first infected rabbit early in March. We shot a modest total of nine of them that year. We shot only one the next year, and it was the same in the next year. Meanwhile the rabbits' food had grown rife all over the place, and instead of the edges of hayfields, cornfields and turnip fields being shaved down by their destruction, and the grass on the moorlands and heathland mown like a bowling green, now there was absolutely no difference round the edge of the fields and the rest of the crop, and moorland grass was growing more than a foot high. In 1958 we accounted only for three rabbits. It had been slow in spreading. We found it first in the dunes, and in a rabbit that we found in *extremis*, in the long drive. But the disease was slow in crossing our little burn. One side was cold and silent and mute and odiously full of bodies. On the other side of this burn, not five feet further, the rabbits were running and frisking everywhere. Then, as nature does these things, the circuit was made, and there were no rabbits at all. The feed for rabbits, their carrying capacity, built up without them. And in 1959 a page was turned, the disease was gone, and the rabbits came back to enjoy all the extra supplies of food that had burgeoned during their absence. We shot the unprecedented number of ninety-eight that year. And then the disease came grumbling back. We shot only thirteen in 1960, and eleven the next year, and thirteen the year following.

The effect of the disease went far further than the fortunes of the rabbits. It had been one of the great attributes of Potterton that the owls hooted and hooted on moonlight nights, starry nights and on almost every night. Then the owls' hooting died away and we heard no more of it. For the owls when they are feeding their young require a lot of young rabbits. When there were not any more young rabbits there were no more owls. Our extraordinary anomaly, our colony of long-eared owls, normally unclubbable birds, took themselves off and disappeared and we have rarely seen them since. There is a village not very far away where the last fox was seen somewhere in the 1880s. But this disease of the rabbits set the foxes roving searching for anywhere that they might find food, until they got to a point, at that particular village and at Potterton itself, that they had to have a weekly onslaught on the foxes, with guns. The buzzard, who was then unknown among us, has become not common but a regular visitor, searching for what he can find. The stoats, who once lived largely on rabbits, cleaned out two complete nesting seasons of birds in 1961-2. For they are expert climbers and can reach any nest. The absence of foxes has a curious effect on certain kinds of bird like the pheasant and the mallard, in fact upon all wild duck. The pheasants in country where there are foxes will always roost up trees. In country where there are no foxes they will roost happily on the ground, as they used to do with us, but they have latterly started to roost in the trees which suggests that foxes are more than an occasional visitor. The duck are much more approachable here than they are at any other place that I have known in Britain. When we had the low ground shooting of Mar Lodge in our Braemar days, they used to put out a sentinel, as they always will in a country where there are foxes. The vigilance of the sentinel made them very difficult to approach. But here they have only recently needed to take that precaution, which is, incidentally, one that wild geese never relax.

Then, of course we have the smaller animals. We have moles in great plenty. One of the wonders about the mole is that he manages to run his long galleries without drowning. Often, starting a ditching scheme, I have come upon a gush of water coming out of a hole, perhaps $1\frac{1}{2}$ or 2 inches in diameter. This is a mole's hole and you find it acting as a direct channel of drainage, and what the mole does about it no-one can say. You will see a piece of flood water in a hollow. You will see the water level fall and you will think that any moles underneath it must have been drowned. You are entirely wrong, because when the water goes, the molehills appear again. These galleries are not passages in the mole's dwelling house but places where he can find food such as insect larvae and worms. And there can be as much as two tons of worms to an acre. From time to time we set a lot of mole traps. In one of these we caught a weasel, a long way from the nearest hole whence he could have entered the ground, and a long way from the nearest hole he could have come above ground again. How he had squeezed himself into this hole and into our mole trap it is very difficult to say. But weasels do this. You can tell when a spell of hard frost is going to break by the first loose earth that the moles throw up.

At Potterton we are a long way from the high hills, the crags and the heather of the deer country, but it is a curious thing that roebuck, and occasionally red deer, make their way to the sea during the summer months. For they have miles of road that they must have to cover, and a great many fences and stone dykes to jump. They do it in the darkness, and they come to the sea to cure some sickness or heal some deficiency. Red deer have been seen coming through the village of Belhelvie in the moonlight heading for the sea, and, only a few years ago one was seen swimming off the mouth of the Don, almost in Aberdeen city. It was sub-sequently caught in a wire fence and destroyed in its very purlieus. The roebuck do the same, and my friend Charles Buchan the farmer always rings us up when he sees a roebuck in the dunes. We have every reason to be afraid, because that same roebuck will almost certainly take up quarters in our horseshoe of woodlands and do the most fearful damage to the trees. Our kirk session records that on November 28th, 1669 "James Abernethie con-fessing to prophaning the Lord's Day by killing and shooting a Dear(?) sharplie rebuked before the Session and ordered to remove the scandall before the congregation." I have been sorely tempted to do the same thing.

All animals, and indeed the human race too, have their own particular weapons. Those whose weapons are the brain, or tooth or claw, such as humanity, or the lion or the leopard, or the dog or the cat, have young which mature very slowly and are abso-lutely helpless for a very long time. The human young are more helpless, and for a longer time, than any. Then there are the animals whose only weapon is flight. Those like the horse and the deer, have young who are fit to walk and run and take cover within an extraordinarily short time from being born. The smaller ones, like the rabbit, are born down a burrow and do not emerge until they can give a tolerable account of themselves. Then there are the birds, who cannot leave the nest until they can fly. That is, of course, those who do not nest on the ground. The ground nesting birds grow up ready to walk almost as soon as they have broken out of the egg. The young duck must get into the water, and swim, after it has been in the world for only a matter of hours.

In the Canadian Arctic, you see a perfect pyramid of Nature. You find at the base of it the most numerous animal whose unenviable task is to convert herbage into flesh to become the food of the next most numerous animal, or group of animals. In the Far North the base is the lemming. It is the food of the ermine and the white fox and the great snowy owl, and even the raven.

The Eskimo has traditionally lived on the beasts of the sea, the seal and the walrus and, to some extent the polar bear, as well as the caribou of the inland. But when the lemming die out, every five or six years, the foxes die out and the ermines die out, and the Eskimo suffers economically. It is a much more directly geared process in the forests among the Indians, where the snowshoe rabbit dies out every two or three years. Not only do the foxes die out with it, but also the coyotes, instead of singly hunting the rabbit, gang up in big packs and hunt the deer. This scatters the deer and reduces their numbers and deprived of a staple food, the Indians in old days used to die out as well. The Indian population rose and fell with this cycle of the snowshoe rabbit. Far more Indians died that way than ever were killed in battle.

But, by and large, what changes the balance and population of Nature today is man and his methods. In East Africa, when I first went there, over thirty years ago, there was an abundance of game that is almost impossible to describe to somebody who now visits East Africa for the first time. But it is not the killing of the game that has made the difference. It is the presence of so very many more human beings, and the hundreds of miles of new wire fences and roads that they have created. Many species of African big game have a long migration line, where the two sexes meet and sort themselves out. But if they find a new tarmac road and wire fences in their way, they are only too likely to turn back and there will be no progeny that year.

Priscilla has always been a very keen deer stalker, and, although I say it myself, is a remarkably good shot. Some years ago we were out in East Africa on business. We had the chance of a short safari in the Northern Frontier Province of Kenya, where there was still a great deal of game and both men and animals are still very close to their historic balance of Nature. Looking at herds of sleek impala, among many other antelopes as well, she was continually exclaiming about their wonderful condition. Their condition was supreme, because theirs was a world of the survival of the fittest. Anything that man touches tends to the survival of the unfittest. There is only one kind of big-game hunting which is real hunting, and there is nothing to beat it. And that is to go to a water hole and look for the spoor of your quarry and follow it, for days if necessary, until you get within shot of it. That is what the lion and leopard do. They do not look for the biggest antelopes. They look for the one whose spoor tells them it is unfit, perhaps wounded, or is getting old, and they follow it. They are continually purging away the unfit. Man is quite different. He keeps people alive in hospitals and asylums to the greatest possible age. In wars over the centuries the bravest and the strongest have rushed to the front and have been slain. If you let a deer forest to many tenants they will shoot the best stags and leave the worst. If you walk up grouse or partridges you are probably shooting those who rise nearest, which are probably the youngest. Though, in the most man-made of all sports, which is driving, the covey comes over led by the eldest which is the one at which you will probably aim. Only now that war has become so indiscriminate have we got away from the working of the dread formula by which the fittest were those who inevitably fell. But that then raises the question to us as the human species— Who are the fittest? Because we regard every living human soul, however bodily or mentally decrepit, as being saveable and worth saving, and it being right to save them.

Over the world of living things is poised a threat becoming more indiscriminate as time goes on. The birds that survive a very cold winter are the strongest birds. But the random use of toxic poison sprays has come to level that difference. In my year spent with the Eskimos in the Canadian Arctic, thirty years past, they still used to expose the old people upon the ice to die, when they had, in fact, ceased to be fit enough to contribute to their families and could not help with hunting. All that has changed now, and rightly so, because we put a different meaning on the word "fittest". This gets us back to our old difficulty of equating man and animals in the same comparison. We put the instinctive beings and the reasoning beings in the same bracket, and find ourselves with an analogy that can easily be taken too far.

The little estate of Potterton lies in a hollow. When we moved in, just before Hogmanay, in 1952, the slopes of the hollow were covered in thick forest. The trees had been planted some forty years before, and never thinned. They made just that kind of jungle which pigeons love. Particularly do they enjoy it on a frosty night. A careful investigation failed to reveal any sign of pheasants. What looked like a woodcock turned out to be an owl. But on the first voyage of exploration that we undertook, a single cock pheasant crowed loudly from the hill above us. In some years we do find a handful of pheasants on this little bit of land. But for years we never shot at a cock pheasant, lest we should be shooting the one who welcomed us originally. The big field at the bottom of the bowl, at the back of the house, on the seaward side generally held several hares, and ducks would flight over high of an evening. We plainly had to go further afield, if we wanted to shoot at anything except pigeons. In this part of the country every bit of land that can be used for agriculture has been in use for a long time. There are rocky and boggy outcrops, some of them full of heather. Here where the bare knuckles of the earth show through and the plough has been defied, some of these heather mosses held a few grouse. We soon made contact with the farmers who owned the little marshy pools towards the dunes. But the pigeons were so close at hand it was on them that we concentrated originally. That forest lasted exactly a month and blew down on January 31st, 1953. Since then we have been steadily and slowly replanting.

For two or three years after the big gale a good number of pigeons used to come back to what trees we had left. We still had one stand of Scots pines about three acres in extent. But latterly some big plantations have grown up further inland and they over-fly us of an evening on their way to them. But if nature played us a scurvy trick in blowing down our little forest, it did us a good turn the following year. Quite suddenly in the big field a pool of water appeared and it spread until it became about an acre and a half in extent. An agricultural drain underneath the ground had become blocked. That happens a lot in this part of the world where you get that fine limestone gravel in the drains, which sometimes fills them up and hardens like cement. No sooner had the pond appeared, when the ducks appeared with it. We were first aware of it by waking in the night and hearing a most prodigious quacking. An investigation of the pond showed teal and mallard feathers where they had been preening. And then for three years we had our own duckshoot at our own back door. It was an ideal duckshoot for one person. You could do an afternoon's work and then put on a pair of Wellington boots, walk out of the back door, throw your leg over the fence, walk three hundred yards and there you were. I had been given for Christmas the previous year a decoy duck. It was a beautifully painted mallard made of wood. I set him out when I am flighting. I have never really known whether he has any beneficial effect in attracting in duck. But I value his companionship.

I would anchor him in the pond in the field, crouch down on the side where a few pines, about thirty yards away, made a blot of darkness. Anything or nothing might happen. My bag was never very big. But it is not everywhere that you can shoot three mallard or a brace of widgeon within sight of your own back door, and be absent from your own house for not more than half an hour.

Sport is always more enjoyable on a piece of land that you own or rent. Because you can study how to improve it.

At first sight the country around Potterton would seem ideally adapted for shooting, with its gentle rounded rolling hills, ploughed or in pasture. But I have always noticed that the game there, meaning the pheasants and partridges such as they are, are always to be found on the slopes facing the sea. In other words facing eastwards, whereas our slopes face northwards or westwards. The reason must be that love of the morning sun. They are never numerous, the nesting conditions hardly exist in fields where they plough right up to the fence or the dyke, and they must nest in the mosses or in the little pieces of woodland such as we possess. And also it is rather too near a large city for game to be very abundant. The duck pond after three glorious years of existence came to an end as suddenly as our forest had. The farmer decided to lay out considerable expenditure and drain the field, and the pond disappeared as if it had never been. But we get wonderful flighting on the burn in hard weather. And kind neighbours allow me to pursue duck on their patches of water. The geese fly over us at a great height but never land except in very hard winters when they were very reduced in condition.

We started to extend our range to the estuary of the Ythan at Newburgh. There must be several thousand geese at Newburgh, when they have all come down from Iceland towards the middle of October. And they flight to and fro between the fields and the estuary. There are great flocks of widgeon there, come perhaps from beyond the Urals and you find, strangely enough, fair numbers of snipe feeding in the tidal marshes. Under certain conditions it is possible to drive them but you need a very good dog to pick up a snipe which has fallen in sedge seven feet high. We do a lot of what we call goose shooting. In fact, geese very rarely get shot. But it is a wonderful excuse to be out on the banks of that beautiful estuary when the afternoon light is turning to the glory of a winter sunset.

It needs a first-class retriever of heavy build to retrieve a wounded goose that has fallen in the water. And not possessing such an animal we can only shoot them over the land, where we know we can pick them up as they fall. If you are really serious about geese on the Ythan estuary you must go out of an evening and listen to them calling and find where they are feeding. Then come back early in the morning and lie in wait for them.

There are several places that I know of to the south of us where geese can be shot in numbers, in complete comfort, sitting on a shooting stick. But in the main geese must be hunted and you must really know their habits if you are not to come back empty-handed from most of your sorties.

The true wildfowler are those who shoot in the sea marshes. They have to contend with treacherous and dangerous tides and steer in the darkness, as often as not by a compass. Ours is somewhere between the two.

Geese are always regarded as being extremely clever birds. But I question whether they really are. I wonder whether really clever birds would follow very much the same flight line every night in spite of being shot at again and again. Mallard and pigeons would never do that. But geese possess amazing eyesight, a knowledge that man is dangerous, and the power to recognise his presence from signs like his fresh tracks across a sand dune. Just every so often you get the better of them. In November a few years ago I was out with a friend of mine, who is now a forester but was previously an officer in the Somaliland police, in search of geese. We heard a great clamour of geese feeding on the stubbles after dark had fallen. We found out exactly where they were and put them up. They went clamouring off towards the sea. We came back early the next morning and as we arrived so did the first echelon of geese and saw us and sheared off. We threw ourselves down beside a wire fence on our faces in the frost. There the geese came over us line after line. We had to wait until they were right over the top of us and then leap to our feet and shoot, and we shot very badly. At last no more would come over but a big lot came and pitched to one side, about three hundred yards away. There was a croft just beyond where they had settled, and out of the croft came a man and started calling to his dog. The whole pack of geese got up and flew straight and low over our heads. My friend and I fired at the same moment and two geese came down with a crash. I was just pulling my second trigger when the goose collapsed in the air and I was too late to transfer my aim to another one. If you are ever standing very close to someone shooting geese, and indeed, even duck, it is extraordinary how often you tend to pick the same bird. The ten geese that we got that morning satisfied me for the whole of that season and the next.

Some people work a hard day at business or in professions or politics and manage to remain pretty good shots. When they do get a day's shooting on Saturday they probably get so much to fire at that they can maintain a high pitch of skill. But it is very difficult if you have got a 500-mile train journey from London and you are only firing a handful of cartridges at each weekend, to remain in even reasonable practice. This tends to make one a very pokey shot, shooting only at what you know you can get. Lacking a retriever dog I can only shoot at birds that I know will fall where I can pick them up, which precludes shooting over water or over long rushes. That makes one pokier still. And it may be the advent of middle age or something else, but my dislike of wounding a bird, and it escaping winged, has increased to the point where it can spoil not only an afternoon's shooting for me but it can spoil the whole idea of shooting for me for quite a long time.

Rory accompanies me on my evening vigils. He loves adventure of any kind and likes to be out when it is getting dark. He is very useful if a bird comes down and still has a flap left in it. He rushes up to it and wags ferociously, and is awarded with a piece of chocolate. This sounds very unprofessional, but he has found many a bird for me which I could not have found for myself. Although he possesses a wonderful nose for animals he finds it practically impossible to discover a bird by its scent. But he does his level best.

My great-uncle Archie Stuart Wortley, who was one of the most famous shots of his day, speaks in one of his books of gripping his gun like a vice. There are days when one simply cannot shoot at all, and it is nearly always the days when you find that you are gripping your gun slackly. If you are going to have a good day you are automatically gripping it tightly. In wildfowling you almost never get a shot standing upright on the level ground. And it means if you are firing kneeling or sitting or lying that your swing is sharply curtailed. I find one of the best ways of keeping in practice is to carry an empty gun under your arm when you are at home, constantly throwing it up, to draw a bead on birds or anything moving. You keep that familiarity of touch which is so important. By the same token a really good rifle shot, in the old Africa that I knew, would never allow anybody to carry his rifle for him and would handle it all day.

Nearly all shooting is good sport. But flighting is my own favourite. The clonk of cartridges falling into the breech, the smell of gun oil and the shape and feel of a gun are just as exciting as they were to me as a child. I always make a point of being out whether with or without a gun, when dusk is falling. I return from the darkness, throw open the back door to be momentarily blinded by the light in the wash-house, take off my heavy clothes, and boots, and lay down two mallards which I have been clutching by their long green necks. You can think about that evening for a long time afterwards and carry the recollection of it down to London, to keep you going until the following weekend.

I tried to teach Priscilla to shoot with a .410 but she never became keen, although she showed a lot of aptitude. My step-daughter Anne shot with a little old bolt-action .410 that I have had for nearly forty years. She made excellent shooting with it and if she had got more practice would have been a good shot. She has never wished to graduate to a larger weapon.

Just under fifty acres of land of blown-down woodland or very young plantation trees and fields does not amount to a great estate. But we have shot nine varieties in our big field and ten if you count a Jack Snipe as being a separate variety. As far as I am concerned that is enough to keep me absolutely happy. Priscilla and I have varied our shooting or "hunting" in Canadian terminology. In 1957 I had long and abortive, but happy, day hunting, on one and the same occasion, Alpine chamois and Himalayan mountain goats. While I sat down to eat my sandwiches in the middle of the day beside a rushing torrent, a blackbird sat down beside me and began to sing. I always ask my big game hunting friends, having told them that to tell me where that could be done. It could be done in only one place in the world and that is the Mount Cook range in New Zealand.

The two years before that, Priscilla joined me in British Columbia. I had just been doing a pioneering job in Labrador on the other side of the Continent. We went up to what is known as Tweedsmuir Park that wonderful stretch of pristine wilderness in the northern part of the Province and hunted grizzly. We got a shot at a grizzly, missed him and it is strange to say he did not come for us as they nearly always will do. Priscilla got a moose and a beautiful caribou and rocky mountain goat. We climbed the 7,000 feet of Tweedsmuir peak and on our way back we passed along the top of its steep cliffs and there, on a ledge were five mountain goats. Priscilla fired and the largest one folded straight over into the void, turning over and over. We crept down on a moraine and picked it up, the horns were smashed and we brought back the skin which is on our bedroom floor. I am much afflicted with vertigo—I hated every moment of that climb. Two days earlier we had come on a band of caribou. We got off our cow ponies, the guide who was with us had gone on to a little rise and looked over. I can still see him standing completely still, his sombrero hat rammed down on his head, unconsciously turning his back to a cold wind coming from the glaciers. He turned round with a broad grin to Priscilla and said, "You can't miss," and she changed places with him. Priscilla fired three times and when I looked over the top a great bull caribou was lying in the trickle of water that ran from the toe of the glacier that bears our name. The hobbled ponies looked up at the shots and started to browse the tundra plants again. Perhaps we are too amateur to do any of these things well. We are unlikely to change, because we do them for pleasure.

17   *Cold Winters and Wet Days*

WINTERS are harsh in the Cairngorms. We had four of them at Braemar. Generally it was mild until Christmas, and we usually managed to plant trees in Christmas week. Then winter would begin in earnest. The autumn colours had been with us since September, for the first frosts come early in the mountains. The gean, as we call the wild cherry, turned crimson. The birches yellowed. The poplars in the steep narrow glens, with their restless leaves, looked like a shower of golden coins. The Norway maple went a subdued scarlet. At Braemar our Canadian trees from Ontario were completely at home. Now they had the climate that they liked, a short summer and a harsh winter with the mercury going several times below zero Fahrenheit. When we moved to Potterton we arranged for their transfer. They were dug up and sent to us, one cold winter's day, with their roots exposed. The maples paid us out by refusing to grow up in our uneven season, or colour in Autumn. At Potterton we very often had a few very warm days in January and the Canadian trees, believing that Spring had come, straightaway started growing, only to find that the worst part of the winter was to come. They have since relented; several are now tall, and a few of the maples glow gloriously in September.

At Braemar the deer, at times, would come right up to the castle walls. They went up to the high tops in summer, to get away from the flies, and came back to the valleys in September. In the autumn they roared incessantly, and there is in that strange cry all of Celtic melancholy and the mystery of the hills, and the fall of the old Gods. But with the rutting over, the roaring ceased. Growing gaunt and hungry, they would prowl listlessly up to the walls. Our couple, James Thom and his wife, had the cottage which was added like a limpet to the back of the castle wall. Their little daughter had been put to bed one winter's night, with a fire burning merrily and chasing the shadows round the pitch-pine walls of her ground floor bedroom. A great stag came right up to the window and looked in. The child lying in bed looked up and saw the outline of its head and horns at the window with the moonlight behind it, and the flames of the fire reflected in its eyes. She had the most terrible fright which we succeeded in exorcising, as time went on, by taking her down to see the herds of deer beside the river and for her to watch them running away in front of her.

The river would shrink with the frost. At dusk it was black between its snow banks, and the deer were dark shapes along its margins. By day it ran the cold colour of pale amethyst. Winter never seemed to lift from the valley, but rather to run away down it when the spring came. That is why the sight of the jostling grinding icefloes careering down-stream in the green snow water of February was so exciting. Gradually the rivers emptied of everything except a few lean brown trout. When the old spent salmon of last year had gone downstream with the ice, the river had emptied of winter, and in a month's time the birds and the fresh salmon would be making their way up.

Although the Aberdeen road is kept clear, the road that runs from Braemar, up over the Devil's Elbow to Perth, is regularly blocked for a large part of the winter. It happens with unfailing regularity, but is none the less highly esteemed as an item of news. I have even read that the Devil's Elbow was blocked on a prominent position on the front page of a famous newspaper in Buenos Aires. This is completely logical in a country like Britain where our clothing is unsuitable alike for winter or summer and we put the water pipes on the outside of our walls where they can freeze immediately. Even a modest snowfall can bring industry, commerce, and recreation to an abrupt halt. But, even in the midst of the North American continent, where they are extremely expert at dealing with snow, the New Yorkers are little better than ourselves.

However, the road to Aberdeen was kept open by snowploughs, and we were seldom completely cut off. It could be a long, wild drive back from Aberdeen, sixty miles away, after fulfilling a constituency engagement in late evening, when there was snow on the roads and snow falling. After miles of road winding through a white world we would cheer when we saw the tower of the castle as a line of lights, one above the other, in the staircase windows. It was an exacting life. We were hardy, or so our friends told us, and it was worth all that effort to get home to the mountains to snatch a weekly respite from the furious cities.

When we left Braemar and went to Potterton, we might have gone to live on a different planet. Mountains and deer, crags and heather, and a great rushing river were exchanged for rolling, closely farmed country a mile back from the sea. The ocean on the western shores of Britain brings a mild, wet, relaxing climate. Argyllshire is the mildest county in Britain, and trees there grow at an embarrassing rate, too fast for their good. But the east wind that comes across the North Sea to Potterton comes straight off the Russian steppes. Its transit across the sea puts no moisture into it, merely some salt, and it blows hard and keen and bitter, sometimes for days, sometimes even for weeks at a time. Snow does not commonly lie long, close to the sea, unless it is a severe winter. But since 1952 when we first went to Potterton we have had three snowy and really severe winters. The bowl in which Potterton lies still has a gread deal of the clay with which the potters of Potterton once used to work. It seems to hold the frost and snow, which stays on in the bowl after it has gone from the country round about.

The first of them was 1954. It was the year after the great gale. It soon told on the birds. Pigeons flocked for the warmth of our few remaining pines and spruces. You can always tell when pigeons are reduced in condition because they then seldom land on the top branches of a tree, and their perching is attended by a great deal of noisy flapping. You find out even more certainly when you try to eat them. The snow was deep that year, and I did my best to build five-year-old Susie an igloo. There is igloo snow in the Cairngorms, but not at Potterton. In the Arctic, when you want to make an igloo, you must make a careful search for the right kind of snow. On snow, which is wind-packed and frost-hardened, neither you nor your dogs nor your heavy sledge will leave anything but the barest of tracks. That is too hard. And the soft snow is clearly no good. You must find snow of exactly the right consistency, to be cut up into blocks that are about a yard each way and four inches thick, and can be lifted and put into position. It is built round and round, like a snail shell, and all the blocks that build it come from beneath it. When you put the last block into the hole in the top, a strong cantilever structure is complete. You can walk right up to the top and stand on it.

Every time that we had snow we used to try to build an igloo for Susie. We always failed, but ended up by making quite a creditable snow shelter with an open top. The snow was with us for weeks. The birds suffered, but the routine of living went on.

A very much harder winter came in 1962. We had a white Christmas and after Boxing Day there was a steadily hardening edge to the weather. There appeared over the sea a pattern of mauve snow cloud like the outline of a mountain range. When the sun was out, the land was painted in rare colours and then the snow came back and fell, and fell, and fell. The frost hardened. That is always an exciting time because the duck, finding that there is no open water, flight up in the burns and give us a wonderful opportunity. We had an exciting pilgrimage to the burn every evening. Gradually the roads were blocked. The mail was delivered by our postman driving a tractor. He would descend from the driving seat, red-faced and muffled, and tell us the news. Our telephone lines were covered with snow an inch thick, making them look like white bell ropes. One of them began to sag and touched the other, which stopped the telephone working, though it would tinkle happily to itself. This was ideal, for it meant that no incoming call could reach us. But by tying four delphinium poles together, and reaching up and separating the two wires, we could send a call out and then let the wire fall back afterwards. As is our custom in the north of Scotland, we had ensured adequate supplies of food in our store cupboard. By going down the slope to the burn and over the stone bridge up to the home farm just beyond, we could keep ourselves in milk and eggs. Occasionally we would run out of butter or sugar, and that would mean a long trek in Eskimo clothes across the fields to the village shop. But we lived in happy isolation and enjoyed ourselves thoroughly. Because winter conditions in Aberdeenshire were painted in such lurid descriptions by the newspapers, no-one had ever expected me to return to work and happily it was the parliamentary recess.

The winter of 1963 was far harsher. It started at about the same time. The cold bit deeper and deeper as the days went on. Duck were still flighting inland in fair numbers. If they fly high one knows that they are in good condition. It is when they begin to fail that they fly low, and only for short distances at a time. Colour values seemed to change. The silver birches were no longer white but pallid against the whiteness of the snow, in very much the same way as a polar bear does not look white against the snow of the far north, but the palest of all pale gold. I would walk up the valley in the dusk of those winter days, to my neighbour's stretch of the burn, looking at that still sky with mauve clouds of unshed snow against the orange light of the evening. The sky seemed to stand still and this strange cold world with it. It was half a mile, perhaps, of Wellington boots going thump, thump, thump, thump, on the snow, the cold reaching through my mittens to my hands, while my breath rose like steam in the frost. And on up the little country road I would trudge watching the lights coming on in the cottages, until it was time to leave the road over a gate and down the side of a dyke, beneath the spindly tracery of beech branches on which snow was etched. There would be a skyward rush of darting teal and a squeaking snipe at the burn at the bottom. Then it was a matter of taking stock, of setting out the decoy, leaning against the dyke to wait, and watching the sky grow darker, and outlines dimmer. Without warning a whole section of the world would disappear as a snowstorm blotted out everything, with the whisper of falling flakes for company, audible above the muttering of the burn. By that time the cold would have reached through Wellington boots and two pairs of socks to my toes and I would have to stamp and walk about, only to discover too late that a batch of duck had come out of the snowflakes, passed within easy range of where I had been

P

standing a moment ago, and were disappearing into a falling curtain of white. I always wear my old Eskimo koolituk for such expeditions. I pull up the fur hood round my head to keep it warm, as it did for nearly three thousand miles of dog-team travel in Baffin Island. But it blankets your ears and you cannot hear that whistle of the ducks' wings or distant quacking. When the cold became sufficiently intense, I would leave my gun against the dyke, putting my hands in the ample sleeves of my koolituk and execute a cumbrous dance to keep my toes warm. Climbing up the hill again, perhaps swinging a couple of duck by their long necks, my feet would be so cold that footing would be uncertain, and I would stumble and stagger on the frozen clods underneath the snow. It was a relief to return to the firmness of the country road and see the light between the curtains of the window of the croft that stood beside it. Feeling would come back to numbed feet in the walk down the road to the lights of the farm beside the mill. The lights of Potterton would just be showing a few hundred yards beyond, across the snowy fields. The light between the join of the curtains would flicker as I drew close to them, from the flicker of the warm fire within.

Fresh snow is always exciting. It carries the news. Where pheasants are scarce the big precise print of a cock pheasant's foot is an event. Treading in the tracks of the animals who have passed there since it fell is absorbing. Rory has always loved snow. He capers in it, he rolls in it, he eats it, he cleans his whiskers in it. But the snow attaches itself to him in balls of ice like so many ping-pong balls, hanging from the rough hair of his legs and his underside. We used to go to enormous lengths to get these balls out. We now streamline the process and put him into a basin of warm water, melt them out and dry him. Always we went over the tops of our Wellington boots in the snow, which meant that the booted foot was numbed by an icy mush. At night our boots stood in rows round the cooker, packed with old magazines to help them dry.

As the cold intensified the birds fell into deepening distress. Susie went out every morning to feed the blackbirds in the field, clad in a red koolituk and carrying a pail of grain. They were part of the large batch that had come over from Norway, and there must have been a hundred of them. She fed them religiously and must have saved the lives of many. The Wildfowlers' Association broadcast an appeal to people to stop shooting duck and geese.

This we immediately did. Though the duck still looked sturdy, the geese were palpably flying lower and lower. They had gone, as they sometimes do, when cold strikes the north, south to more clement conditions. They had found the conditions there at least as bad, and came back again. Many of the duck moved to the continent and roved as far as Sardinia in search of warmth and food. The geese never land round us in a normal year. They rarely land this side of Newburgh. But they were so reduced now that Susie was able to walk up to within twenty yards of a flock of a hundred grey-lags. The goose is an enormously powerful bird, with thousands of flying miles behind him. But his engines must be fully fuelled. When snow blankets the grass fields for long he deteriorates rapidly in strength. The long-billed birds seemed to be suffering everywhere. The woodcock sought the edges of the burns, looking for soft ground into which to put their bills. The snipe became fewer and fewer, and tamer and tamer. We didn't even bother to shoot the pigeons. They were half famished and quite uneatable. We did not have any Brussels sprouts that we had to defend.

The world had become quite different. What the snow covered was compensated by what the snow discovered. The low slanting rays of the sun across the snow illuminated our only two pictures of any antiquity, until one could see details in them which we had never known existed. It intensified the silence of a room. We could listen to the sound of the fire burning, and the clock ticking, and look out at the white world outside. There was little noise of traffic. The sound of the few vehicles passing on the road was muffled. Walking to the shop one met red-faced children, to whom all this was a great lark in contrast to their muffled and serious elders, who clearly did not think that it was.

In January, Susie and I were down on the sand-dunes. I did not shoot at the duck who rose from the pools there, flew round, and settled again, the wigeon looking the poorest of the lot. But we walked along the beach in the gathering dusk where the cold tide was crawling up to meet the snow, and to our amazement we met a baby seal. Rory paid no attention to it until it let out a hiss. This he deemed to be a hostile act and we were thankful that we had brought his lead and could restrain him. The little seal stared at us with whiskered gravity, for almost a minute. It slowly turned itself round. Then plunged its way slowly down the twenty yards to the edge of the tide, and the cold sea engulfed it.

It was a time of portents. We would not have been surprised at anything we saw. By the time the cold let up in March, it was estimated that more than half the birds that had been in Britain before Christmas were either dead or had migrated. It was also estimated that probably a million birds had been kept alive by being fed by human beings.

Perhaps we are going back to an era of cold winters. My father used to describe his boyhood and what was called "the sixteen drifty days," when the snow began to drift and the shepherds wondered how many sheep were going to be left to them. Most of us would not mind the cold winters if only we could return to the hot summers, that used to go with them in my father's boyhood. Cold winters change the face of the countryside. Before the frost set too deep a neighbouring farmer was doing some ploughing. Not merely the gulls were following the plough. There were all kinds of strange birds trying to find a living. I noticed a hungry redshank among them.

A friend of Susie's came to stay. We met her bus on the Ellon road hauling a sledge to carry her luggage. But when the cold really set in there was so little that the farmers could do they turned to their old standby of enforced idleness, which is sawing wood, and the silence would be broken by the high whine of the saw. Our nearest neighbour sawed wood incessantly. The windows of his farm standing opposite across the burn, would be turned to golden squares as they caught the last of the light of the sinking sun. We sawed wood too. The two saws worked in duet, and we both had bonfires whose blue smoke mingled with the haze of the cold evenings.

In London these winters were far less tolerable. The paving stones in the London street where we lodge were raised by frost-lift so that they were all at different levels. As there was no rain to take the soot away down the gutters the pavements were black, covered with layers of black snow. People became bores, about their influenza and their bronchitis, in the way that some people had been bores about bombs in the war. The birds in St. James's Park were reduced to a small patch of water which they stubbornly kept open. They were bitterly hungry and some near famished. The grass in the parks where it showed through the snow was like green concrete to walk on, with the frost in the ground. The weather forecasts on the wireless were the dreary monotony of "more snow, more frost, icy roads" and warnings pertaining to these things. One came to sympathise with the medieval practice of putting the bearer of bad news to death. Even the children grew tired of snowballing and tobogganing, and the whole human race not only in this country, but all over Europe, started to long for winter to end its over-long act and allow spring to take its place on the stage.

If one cuts a tree in the years to come one will always be able to tell when these winters were, because one will see large rings of growth which have taken place in the summers following them. Only the hardiest birds survived. And it was not very long before they had bred up to the numbers which made these winters something about which Nature has forgotten.

The climate is changing. The climate is always changing. That is why deserts are always in transition, becoming wetter or drier, or hotter or colder. Boyhood recollections of long, torrid August days, with the bees buzzing in the heather belong entirely to boyhood memories. August is now the wettest month of the year in our part of Scotland. And you can tell how old a man is by the number of reasons to which he has heard the change of climate attributed. Today you hear people muttering that it is all the fault of nuclear explosions. If you were alive in the late twenties you invariably heard it attributed to the invention of wireless. I am just old enough to remember it ascribed to the artillery barrages of the 1914 war. It is, in fact, due to changes in the circulation of air currents mainly over the Atlantic. Nowadays your best chance of smelling sun-warmed moorland, and hearing the buzz of bees, in North-eastern Scotland, is in June or September. "So much for our degenerate climate!" wrote Osgood Mackenzie* (in 1921) recalling that in his native Ross-shire in the 1860s his shepherd's dog had found for his master some thirty wild bees nests in a short space of time—"Some of which contained quite a saucerful of honey and bee-bread. Nowadays an egg-cup would hold all the honey one could find in a long summer day." But, mind you, this is challenged by that cosy and consistent character the ground hog of North America. He comes out of his burrow on February 2nd to watch the approach of spring. If he sees his shadow he goes back for six weeks, if not he stays above ground.

When I lived among the Eskimos, in the year before the last

* Osgood Mackenzie, *A Hundred Years in the Highlands*. Edward Arnold, 1921.

war, the climate of the Arctic had become about 14 degrees warmer since the century began. If that trend had continued to the point of melting the north and south polar packs, more than five million cubic miles of ice in the Antarctic alone, the sea level would have risen something like 200 feet all over the world, destroyed every major port and many of the world's capital cities —and Potterton. Somewhere in the mid-1940s this trend was reversed and is likely to continue on this tack until the end of the century. Spread over the earth's surface, in these later 1960s are wild contradictions of climate. There have been desperate droughts in Basutoland and Bechuanaland with the old trees dying in the Northern Transvaal, while Lake Victoria to the North has risen several feet above the highest level ever recorded. And in Australia two and a half million sheep have perished in the greatest thirst since 1902, which was the most severe ever known in that country. While Italy has had the worst rains for eight hundred years.

Ours is a wet, temperate country. We live with rain. We do not greatly mind it. But there are some days that even we find hopeless. Those days may come at any time of year and the rain falls steady, even, and remorseless from low clouds that are dirty-grey with the torrents unshed within them. No wonder that Australians, and other peoples of the dry countries, marvel that we can ever have a water shortage.

Rain seems pitiless if the harvest is near to gathering, and pointless when the growing season is passed as it only serves to soak and sour the ground. But in the dry countries it can feel like a miracle and you jump for joy at the sour smell of wet dust and, in spring and early summer in Britain, it can be one of the most exhilarating of all sights and sounds and smells. When you stand and listen you hear it pattering on the puddles, and just audibly chuckling as tiny streamlets gather on the sloping paths, while the trickles grow into a steady splashing from the gutters and the drain-pipes on the house. And the green grass grows while you watch, and buds open, and rising waters scour the rivers of weed and set the salmon moving, and the trout search the brown flood for worms washed down. When the clouds press low we hear the distant mooing of the fog-horn at Girdleness lighthouse. The "Torry Coo" as it is always called, sends its long grinding call through the miles of sea mist. The place to hear it from is your fireside, just as the place from which to hear the morning plane take off for London is your bed.

Now when you get a hopeless day, a day when it is going to rain from dawn to dark, you might as well keep to the house, for the most of it. At some time, according to the season, you can go out and turn a mackintosh into a sodden rag scything willow herb or bracken, or waiting for duck or pigeons who are a great deal less observant when they fly in against rain that is slanting into their faces. But if you decide to spend the day indoors among the books, when the light begins to fail, there comes a yearning for the fresh wet air and for exercise. And your dog must go out sometime. Then it is worth the effort to look out your oldest clothes, the kind that are too disreputable to be worn in normal times, which can be cast off in heaps on your return, and thrown on radiators without regard to folds or creases. And you can revel in the rain and the excitement of defying it. And you have the countryside all to yourself. The cattle are under the shelter of our few trees and there are no men in the fields, only the sodden sheep. Rory looks as if he had changed a rough black fur coat for a suit of shiny black ringlets many times smaller. He takes a great deal of towelling when he comes home, before the fire, before his shaggy, and slightly heraldic appearance, is restored.

It is only when you step out into the rain and the wet air that you can savour the smell of the fire beside which you have been sitting. It is part of the art of making fires that you make them smell attractively, a four-dimensional attraction of sound and sight, smell and warmth. A handful of twigs, particularly wet ones, make a rich smoke if you lay a single piece of peat on top. So do a handful of wet leaves. Smoke hangs in wet air, and it comes the stronger and the sweeter from the chimney out of doors. It is to get the best of it that many people take a peat off the fire, and carry it several times round the room to fill the room with its smoke.

If you look through the misty window panes you see steady rods of rain falling pitilessly and without hurry. When the wind slants it sets the windows streaming. In boyhood I saw it thus in Highland shooting boxes, on our family summer holidays, often against the background of an angry Loch. In the glens the rain seems to march down the valleys. In the Canadian forests you hear it pattering in the silence of the tall pines and, from the door of your shack or the opening of your sodden tent, you see fronds of mist wreathed like smoke, round their tops. Nothing breaks the silence but the occasional crystal note of Le Rossignol, the

Canadian nightingale, which takes you halfway to Heaven. But rain, in early autumn and late summer and when we get all too much of it in the North-east of Scotland, robs the faded greenery of all real colour. Only the moss shines vividly and the lawns look as they look in the tropical rain countries. Most peoples' first impression of Singapore and Malaysia, is the astonishing green of the grass. When you have a very rainy month as we had in September 1966, some of the trees loved it, and others were indifferent. On that occasion the English oaks, Lawson cypress, Douglas fir, and the larch all flourished. There was little change in the pines, and the spruces seemed not to heed it. A long spell of rain nearly always means that mice invade the house.

Looking up from a chair and out of the window at the rain you become pleasantly sleepy. You wonder, reflectively, when it is going to stop. You only know that it is going to stop when all the birds start to sing. And some of them seem to think that they can stop it by raising their voices. The blackbird calls brassily, but none of the others pay any attention to him. He is the bird who always goes rather too far, then realises it, and falls into embarrassed silence. The pigeons start their murmuring. In Scotland they say:

> Tak' twa coos. Davie
> Tak' twa coos
> Tak!

Pigeons in England are supposed to say:

> My toe bleeds Betsy,
> My toe bleeds,
> Look!

Although the grammar of the Scottish pigeons may be open to criticism, they have a much more agreeable version. But they too fall to silence, and the only noise is the slowly increasing patter of the rain and the chuckling of the drainpipes.

If you are on holiday, or it is a weekend, and I am only at home at one of those two, you sink deep into a chair and watch your log fire with the sod of peat on top, it is a chance for a real rest. You can easily suppress the little stirring of guilt about leaving papers and briefs and figures that you packed so dutifully in the South, to be read at some other time. Look at the fire and listen to it. I always prefer wet wood to dry, as I love the bubbling of the logs. Priscilla and I disagree about it. Sometimes, if we throw on a piece of driftwood, strange tongues of green and violet flame light up the room eerily and we stare at them, and listen to the rain, and fall into a delightful lethargy. Green ash is supposed to be the best firewood, but we love birch with its bark. And if you have an old apple tree that has fallen it burns like incense. We relax from the clangour of the cities. You can only be sure that you are relaxed when you can hear the clock ticking. In our drawing-room we have a small simple, and hard working clock. If we sit in our other room, that we call our study, the ticking of the grandfather clock, in the hall, mingles with the precise, metallic tick of the ship's chronometer that lies on the mantlepiece. This is no mere clock, but a superb precision instrument which requires winding once a day. I had it from the Eskimos, when I lived among them, who had it from a wreck in the Eastern Arctic, and for close on three decades it never ticked, until I had it repaired and polished up recently at a good deal of expense.

The sound of wheels at the back door, accompanied by a toot, a rather sportive note like a small hunting horn, means that the baker's van has arrived. It is a matter of rushing out in the rain, jumping on the back step of his mobile shop which has that wonderful smell that Scotch bakeries always have, and stand momentarily under its cover while building an armful of loaves, topped with a tray of meringues, which are a lifetime weakness of mine. This weakness is shared by a robin who comes and chips away at them if we forget to shut the back door. You carry out the warmth of the house with you, and return with your face splashed with great cold raindrops. Once back inside the house, when everything has been put away, the red glow of the fire not only calls you back to the armchair, but reminds you that it needs another piece of peat on top of it.

We have all enjoyed wonderful expeditions in the rain. Some of my happiest and most successful days with a rod have been spent in clothes which clung sodden but unnoticed. Those days when your fingers become smooth and pink with wet. I so well remember my father's shape on the banks of many rivers and in boats and many Scottish lochs or Canadian lakes, his lean figure outlined in drenched tweed. And not a few happy days have been spent in shooting in the rain, particularly deer stalking, as well. But on the back of a horse, wet clothing does not marry well to a leather saddle, and a great deal of rain seems to go down your neck. As for hawking, the bird sits upon your left wrist, becomes steadily more morose, looking skinnier as its sodden feathers seem to shrink and turns his unwinking eyes on you, baleful with blame. Hawks blame you for everything that goes wrong, which dogs never do.

There are two or three favourite books that go with a wet day indoors, and all to do with sport. For this would have been a day of sport had it not been debarred by the weather. There are musty, foxed pages, of the Badminton Library, on Fishing, which have a smell all of their own. Among the meticulous drawings of hooks and baits, and shaggy salmon flies, drawn to scale in black and white, there are a handful of illustrations of splendidly turned out and bearded Victorian gentlemen playing large salmon on vast rods, and with occasionally a kilted ghillie in attendance. And sometimes the smell of these pages brings back a whole vanished world with a lot of my youth mixed up with it. Then there is the volume on the salmon in the "Fur, feather and fin" series, which is about the same vintage. No true fisherman can tire of re-reading the chapter called "A night with a Salmon" in which the Bishop of Bristol of the day, described hooking a monster where the Earn joins the Tay, and playing it for more than twelve hours, which involved two changes of tide which set the fish frantic. And how he spurned the devil, thinly disguised as his ghillie, who suggested he should hang a lantern over the stern of the boat which would have attracted the fish to the surface, where it could have been gaffed. Eventually it broke him, and it was caught a year or two later in the nets, and identified, with its hook in its mouth. He had related that when the salmon jumped it was the size of a full-grown boy of fifteen. He had not exaggerated.

It is an interesting fact that nearly all the good sporting essayists have devoted themselves either to the chase by hound and horse, all through history, or to fishing which has attracted so many writers of real skill and poetry. My father's fishing companion, the poet Andrew Lang, being one of the greatest. Shooting as we know it dates from as recently as the seventeenth-century. But Roger Ascham, in his *Toxophilus, The Schole of Shootinge,* writing a century before, sets out to explain why nobody at that time had ever written a book on shooting—by which he meant archery, "Menne that used shootinge most and knewe it best, were not learned; men that were learned, used little shootinge, and were ignorant in the nature of the thinge, and so fewe men have been that thitherto were able to write uppon it." Ascham was tutor to the first Queen Elizabeth, in her girlhood. He was one of a series of sporting writers who wrote to show the world how much excitement there was to be had from the pursuit of birds and beasts and fishes. Izaak Walton followed him a hundred years later with *The Compleat Angler* (1653) and Richard Blome thirty years later with *The Gentlemen's Recreation* which deals with every sport, and nearly all main branches of knowledge, but give detailed instructions on fowling-pieces and shooting flying. In the next century the Reverend Gilbert White of Selborne, and his correspondent Daines Barrington, produced the classic of the enjoyment of the English countryside, in simply watching nature at work.

There is one magnificent anthology, from which the foregoing and the following quotations are taken. My father gave me a copy of it when I went to school in 1925. I have thumbed through it countless times. It is called *Game Pie** and was put together by that splendid sportsman and writer the late Eric Parker. He was a true sportsman in every sense of the word. When he was dying he had himself wheeled in a bath chair down a wooded ride to see a woodcock sitting on its nest. Together with Patrick Chalmers he was one of the great sporting writers of my boyhood. The debt of sportsmen to these two is immense. Probably the best single chapter ever written on shooting was John Fortescue's "A day on the Yellow Clay".† They, and one or two others like them, were the successors of the writers at the beginning of the nineteenth century and this handful are the writers of the few shooting classics. Their predecessors were three ferocious Colonels, who all wrote tomes at before, during or after the Napoleonic Wars.

Colonel Peter Hawker was a soldier, squire and musician. His *Instructions to Young Sportsmen* published in 1814, had gone through ten more editions by 1859. As a captain in the 14th Light Dragoons he was badly wounded at Talavera in the Peninsular War. He left the Army, devoted himself to sport and, broken hip or no, would shoot from dawn till dusk, and pound down the Hampshire roads on horseback from his home on the Test at Longparish, to shoot wildfowl at Keyhaven, some forty miles away. He kept up a continuous warfare with the local shore gunners ("the Milford snobs" he called them) and usually sent

---

* Eric Parker, *Game Pie*, Philip Allan & Co. 1925.
† From *My Native Devon*.

his bag of wildfowl to his friend King William IV, who had long befriended him and advanced him to the rank of colonel in the North Hampshire Militia. His pen runs like a cavalry charge. He describes Christmas Eve and Christmas Day of 1843 in his diary:

"Weathercock with head where tail ought to be; dark, damp, rotten, cut-throat, looking weather; flowers blowing; bluebottles buzzing; doctors galloping in every direction; a Philharmonic of blackbirds and thrushes; an armistice from guns and shooting; the poor punters driven to oyster dredging, eel picking, day labour, or beggary; not even the pop-off of a Milford snob to be heard in that unrivalled garrison of tit shooters." Let me add that he was one of the first sportsmen to become converted to the use of our Belhelvie minister's percussion musket. He wrote the great shooting motto that, "He would rather see a man missing in good than killing in bad style." He wrote of a day when game was not precisely preserved on the borders of sporting estates, respected as they have since become. He set out early in the morning with a band of retainers, shooting anywhere and at anything and with his band of retainers beating off his neighbours who tried to do the same thing on his own land.

Colonel George Hanger produced his book *To all Sportsmen* in that same year 1814. He must have been an extremely ferocious man who laid down exact rules for preserving a covert near the owner's house by planting a 6-pounder gun on the top of it, loaded with a bushel of marbles and clay balls, to be fired through the treetops at any sound of nocturnal movement. To bring flanking fire, he recommends the building of a martello tower for the gamekeeper on the opposite side of the road with another six-pounder mounted on top. He always said that, if anybody was to shoot his dog through carelessness, he would immediately shoot that man's horse and stand prepared to defend his own person with his second barrel. In order to be fully prepared for this eventuality, he carried a selection of lead balls sewn up in greased linen, which could be quickly rammed home in place of the charge of shot. He saw a lot of soldiering, a lot of sport and wielded his pen furiously. As an ensign in the 1st Regiment of Foot Guards he was serving with the Hessian formation when he was wounded fighting against George Washington at Charlottown and had afterwards become a major in Tarleton's Light Dragoons. Imprisoned for debt he endeavoured to recoup his fortunes as a coal merchant. He had a long friendship with the Prince Regent, who grew more refined as he grew older and began to find the Colonel a little too crude for his taste.

The third colonel, Thomas Thornton, conducted an astonishing journey, of a kind that would now probably be called a safari, through the Northern and Western Highlands, which he described as "a sporting tour". His expedition was accompanied by a sloop called the *Falcon* which he had chartered. This was a highly appropriate name as he did a great deal to make falconry popular again. He wrote ten years earlier than the others. He seemed to have wandered on foot and on horseback through a large part of Scotland destroying everything that he saw, and drawing on himself and his book a blistering criticism from the pen of Sir Walter Scott, in the *Edinburgh Review* of the following year. Scott thus described the book: "The performance is termed a Sporting Tour . . . a long, minute and prolix account, of every grouse or blackcock which had the honour to fall by the gun of our literary sportsman—of every pike which gorged his bait—of every bird which was pounced by his hawks of every blunder which was made by his servants—and of every bottle which was drunk by himself and his friends. Now this, we apprehend, exceeds the license given to sportsmen." It may have annoyed Sir Walter, but it makes capital reading on a wet afternoon in the unquietness of the 1960s.

Dusk is falling. You must get up now to turn on the light if you want to go on reading. So you may just as well put another log on the fire, and put back the books on the shelves, open the French windows and listen for the birds. They will tell you if they think that the rain is going to stop.

You do not have to read far in the press of today to be told that everything that is traditional and pleasant, and mellowed in the countryside, is coming to a speedy end. Before closing the green-bound covers of *Game Pie* I generally turn up one last passage.

"The palmy days of shooting, if not gone by are fast going; moor after moor is enclosed—marsh after marsh is reclaimed. . . soon there will not be a quiet valley, or an *unbricked* hill in the country . . . The present generation may not live to hear of the total extinction of grouse in England; but the next will find few south of the Tweed . . . ." This might be the Sunday papers of today, it is actually taken from the Oakleigh Shooting Code of 1833.

18 *The Parish in Pawn*

WHEN we lived at Braemar the nearest building, and the largest in the village, was the Invercauld Arms Hotel. Smoke rose from its chimneys against the dun background of the mountain or lost itself in the rain. On the ground in front of where the hotel now stands, the Earl of Mar had raised the standard of the rebellion on September 6th, 1715, just five weeks after Queen Anne's death had given the chance to a Hanoverian king to ascend the Throne of Britain.

Mar and his little group of followers must have believed that a miracle was going to happen. For only by a miracle could they have hoped to march the length of the island, destroy the large and highly professional armies that stood in their way, and create a climate of opinion strong enough to bring about and sustain the restitution of a Stuart king.

But there is always a feeling of change and excitement and adventure at this time of the year in these mountains. The first frosts have come, and the mountain air is full of vigour and the world is ripe for change.

The Earl of Mar was gifted and his bravery was proven, but he was not a skilful soldier. He seems to have been one of those men whom history has cast for defeat. At first all went well. They marched from Braemar over the Devil's Elbow and Perth was captured within a fortnight. Then, as with all Jacobite ventures, the leaders disagreed and argued needlessly and endlessly while their opponents built up their strength and deployed their armies. A rebellion can never defend but must, like a snowball, grow in size as it rolls until eventually it starts a tearing, irresistible avalanche. Against them was Argyll, one of the ablest men in Scotland, who had learned soldiering with Marlborough. Events drove them to battle and Mar took up a position on high ground at Sheriffmuir on the early morning of November 13th. It was a good position on the flank of the Ochils and close to Dunblane. The Highlanders were afraid of nothing except cavalry, of which they had a very reasonable dread. But they were safe from them here in this rough ground and Mar's forces outnumbered those of Argyll, by more than two to one.

Battle was joined. The Jacobite right sent Argyll's left flying and the pursuit did not end until they reached Stirling. But on the other flank Argyll, after an unsteady start, put the whole of Mar's left wing to flight and the pursuit lasted for three hours. About 500 had been killed on either side when the forces drew apart. Well might old Gordon of Glenbuchat cry bitterly, "Oh for one hour of Dundee."

The Jacobites returned to Perth, while their enemies received increasing reinforcements. It was with mixed feelings that they learned the Chevalier had at last landed in Scotland, and with dismay that he had landed without an army, no treasure chest, and only a few attendants.

He had landed at Peterhead and spent his second night in the Earl Marischal's house at Newburgh. At Fetteresso Castle, which was lived in up to a few years ago and is now a sad and lifeless ruin, he held his first Privy Council, composed of the Earl Marischal and the Earl of Mar.

The ninth Earl Marischal of Scotland had served under Marlborough. He was twenty-one years of age, and his 19-year-old brother James Keith, who had been in battle beside him at Sheriffmuir, was to become what many regarded as the greatest soldier in Europe. The Chevalier received an effusive address from the Episcopalian clergy of Aberdeen. Jacobite Dundee kept him sitting an hour on his horse while the crowd pressed round him to kiss his hand. But his army at Perth saw only a dour man who lacked any spark of military leadership, and their spirits went to their boots. They learned that the day after Sheriffmuir the other Jacobite force, under the incapable Forster, had surrendered at Preston. The Jacobites had to move fast now to get away from their enemies and, when they reached Montrose, they discovered the Government forces had got as far as Arbroath. The Chevalier, together with Mar and one or two others, quietly took ship at Arbroath, bidding leave of their Army by letter. Their soldiery made their way back to their homes in the Highlands. An Act of Attainder was drawn up and nineteen Scottish peerages were forfeited and the lands of their owners became the property of the Crown.

But the attainder that cost the Earl of Mar Braemar Castle, among his vast possessions, cost his followers equally dear. Into the fight at Sheriffmuir had ridden with him another famous pair of brothers, James fourth Earl of Panmure and his brother Harry Maule, the "gallant Harry" of the ballad. The Panmure estates were the largest of all those forfeited. They included the lands and barony of Belhelvie. They were all put up for sale by the Government under the control of councils for forfeited estates. But there is a pendulum in British politics and this made people shy of offering for them. They knew that one day that pendulum would swing back from the Whigs to the Tories. As the Lord Advocate Dalrymple pointed out, it was one thing to declare estates forfeit and another to turn them into money. It was therefore a matter of great congratulation to the Commissioners when they received an approach from the York Buildings Company, to whom for more than sixty years Belhelvie parish was to belong.

The York Buildings Company had been incorporated in the reign of Charles II, with a licence under the English Great Seal, to erect a waterworks in the grounds of York House, and supply Westminster with water drawn up from the Thames. The site was on the north bank of the river, near the meeting of Whitehall and the Strand, and had once been the house and grounds forming the town residence of the Archbishop of York.

Q

An Act of Parliament in 1690 incorporated the company under the title of "The Governor and Company of Undertakers for raising the Thames Water in York Buildings." There was to be a Chairman or Governor and six assistants. Water was to be drawn up by some strange forerunner of the steam engine, but as it quickly proved so expensive, they soon abandoned the idea. The position of the waterworks was given as equi-distant from the water engine at London Bridge and that of Chelsea.

Speculation was in the air in the first half of this century and the South Sea Bubble had set everybody thinking about getting rich quick. The £10 shares in this enterprise rose to £305. But their manifest lack of success led them to search for other fields of activities. So it was that in 1719 they decided to raise the vast sum of £1,200,000 to purchase forfeited Jacobite, and other, estates to constitute a fund for granting annuities and life insurance. Most of these estates were in Scotland, the principal exception being the estate of Widdrington in the North of England. The Governor and all his court of assistants but one were English and they had acquired a lot of Scotland. It was a measure of the gambling mania that prevailed that by the following year they had raised that very large sum and nearly £60,000 more. For £207,091 14s. 1d. they acquired the estates of Panmure, Kilsyth, Winton, East Reston, Marischal, South Esk, Linlithgow, Fingask and Pitcairn.

They spread their activities to lead and silver mining and acquired a sub-lease of the mineral deposits at Strontian in Argyll from the lessees, who strangely enough included the Duke of Norfolk.

They agreed to pay £3,600 a year in rent for thirty-three years. This venture was a total failure although at the beginning of the nineteenth century, the mines were to provide nearly all the lead for the bullets which were fired by the Duke of Wellington's Army at Waterloo. It must then have been a low-cost producer as it was worked by French prisoners of war. A century and a half later I acquired the lease of the mines, with a Canadian mining syndicate from the Scottish Department of Agriculture. It seemed appropriate, that since Scotsmen had done so much to pioneer Canada, the Canadians should come to help pioneer Scotland.

The first President of the York Buildings Company was the Earl of Westmorland. The Court of Assistants decided to come

north to inspect their properties. Like so many visiting strangers
to Aberdeen in the eighteenth century they received the freedom
of the city. The earl of Westmorland's scroll described him as—

*"Gubernator Societates Susceptorum pro erigenda aqua fluire
Thamensis in edificus Eboracensibus, Londoni."*

Each director was described as *"Unus directorum Societates in
Edificus Eboracensibus."*

The year following, Provost George Fordyce, of Eggie in our
parish and of whom more hereafter, leased the greater part of the
parish from them. He agreed to pay £500 a year for a term of
twenty-nine years. But the Company was faced with the difficult
problem of finding competent people to administer and improve
these estates and collect the rents. Many tenants, throughout the
exile of their lairds, paid one rent in Britain, and another rent
clandestinely to their leaders living abroad.

The company had its first real stroke of luck in enlisting the
interest of Sir Archibald Grant of Monymusk and his brother-in-
law Alexander Garden of Troup. Sir Archibald was made factor
of Monymusk by his father as a very young man, became an
advocate in Edinburgh, a Member of Parliament for Aberdeenshire in 1722, being re-elected in 1727, but was forced to resign
a few years later as a result of a Parliamentary inquiry into the
affairs of a charitable corporation. He is believed to have lost
heavily in the speculation fever of the day, and further lost as a
big shareholder in the York Buildings Company. He returned to
Monymusk in 1734 and began a twenty-year struggle with debt
during which he became one of the greatest agricultural improv-
ers of the century. When he died he had several million trees
growing, and left the derelict estate that he had inherited, planted,
drained, financed and carrying crops like the turnip which had
never been seen before in that part of the world. He leased
considerable stretches of the forfeited estates from the Company
and no doubt ran them extremely well.

In the summer of the year 1725, the company was burdened
with difficulties from which it never could free itself and decided
to try a new venture in waterworks in London. This time they
made a bargain with the Duke of Chandos and the Earl of Oxford
for a ninety-nine-year lease of an area of London, which they
proposed to convert into a vast reservoir. In 1731 they abandoned the idea, well in arrears of the payment of their ground

rent. That site is now occupied by Marylebone Road and Queen
Anne Street. By now the shareholders were getting very restive.
Both sets of waterworks had been a failure. The mining at
Strontian was going the same way and the rents from the forfeited estates, which were the basis of a fund for granting annuities
and insuring lives, were bringing in a very modest return. Having
been set up by Parliament the Directors' persons and estates
could not be seized and attached as if it were an ordinary commercial company. But a Parliamentary inquiry was launched and
the Governor of the company, a certain Colonel Samuel Horsey,
who had succeeded the Earl of Westmorland in that position, was
found to be owing the Corporation some £50,000 and was
arrested on their suit in 1733. But the company still put a brave
face on it. They produced a map of Strontian and an account of
the workings dedicated to Lieutenant-General (later Field-
Marshal) Wade and headed, "A plan of Loch Sunart etc. become
famous by the greatest natural improvement this age has produced." An inset sketch of the workings shows the little village
that they had built for the miners, and called "New York".

The shareholders were all the more disappointed because waterworks normally paid very handsomely and continued to do so
until far into the next century. The *London Observer* of December
10th, 1848 describing the meeting in the vestry of St. Martins-in-
the-Fields of a company called "The New River Company",
notes that the shares which "originally cost £60 each, were then
worth from £12,000 to £13,000 per share."

The company's affairs were now stagnant, and worsened by
the suits of their creditors. The directors decided to try their
hand at something that was completely new. Early in 1747 they
presented a petition to the House of Commons praying that
"they might have liberty and encouragement to carry on fisheries
in Scotland, and upon the coasts thereof, and in the North Seas,
where they proposed to carry on a whale fishery." Nothing more
was heard of this scheme. Their abysmal failure in the field of
waterworks, insurance, estate management, and hard-rock
mining was hardly likely to bring in many subscribers to promote
fishing and whaling under the same control.

In 1763 Parliament passed an Act allowing for the sale of parts
of the forfeited estates on the understanding that the creditors
restricted their claims to about three-quarters of what they were
owed. The estates concerned were those of Panmure, which was

much the largest and included Belhelvie, South Esk, Marischal, and the much smaller estate of Pitcairn.

Arrangements were made for a roup to be held, for that is what we call an auction in Scotland, and the Edinburgh papers carried advertisements of it in 1763 and 1764. The upset price was to be thirty years purchase of the free rent calculated according to the lease which they had had with Sir Archibald Grant and others in 1723. The lands were described as "very extensive and capable of great improvement," and a large concourse turned up at Parliament House on February 20th, 1764. In charge of the proceedings was Lord Auchinleck, Lord of Session and father of Johnson's Boswell. There were many there to bid, but the eyes of the spectators in the gallery saw only three. There was George Keith, late Earl Marischal of Scotland and at the age of 70 on a visit to the land of his birth. Ten years before, an Act had given him the right to inherit or acquire property in Scotland though his titles were never restored. The City of Aberdeen had taken the opportunity of making him a freeman of the city, apparently unaware that they had given him the freedom when he was five years old, and to his brother, the Field-Marshal, who had been two years younger.

When he had left the country after Sherriffmuir, nearly forty years before, the brothers had served many rulers and served them with unswerving loyalty. He had himself taken part in theiabortive rising of 1719 when the Spanish landed 300 troops n the Western Isles who were forced to surrender ignominiously at Glen Shiel where the few Highlanders melted into the mists. The Earl Marischal himself, who was severely wounded had escaped with difficulty. He had attended the Chevalier in exile in Paris and Madrid. Then entered the service of Frederick the Great and served as Prussian Ambassador in Paris, and in Spain, and several years as Governor of Berlin. He had the Prussian Order of the Black Eagle and he and his brother, had been the right and left-hand of Frederick the Great. Voltaire said of him, "when I raise my eyes on his noble features, so full of fire and so expressive of truth, I was struck with admiration."

Four years earlier, Marshal Keith, perhaps the greatest soldier in Europe, had fallen commanding the right of the Prussian army at Hochkirch. After Sherriffmuir he had escaped to Brittany, returned with his brother in the 1719 expedition, and served nine years as a colonel in the Spanish service including the operations against Gibraltar. Finding that he was banned, by his Protestant religion, from promotion, he joined the Russian service and became a major-general and lieutenant-colonel of the Empress's Guards. In the war with Turkey he nearly lost his leg with a bullet in the knee at the battle of Otchakoff. The Empress Anne had said, "I would sooner have lost 10,000 of my best soldiers than Keith." He became governor of the Ukraine and mightily distinguished himself in the war with Sweden in the early 1740s but, when the new Empress Elizabeth came to the throne, her admiration for him aroused so much jealousy that he was stripped of his rank and left the service of Russia for that of Frederick the Great's Prussia. All Europe rang with his deeds. But half-way through the seven years war, on October 14th, 1758, an Austrian army came out of the autumn mists in the early morning and among the dead that they buried that night was the great marshal.

Their glance next fell on Carnegie of Pitarrow. This was the heir to the attainted title of Earl of Southesk which was not to be restored to his family until half-way through the next century.

Southesk had ridden into the fight at Sherriffmuir as colonel of the Regiment of Angus Horse. He had escaped to Brittany and joined the Chevalier at Avignon, refusing to become reconciled to the new régime. He died in Paris at the age of 37 having never set foot again in his beloved Scotland.

The third was an arresting figure. He was 64 years old, a ramrod of a lieutenant-general. When he died eighteen years later at a ripe old age it was as a full general and one who had strangely combined soldiering with forty-seven years as a Member of Parliament for Forfar. He had fought at Dettingen and Fontenoy. In the jargon of the present day he had joined "the new establishment." He had been part of the army which pursued Prince Charles from Derby to Carlisle. But the old lines were getting blurred. Thirteen years after the defeat of the Highland Army at Culloden, Highland regiments were storming to victory at the heights of Quebec, in the army of the Hanoverian King. It was the end of an old song, as we say in Scotland. You can hear the echoes of it today in the Glens. You always will hear them. But a new concept had got into its stride, a concept of Britain, a loyalty to which was compatible with a loyalty to Scotland. And this soldier was none other than the Earl of Panmure and Viscount Maule in the peerage of Ireland, which honours had been bestowed on him to make up for the same attainted Scottish peerages. He was the son of "Gallant Harry" Maule, and the nephew of our old laird, James, Earl of Panmure. His father and uncle had raised a regiment of horse and put up a great deal of money for the preparations that went before Sherriffmuir. Together they had ridden into battle on the right flank. Panmure was badly wounded, captured, rescued by his brother Harry, and managed to escape to France from Arbroath. He had a head wound which prevented him serving any longer in the field. It is said that twice he refused a pardon and the right to return to Scotland because it carried with it the condition of taking the oath to George I. Eight years after Sherriffmuir he died of pleurisy in Paris.

Harry Maule spent much of his exile at Leyden but was allowed to return to Scotland in 1724 and obtained a lease of Brechin.

The roup began. The lands of the Marischal, of Southesk and of Panmure were put up one after the other. These three men stepped forward in turn. Nobody bid against them and they went at the upset price.

The *Scots Magazine* of that day tells us, "that the people in the galleries could scarce forebear expressing their joy by acclamations, on seeing these properties thus revert to the representatives of the noble and ancient families to which they had formerly belonged." The pendulum had swung.

But from the Panmure estates that were bought back that day, our parish was exempted. But the scene was the same, eighteen years later, when the estate of Belhelvie was put up for sale by the authority of the Court of Session. It was said to extend to 8,200 Scots acres. "This property was exposed in sixteen lots varying in size from 227 up to 1,039 acres each. The upset price of the whole was £22,963, being twenty-four years' purchase of the free rent paid by the then occupants. . . . Most of the leases at Belhelvie had expired," the advertisement stated, "on Whit Sunday 1782, and the few subsisting tacks terminated at Whit Sunday 1789. The lots distinctly divided and marched, and each well accommodated with moss, were all disposed of for the cumulo sum of £30,745 Sterling, chiefly to individuals connected with the district of country in which the estate was situated."

From that sale of the remaining possessions of the moribund York Buildings Company, the little estate of Potterton and those others that cover the parish today came into being.

The York Buildings Company sold the last of their property on much better terms. The revolutionary war in America depressed land prices seriously in Britain but when it ended, they rose again. In 1783 the shareholders were so depressed that many were offering their £100 bonds, with fifty years' interest due on them, for less than five shillings each. One shareholder offered his holding for £300 and failed to get it. It later realised £16,000.

But in Belhelvie parish life for everyone improved.

The Rev. Mr. Forsyth wrote of it in 1793 in the *Statistical Account of Scotland* published in that year, (with reference to the York Buildings Company) "Short leases were universally granted and no improvements of consequence took place. If the tenant improved with lime, which very seldom happened, he took care, when his lease was near expired, to take so many crops of oats as to leave his ground in as bad, if not in a worse state than when he got it. And it was likewise a general method to pare and burn the mossy ground which gave a temporary manure at the expense of the soil. . . . Since that time a rapid improvement has taken place in that [the Panmure] estate and other parts of the parish. Long leases, often 57 years, are given; and the ground, of course, is assuming a different appearance. The tenants who have got the long leases are using quantities of lime, and throwing great parts of their ground into grass and turnip. Even the petty crofters, with life rent or nineteen years' leases, have their patches of sown grass, turnip, and potatoes; and winter herding is universally established, which was known of late years only in this country. A great bar to improvement, high multures,* are mostly taken away. . . . The greatest drawback to improvements still remaining is the casting, drying and loading of peats for fuel, which consumes a great part of the summer time that might be much better employed, and will continue to do so while the price of coals is so greatly enhanced by a duty which produces in the north of Scotland very little revenue to the Government, and yet falls heavy on those who pay it, because it is both a partial and oppressive tax." We had paid heavily for our share in the 1715 Rising. Sixty-seven years had passed since that disastrous November day at Sherriffmuir. And now no man could fail to be aware of the surge of Scotland of the late eighteenth century. Our first Rennaissance had ended at Flodden, and we were now in the flood tide of our second age of greatness.

* Charges for the milling of grain.

19

The Fame of the Fordyces

THE grey L-shape of the house of Eggie, stands on the seaward, and that is the downhill side, of Balmedie village which, up to not many years ago was also called Eggie. From its door fields run down to the bald sand and the spiky grass of the dunes, over the dunes to the sea, and then on "up the. sea hill". The straightening of the road to Ellon has been a continuous process since we came to the parish, and has now brought the tarmac and the traffic a good few yards nearer to the old grey house, on whose outer angle you look down. Its present owner, a widely renowned expert on Aberdeen-Angus cattle, has planted a shelter belt of pines but it will be another decade yet before they hide the house from the road.

The eighteenth century had run almost exactly a third of its course when George Fordyce lay dying there. At seventy years of age he could look back on a career of achievement. He had enjoyed just the kind of success that he had sought. Starting life on his father's farm near Turriff, he had moved to Aberdeen and to a business career. In 1710 he was a baillie, and during the ten years after 1718, was six times provost. He would have been one of the City Fathers who gave a welcome of non-committal warmth to the old Chevalier in 1715, when he landed in his fruitless quest for a crown. George was more than once married and records vary as to how many children he had. It would seem that there were over twenty, and some have said that there were all of thirty. Four of his sons, and one of his grandsons, were to leave a deep impression on the history of that century.

Provost George, as he was called, acquired the estate of Broadford, now part of the city of Aberdeen, quite early in his career. In 1721 he got a lease (a "tack" as we call it) of the forfeited Jacobite lands at Belhelvie from the York Building Company. He settled down in the midst of his new property at the house of Eggie. The secretary of the York Building Company, a Fordyce of Ayton in Berwickshire, was probably a cousin.

George was 58 years old when he settled on his new acres, and was to hold the office of Provost several times during the course of the next seven years. Five more children were born to him at Eggie and three were to die there. In 1724 the York Buildings Company gave him power of attorney to present his own minister to our parish. A year later he nominated his own brother-in-law, the Reverend David Brown, who was to hold the charge until 1744.

The minister was married to Isobel Fraser, daughter of the twelfth Lord Saltoun, and had four of a family. For twenty years he was held in high esteem; then came the crash. An entry in the records of our kirk session, on October 21st, 1744, records with awful brevity "Church preached vacant and sentence of deposition intimated against Mr. David Brown formerly minister here for the horrid sin and scandal of adultery."

The General Assembly did not depose him from the ministry but accepted his evidence of penitence and his declaration to go abroad. But no amount of research has revealed whither he went, or what happened to him and his family.

The downfall of Mr. David Brown must have been the more devastating for the powerful stand that he had taken with any of us who showed any trace of unruliness or laxity. His attitude towards "penny bridals", was an example. In the days when men lived the lives of unremitting toil, with little diversion, the "penny bridals" as they were called, were a great source of excitement in the parish. Theoretically, they were the occasion of marriage between two people too poor to pay for a wedding celebration, and the parish appeared in force, each man nominally contributing a penny so that they could have a fiddler and a dance and some merry-making. They came to be denounced by the Church for the unruly scenes to which they frequently gave rise, and in some parishes the possession of a fiddle was forbidden. On May 22nd, 1726, Mr. David Brown delivered a powerful attack on them in which he referred to "one instance . . . in the parish of Deskford where, in the month of June last at a penny brydall there happened such a pleying and fighting that one man was killed on the spot and a great many wounded."

A year later he was denouncing various disorderly gatherings of servants leading to "certain indecencys and abuses" as well as drinking "which things are not to be tolerated in a Christian land . . . none to presume to use such abominable customes."

We always like to keep up-to-date in Belhelvie, and so in 1728 we acquired a new pillory. A month after it had been put up fifteen people were charged, and found guilty of "prophaning the Sabbath Day by going to the sea-side and gathering 'scrows'."* There was nothing like enough room in the pillory for them all, so the Presbytery bound "the first rank to appear in the pillory and the second rank to appear before the congregation and to be rebuked."

Mr. Brown was very severe with all forms of Sabbath breaking. With William Dower who admitted that he had "on a recent Sunday pulled some handfulls of grass among his corns but denied thistleing the same." With Elizabeth Thom who confessed to "prophaning the Sabbath day by pulling Mugwort or Scallick Kail." James Vass made it all much worse for himself by denying the charge of "drying malt and killing, opening and flaying a steir."

In general, in Scotland, we tend to be very tolerant about anything that happens on January 1st, but the kirk officer must have behaved extremely badly on that New Year's Day 1739, for they deposed him on the spot for "carelessness, neglect and insolent behaviour."

---

* Various meanings are ascribed to the word "scrow", none of which would fit this context. As the word is shown in inverted commas in William Harvey's nineteenth-century fair copy of the parish records it may be that the original word was indecipherable.

Otherwise, nothing very extraordinary seems to have happened during David Brown's ministry. There was rather more than the usual trouble with almost worthless foreign coins being put in the collection boxes. But national events hardly touched the parish. The Porteous Riots took place in distant Edinburgh and in Belhelvie we couldn't have cared less whether Captain Porteous, or anyone else, was hanged by the mob there. The news of the coronation of George II stirred few emotions, but probably brought a reassuring feeling of stability. It settled something. The dangerous times were those when men ranged like wolves fighting for who was to wear the crown. Nearer at home was the affair of Alexander Lyper, a white fisher of Torry. He was excommunicated for being an atheist, but the people of Torry have always been very independent thinkers.

After so many years as the watchdog of the kirk, upon the morals of the people, the fall of Mr. David Brown must have shaken the parish with gale force. Provost George Fordyce, his brother-in-law and patron had been in his grave for eleven years by then. His son George had followed him only three years later, just before the birth of his own son, yet another George Fordyce.

This third George was to gain great renown as a man of medicine, a Fellow of the Royal Society, and an intimate of Dr. Samuel Johnson. He was born fatherless and, from a very early age, grew up motherless, although rich in talented uncles. For his mother soon married again and he was sent away to school, under a famous teacher, in the next door parish of Foveran, where the river Ythan winds through its sandy confines to meet the sea at Newburgh bar. In my father's youth it was nothing for Scottish children, himself among them, to walk five miles to school and back every day. The distance to Foveran is a great deal longer. It soon became clear that he was exceptionally clever and he won his M.A. at Marischal College in his early teens. His fondness, which most of us have shared in our time, for looking in at the windows of apothecaries shops at the coloured liquids in the giant bottles, as well as the great caddies full of exotic herbs, was the beginning of his dedication to medicine. He was apprenticed to his uncle John Fordyce who had been a surgeon in the Guards, and was in practice in England.

John Fordyce took his M.D. at Edinburgh, aged 22, and studied at Leyden, under Alpinus, it is said. He returned to settle in London as a teacher and a practitioner. Students all through the ages have had an instinct for the lecturer who can really help them. His original class of nine pupils soon swelled to a legion who jostled each other to hear his lectures on chemistry, *materia medica*, and the practise of physick. He would start lecturing at the chilly hour of seven in the morning, and continue for three hours. He spoke without notes and in an extremely halting and obscure style. But he was the greatest lecturer on his subjects in the country, perhaps in the world, so his contemporaries said. His private practice grew steadily, though his uncouthness of dress and manners probably prevented it from growing even larger. His manner of life was very strange. He had only one meal a day, but that a gigantic one. He loved good food, good wine, and good conversation and all of them in abundance.

The story is told in Boswell's *Life of Johnson*, of his being called one night to the bedside of a lady, who was one of his patients, after he had drunk a great deal too much wine, "feeling her pulse, and finding himself unable to count its beats, he muttered, 'Drunk by God'!" * Next morning a letter from her was put into his hand. "She too well knew", she wrote, "that he had discovered the unfortunate condition in which she was when he last visited her; and she entreated him to keep the matter secret in consideration of the enclosed (a £100 bank note)".

In 1774 he was elected a member of that literary club which had been founded by Dr. Samuel Johnson, Sir Joshua Reynolds, Edmund Burke, Goldsmith and others, a decade earlier. Dr. Johnson informed Boswell, by letter dated March 5th, 1774, that "we had added to the club, Charles Fox, Sir Charles Bunbury, Dr. Fordyce and Mr. Steevens." Charles James Fox had been brought in by Burke. Sir Charles Bunbury, for forty-three years M.P. for Suffolk and the winner of the first Derby, was to be one of the pall bearers at Johnson's funeral.

Steevens was a stranger choice. The son of the captain of an East Indiaman he had become a great expert on Shakespeare and possessed a biting tongue, both of which facilities seemed to appeal to Johnson. By the end of the century, other famous names had been added—Garrick, Gibbon and Palmerston to mention only a few. The membership of "The Club" in Fordyce's day was generally limited to thirty-five, and they dined once a fortnight during the sitting of Parliament. My father was a member from

* Vol. II, p. 274. Footnote quoted from Roger's *Table Talk*.

the 1920s until his death. By this time the existence of a club presuming to call itself, proudly and plainly, "The Club," had stirred up Sir Winston Churchill and some of his friends. They formed a rival establishment, called, "The Other Club," at which Sir Winston was a regular attender until his death.

Dr. George Fordyce was now a famous man, F.R.S. in 1776, and a Fellow of the College of Physicians two years later. In the records of the club his name was frequently mentioned and he is shown by the letter "C" (for Chemist). Others were known by similar symbols, Sir Joshua Reynolds as "P" (for Painter), Richard Brinsley Sheridan as "R" (for Richard) and Gibbon as "I" (for Infidel). Fordyce's great strength supported his robust manner of life for many years, but the good looks and the health that he had once enjoyed gradually deserted him, and he became plagued with gout and a prey to sadness. He died in 1802 leaving a family who were not particularly notable, although one daughter married a General Bentham, the brother of Jeremy Bentham the economist. His four brilliant uncles had gone before him and left their mark but no successors.

Of these sons of Provost George Fordyce, Professor David was the philosopher, the Reverend Dr. James the famous preacher and friend of Dr. Samuel Johnson, Sir William the doctor, and Alexander the banker.

David, the philosopher, was born in 1811 when his father was forty-eight. Alexander, the youngest, was born at Eggie and baptised at Belhélvie Church in 1829, four years before his father's death at the age of seventy. It is sufficiently long since very large families were the rule in this country that most of us have forgotten, or may never have known what they were like. There must have been a rare commotion in the house at Eggie with all those children scuffling about within, when it was too drenching wet for them to go out. On those days when the rain marches inland from the sea, and a soaking sea mist lies low on the land. Those would have been long days for their mother until night fell and they were tumbled into bed, and eventually tumbled out into the world. Several of them went by way of Aberdeen Grammar School and Marischal College, of which two were to be Lord Rector, and where David was to be Professor of Moral Philosophy.

David seems to have had a remarkable intellect. Although

licenced to preach he never did so, but studied and wrote instead. He won his Professorial Chair at the age of thirty. His publications created a stir in the university world and there were many to mourn him when, on his return from a European tour the *Hopewell* of Leith, which he had boarded at Rotterdam, foundered in a tempest with nine other passengers beside himself.

His brother James, in his famous publication "Address to the Deity" in which he penned a long obituary tribute to his friend Dr. Samuel Johnson, mourned David in beautiful prose.

The lease of the house and lands at Eggie now passed to James, who had become the Reverend James Fordyce, D.D., and was the only Presbyterian divine whose presence, Dr. Johnson could abide. Boswell wrote, "Nay, though Johnson love a Presbyterian least of all, this did not prevent him having a long and uninterrupted social connection with the Reverend James Fordyce, who, since his death hath gratefully celebrated him in a warm strain of devotional composition."

James was a famous preacher and had won a great reputation in the North, when he was called to London to the Presbyterian Congregation at Monkwell Street. He soon attracted a very large congregation, but ministers who worked with him found him a difficult colleague and the orthodox thought his discussions, though eloquent, not sufficiently fundamental for their taste. Boswell was persuaded to go to his church one evening, to hear the famous Dr. Blair preach. He wrote of it in his diary on May 15th, 1763. "I thought this would have done me good. But I found the reverse. Blair's New Kirk delivery and the Dissenters roaring out Psalms sitting on their backsides, together with the extempore prayers, and in short, the whole vulgar idea of the Presbyterian worship, made me very gloomy. I therefore hastened from this place to St. Paul's, where I heard the conclusion of service, and had my mind set right again."*

James resigned his charge in 1782 and settled in Hampshire close to his friend Lord Bute, that sensible and undeservedly unpopular Prime Minister, whose library and whose conversations he enjoyed. Fortune was at her most capricious when she threw her dart at Lord Bute, a quiet, reflective man, with a taste for botany and a deep knowledge of agriculture. He had lived in England since the Forty-five. He was attending Egham races in

* *Boswell's London Journal* 1762-1763, p. 259. Heinemann, 1950.

1747 when a downpour of rain prevented Frederick Prince of Wales, from leaving. The Prince decided to pass the time with a game of cards and Bute was summoned to his tent to make up a party at whist. He became an immediate favourite and was promoted steadily up the political ladder. "Poor Fred" died in 1751, but a year after George III's accession, in 1760, Bute became Prime Minister. The King had seen in Bute those qualities of cool tenacity and judgment, which was just what he felt that he needed to break up the old Whig hegemony. As a Royal favourite, an adversary of Pitt and, above all, as a Scotsman, he was hated, more for the last than for anything else. He had to have a body-guard of prize fighters to protect him in the streets. When he retired from his burdensome office he found great enjoyment in the peaceful company of the learned James Fordyce.

Bute's death in 1792, four years before his own, was a great blow to James. For these two men had become great friends and spent much time in each other's company. Bute had given him a silver lantern to guide him across the grounds at any time he felt like coming round for a talk in the evening.

James had a wife well worthy of him, called Henrietta. They had not rushed headlong into marriage, for his long and decorous courtship takes up nearly a quarter of her biography.* She was a great support to him and survived him by twenty-seven years.

In reading the lives of eighteenth-century clergy one is inclined to expect a dourness amounting to a devastating drabness. But the Reverend James enjoyed life and the good things of it. He was married at the fine house of his brother, Alexander the banker, at Roehampton. He is described on that occasion in his wife's biography as follows: "She [his wife to be] observed that the dress of her Cicero was as gay as the sober costume of a Scotch kirk minister would admit; his habit was entirely new and he wore light grey silk stockings; gold shoes, knee and stock buckles; and his full curled wig was newly and becomingly arranged. A smile of chastened pleasure irradiated his serene countenance, while an attempered joy shone in his fine expressive eye." Sir William Fordyce (the doctor) "looked as he felt, de-lighted;" Alexander (the banker) "looked arch."

When he retired he had sold the copyright of his various publications, nearly all of which were his sermons, for upwards of £11,000. As late as the last quarter of that century some four-

* *Memoirs of the late Mrs. Henrietta Fordyce.* Hurst Robinson & Co., London, 1823

fifths of all books printed were published sermons. Thus, without the modern aids of radio, television, and a national press, a preacher could become very widely known. One of his most famous discourses "Sermons to young women" went through several editions and was translated into eight languages.

William was born four years after his brother James, and died four years before him. He did well at his Greek and at his mathematics at Marischal College, studied medicine, volunteered for the army and found himself surgeon to the 3rd Regiment of Guards. With them he is said to have seen a good deal of active service in Europe. He returned and settled in London and built up one of the most lucrative medical practices of the day. He had the pleasant easy manners that his nephew George lacked. (They were made Fellows of the Royal Society at about the same time.) William was kindly. He was indiscriminately generous with the money that he earned. In 1771 he became a freeholder of Elsick in Aberdeenshire, and eleven years later he was knighted. In 1790 he became Lord Rector of Marischal College. He won the gold medal of the Society for the Encouragement of the Arts and left £1,000 to Marischal College to found a Lectureship in Agricultural Chemistry and Natural History. In the year of 1965 the foundation stone was laid for a new building at the Aberdeen University which owes its origin to his bequest.

While these three famous brothers were winning fame in their different professions the land at Eggie was tilled by tenants. After David was drowned, it had gone to James.

Barbara Fordyce, Provost George's fifth daughter, married a certain Lieutenant Robert Hay R.N. in the year 1752, at Eggie. As they christened the eldest of their several sons, Edward Legge Fordyce, it has been suggested that Lieutenant Hay may have served under Captain Edward Legge who commanded H.M.S. *Severn* in Anson's squadron, when that great sailor rounded the globe and captured the annual treasure ship returning to Spain. But poor Captain Legge, after being swept back and forth by a forty-hour gale off Cape Horn, sailed his battered ship northwards believing that he had turned the corner into the Pacific, only to find himself in the Atlantic. To this day this is regarded as a classic case of the complexity of dead reckoning. He managed to limp into port at Rio and patch up his ship and his

R

crew, before making his way back empty-handed to Britain. Lieutenant Hay settled in Old Aberdeen and became a Baillie and when his term of office was up he leased the farm of Eggie. He grew what was called "Siberian wheat" on its sandy acres, and the Aberdeen Journal of 1776 carries an advertisement for the sale of his crop. Siberian wheat was a misnomer. This crop would almost certainly have been that variety of oats, known as "Black Tartarian," which was introduced into Scotland about the middle of the eighteenth century. It was hardy and grew well in peaty, and marshy soils, gave a big bulk of straw and meal of an excellent quality. It was still being grown in the North of Scotland as late as 1950.

The last of the famous brothers was Alexander. His childhood was spent at Eggie where he had been born. He had been four when his father died. He soared like a rocket to riches, but when the burned-out firework fell it blackened thousands with ruin.

There must be many a family today in Britain who have been brought up to regard the name of Alexander Fordyce as synonymous with ruin. As a youth he was put to the hosiery business in Aberdeen, but the trade was too slow, and the town was too small, and he made his way to London where he became a bank clerk. In his early thirties he was a partner in a finance house. Somehow he got wind of the signing of the Peace of Paris in 1763 before the market did. His small competence became a fortune, which was further swollen by the rise in East India Stock in the two years following. In the General Election of 1768 he stood for Colchester and, in spite of spending £14,000 on the election, he lost by twenty-four votes. He determined to win it next time, and built a hospital there to acquire some more local goodwill. Two years later he married the beautiful Lady Margaret Lindsay, daughter of the Earl of Balcarres and whose sister, later to become Lady Anne Barnard, was the authoress of that famous Scottish air—"Auld Robin Gray". A contemporary description of Alexander Fordyce runs, "His eyes were dark, and, though rather dull, they often flashed with a spirit of high thoughts; while every feature spoke impatience of enterprise and acute discrimination; he could smile, and could look well pleased; yet there was a dark meaning seated in the recesses of his mind, which giving a glow to his countenance, disclosed him a man fitted for strategy and wiles. . . ."*

* *Op. cit.* p. 15

Poor Lady Margaret did not have long to enjoy her married life. In 1771 came ruin, from the unexpected direction of the Falkland Islands. A quarrel between Britain and Spain brought fear of a European war. An unsteady market began to sag, and then slide. The Scots bank, Douglas Heron & Company in Ayr, in order to establish itself had gone in for an extensive programme of what was known as "kite-flying." In other words, they had circulated a chain of bills, drawn in succession, to replace one another. It was a symptom of Scotland's acute shortage of actual currency. A worried Bank of England tried to firm up the consistency of credit, but the situation was by now beyond them. Half the land in the County of Ayr changed hands in the ensuing crash. And it was Alexander Fordyce's firm that was the first to go.

The Reverend James Fordyce and his wife were staying at Roehampton when Alexander returned one evening from the City, flushed and wild-eyed. He ate and drank heavily during dinner while his wife and the company watched him in silence. With a burst of laughter he started to peal the bell for the butler; "I always told the wary ones" he shouted, "and the wise ones with hearts of a chicken and claws of a corbie, that I would be a man or a mouse; and this night, this very night, the die is cast. . . . Bring champagne; and butler, burgundy below! Let tonight live for ever! Champagne above, burgundy below! The Gods shall celebrate this night, for Alexander is a man!"*

The public learned of Fordyce's crash on Friday, June 12th, 1772, in the *Morning Chronicle & London Advertiser*.

> An eminent banker was up with his clerks all Tuesday night, to inspect into the state of his affairs; and early on Wednesday morning, set off for France. It is said he has failed for upwards of £300,000.

The same editor added what would now be called a "human interest" paragraph on:

June 15th, 1772—*Morning Chronicle & London Advertiser*—

> A banker, who lately failed, had no less than three houses furnished; one in the city for business; one at the court end of the Town, for seeing company; and a third in the country, for retirement.

* *Op. cit.* pp. 15, 21.

June 16th, *The London Evening Post* recorded—

> Bankrupts—Alex. Fordyce of Clement's—lane, London, banker, to surrender June 20th, July 4, 25, at Guildhall.

The news was in Edinburgh in forty-three hours.
Saturday, June 20th, *The London Evening Post.*—

> The moment a late great failure in the City was known, a gentleman rode off express to Edinburgh to the bankers there, and back again, which is near 850 miles, in so short a time as 103 hours.
>
> In consequence of that gentleman's return, the Bank of England on Wednesday advanced £400,000 to the bankers there, who, but for this timely supply, must have all become bankrupts.

The city of London lurched towards chaos.
Tuesday, June 23rd—*The London Evening Post.*—

> Bankrupts: Henry Neale, William James, Alex. Fordyce and Richard Down, of Threadneedle Street, London, bankers and co-partners to surrender June 26, July 3, August 1.

> London, June 23rd.—It is beyond the power of words to describe the general consternation of the Metropolis yesterday. No event for these thirty years past, has been remembered to have given so fatal a blow both to our trade and credit as a nation. An universal bankruptcy was expected; the stoppage of every banker's house in London was looked for. The whole city was in an uproar; the whole city was in tears. This melancholy scene began with a rumour of *one of the greatest* bankers in London having stopped, which afterwards proved true.

Sir Richard Glyn had been Member of Parliament for Coventry since 1768, his partner Hallifax expected to receive a knighthood shortly. They were the soundest and most respectable of banking institutions, but their Scottish connections had involved them heavily within the Fordyce sphere of operations.
Thursday, June 25th—*The London Evening Post.*—

> Bankrupts: Sir Rich. Glyn, Bart. and Thos. Hallifax, Esq., of Birchin Lane, London, bankers and partners, to surrender June 27, July 6, August 4.

But happily they managed to turn their corner, and good Sir Richard did not have to resign from the House of Commons. Mr. Hallifax received his knighthood and the following item in the newspapers cleared their credit:

Friday, August 7th—*The Morning Chronicle & London Advertiser.*—

Yesterday the house of Glyn & Hallifax opened for the dispatch of business.

In the midst of this earthquake the figure of Alexander Fordyce seemed to have become temporarily obscured. He had left the country.

Tuesday, June 30th—*The London Evening Post.*—

Despatch, date-lined Dover, June 26th.

Mr. Fordyce, the Banker, embarked at this place for Calais on Monday last.

Horace Walpole picked up his pen and wrote to his friend Sir Horace Mann:

Strawberry Hill,
July 1st, 1772.

. . . Will you believe, in Italy that one rascally and extravagant banker had brought Britannia, Queen of the Indies, to the precipice of Bankruptcy. It is very true, and Fordyce is the name of the caitiff. He has broke half the bankers, and was willing to have added our friend Mr. Croft to the list; but he begged to be excused lending him a farthing. He went on the same errand to an old Quaker, who said, "Friend Fordyce, I have known several persons ruined by *two dice*, but I will not be ruined by Four dice."

As the fellow is a Scotchman, and as the Scots have given provocation even to the Bank of England, by circulating vast quantities of their own bank's notes, all the clamour against that country is revived, and the war is carried very far, at least in the newspapers. This uproar has given spirits, too, to the popular party in the City, who are recovering some of the ground they had lost, and will best the Court in the election of sheriffs, which I think was to be decided this morning; but to say the truth, I know little either of this matter, or of the history of the bankers. . . .

3rd.

Four more bankers are broken; and two men, ruined by these failures (which are computed to amount to four millions) shot themselves the day before yesterday. It is now thought that Fordyce only advanced the crash, and that it would have happened without his interference, for the Scotch bankers have been pursuing so deep a game by remitting bills and drawing cash from hence, that the Bank of England has been alarmed, and was not sorry to seize this opportunity of putting an end to so pernicious a traffic. In short it has given a great shock to credit, and it will require some time to re-establish it.

Arlington Street,   To Sir Horace Mann
August 3rd, 1772.
    . . . The crack in credit is not stopped; two more persons broke
last week; the lesser for two hundred and forty thousand pounds.
There are some great Scotch lords in violent danger of becoming
de tres petits seigneurs.

Alexander Fordyce returned and faced his bankruptcy proceedings. Some say that his life was in real danger from the
London crowd. That may well have been true. His brother James,
and his Henrietta, suffered cruelly. They lost heavily, not only in
money, but in friends and in repute. Alexander was not reduced
to a pauper. He managed to retain enough from the crash to live
a reasonable life, supported by the splendid loyalty and affection
of his wife. He died in 1789, a year in which so much was engulfed;
the year of the French Revolution. We have seen others of his
like since.

The summer following the Fordyce crash, Dr. Samuel Johnson
had appeared at Aberdeen accompanied by the faithful Boswell.
He had just received the Freedom of the City and, on August
23rd, 1773, he set off for the North. Leaving Aberdeen at 8 a.m. he
breakfasted at Ellon. He must have been hungry, because even in
the present state of the roads it would take a horse-drawn rig
some time to cover those eighteen miles. But although turnpike
trusts were then bringing tremendous improvements, through
making farmers and landowners responsible for the upkeep of
the highways, it must have been a bumpy ride between the fields
of ripening harvest. He passed through Belhelvie parish out of
sight of the little house at Eggie, which had been the home of his
colleague of "The Club" and of his friend the Presbyterian divine,
and following the inland road clattered over the bridge beside
the mill, neither of which has changed since. He made the usual
comments about there being no trees, and generally behaved as
if he was travelling through darkest Africa. When he got to
Ellon the Innkeeper mistook him for a doctor of medicine and
said he wanted Johnson's opinion on his child's earache. But he
cheered up the eminent man by telling Boswell that he had heard
that Dr. Johnson was the greatest man in England, after Lord
Mansfield. Johnson enjoyed the exception.

    Ten years later the York Building Company sold off the
remainder of their Belhelvie property. Arthur Dingwall Fordyce,

the great-nephew of Provost George, acquired Eggie and Bal-medie. He never lived there. His fourth son, Alexander, helped him manage the property and the salmon stake net fishing on the shore. After his father's death in 1834, Alexander emigrated to Canada and the lands at Eggie and Balmedie were sold. There have been no Fordyces in the parish ever since. But the smoke has gone on rising from the stone chimneys to lose itself in the wet sea air, and in the dusk the graceful windows can be seen as oblongs of light from a long way off, a mark for ships at sea.

20

Explosive Genius

IF YOU attend Church at Belhelvie, which you are very welcome to do, you will now come to what we have always called
the North Church. Books of reference record that it was
built in 1878. No book will explain the purpose of that tiny
anvil on a shelf that you see as you enter. But it helped to bring
about a revolution in musketry and consequently in warfare.

Our minister lives in the charming eighteenth-century manse,
with bow-windows added in Victoria's day, that lies on the
seaward side of the main road and down the slope from the old
ruined kirk. This kirk became famous during the ministry of his
namesake, the Reverend Alexander John Forsyth, which extended
for over fifty-two years from 1790 until his death at his own
breakfast table in 1843. That manse had been his home for
seventy-five years. And they must have been very happy years, for

a man with so many friends and so many interests. In 1912 an American Presbyterian minister, in Milwaukee, published a long article about him entitled "Forsyth of Belhelvie, the father of modern firearms." It is written with that splendid, if not always discriminating, enthusiasm that is one of the most endearing qualities of the American people and is not the least of the reasons for America's rise to world power. Our parish, even nearly two hundred years ago, was hardly "one of the most out-of-the way corners of the globe" as he describes it, but why cavil at that? Let a world that coldly disregarded our Minister alive paint him now in high colour. The American minister begins:

> What follows is history—aye, and history worthy the pen of a Macaulay, a Fiske, or a Froude. For it is the story of the all-but-unknown man who, in one of the least likely of all professions and during a life-time spent in one of the most out of the way corners of the globe, nevertheless more determined the armament and (to that extent, at least) the battles, the victories, and therefore the history, of the nineteenth century, than a Napoleon or a Wellington, a Grant or a Lee, a Moltke or a Bismarck, a Nogi or a Stoessel, or than all these together. Yet he never wore a uniform or heard a "shot fired in anger". He refused a bribe of a life-time's affluence rather than reveal to any save his own country the secrets of his great discovery, and that country appropriated his work without bestowing upon him one ha'pence of reward.

Now the Reverend Alexander Forsyth took his hobbies seriously. Among other things he was a very keen wildfowler. We know that he used to shoot ducks on the water, and that the flash of his flintlock often made the ducks dive before the shot reached them. And this began to annoy him more and more. Probably the fastest diving ducks are the tufted, the golden-eye and the pochard. None of them is particularly common on this coast nowadays, but they may well have been plentiful in the past. Occasionally on a windy night the priming would blow away, or on a wet night become sodden and useless, and the hammer would fall with a sterile click. Mr. Forsyth was a clever and meticulous man. He was determined not to be beaten. He made a hood with a sight on it, to fit over and shield the lock. But it was not the real answer and he knew it. He then conceived the idea of a percussion powder that could be detonated by a blow struck, and did not need the spark of fire from the flint. That was the touch of genius. He worked in a little smithy in the grounds of the manse, grounds which would have been well kept, for he was a keen gardener. No sign of the smithy remains, but the anvil in our North Church today is the only part of his modest equipment that survives. With it he worked to produce his percussion powder, and then a lock with which to fire it. And he was finally successful, as all the world now knows. But they do not know that had he accepted £20,000, offered to him by the French, for his invention, we might never have beaten Napoleon's army.

In that manse he had been born in 1768, and from it gone for his education to Aberdeen University. He was licensed for the Ministry in 1790 a few weeks before his father, the minister of Belhelvie, died, and he was called upon to succeed him.

Not many a son of the manse, [writes the American minister] has been chosen by the very people among whom he was brought up and while himself little more than a boy, to succeed to his own father's place in their eyes and their affections! If naught else than this were known of Forsyth of Belhelvie it would suffice to demonstrate the manhood and the virtues of him who, for more than half a century led by the Sword of the Spirit a tiny parish, and by his inventions startled nations, revolutionized warfare, effected peace, and energized the arts, for all humanity while Time shall endure.

It came about through his beloved and life-time passion for hunting. The quenchless delight of the young minister's every leisure hour lay in scouring the fens for rabbits or the gorse for grouse, or in stalking amid the sand dunes the great flocks of sea fowl as they gathered to swim inshore with the surf or dive in quiet spots for food. In these pursuits the zest of the sportsman could not annihilate the instincts of the student, and as the young preacher lay wrapped in his plaid among the sedges to await the long lines winging in over the German Ocean, they were the researches of the scientist that his remarkable mind called to aid the designs of the fowler. In his notes of those early days he has left a description, vivid to the appreciation of every duck-hunter, of how he turned to the problem that he was to solve as the years went on. Many a long stalk through the wet marshgrass into range of some fat "Brent-goose" resulted only in disappointment, and perhaps in a meal of porridge instead of roast gander, because the flash in the pan that inevitably preceded the discharge of the flintlock acted as a warning which sent the bird diving, and the whizzing charge only splattered vainly across the ripples where the coveted game had been.

His work in the smithy in the manse garden was by no means exclusive to other interests. Like so many of us in the North-east Lowlands he had a strong streak of pioneer in him. He started a local Savings Bank when such things were virtually unknown. Directly he heard of Dr. Jenner's discovery of smallpox vaccine he became his earnest disciple, and a pioneer of its use in Scotland. He was a close friend of James Watt, one of the pioneers of the steam engine, and was a first-class scholar into the bargain. He loved new thought, new ideas, and inventions. In later years he took up gardening seriously. And he enjoyed a hand at cards with James Adam of the *Aberdeen Herald,** and some of his other friends.

He did not lack for stimulating company. The number of wrecks at Belhelvie has always called for a responsible coastguard. The parish had a welcome addition when a Royal Navy officer was appointed to the job, who had served under Nelson at Copenhagen and the Nile. In 1817 Captain Colley, R.E., working on the check base line for the Ordnance Survey of Great Britain, for as long as it takes to measure a line of 5 miles and 11.753 feet, was an interesting visitor. There was his old university only a handful of miles away. As he paced up and down outside the manse, his mind on invention or his Sunday's sermon, his pet goose would keep pace with him and was often, with difficulty, prevented from following him in to church. His housekeeper said that he generally came back from the seashore with wet feet, too deep in thought to notice the edge of the tide.

It was now several years since he started work in his smithy with so few tools and so little apparatus. It was exacting work. He worked steadily on his experiments with blendings of powder that were often dangerous to handle, and on a lock to fire the powder which he had chosen. He was self-taught, but intensely gifted. Repairing locks and making pocket knives from ironstone were his earliest achievements. It was 1805, the year of Trafalgar, that he produced and perfected a reliable percussion powder and fitted a lock to fire it on his own flint-lock fowling-piece. The Encyclopaedia Britannica (1945 Edition) describes the workings of the flint-lock and continues: "Forsyth made obsolete this relatively complicated system through the provision of a medium

---

* The Statistical Account of Scotland 1845 says of this newspaper that "the principles which it advocates are . . . partly infidel." But a slip at the end of the entry under Errata carries a retraction of these words and an apology.

(his 'percussion powder'—composed largely of potassium chloride), a pinch of which placed in a tube communicating with the bore and crushed by mechanical means (the falling of a hammer) would produce a flash strong enough to ignite with certainty the powder within the chamber of the piece." We should remember that he did not invent the percussion cap. This is generally agreed to have been discovered by a certain Joshua Shaw in the U.S.A. who invented one made of iron in 1814, a second made of pewter in 1815, and a third one, which the world adopted, of copper in 1816.

Our minister shot all through the season of 1805 to 1806 with his new powder and lock, and was sufficiently satisfied to take it to London, the year following, to show it to his friends. He must then have realised that he had found not merely a means of getting even with the diving ducks, but an invention that could revolutionise small arms. Then others began to realise it too. He was related to Henry Brougham, who twenty-five years later became Lord Brougham and Vaux and Lord Chancellor, and who referred to him as "my honoured and dear relation." Brougham had no influence at this time. But the invention made its own headway. Forsyth showed it to certain friends, who showed it to a certain Sir John Banks, who showed it to Lord Moira, later Marquess of Hastings and Governor-General of India, who was then Master-General of the Ordnance. This wise man realised that here was a potent idea. The military mind of that time was only too often a barnacled mass of resistance to change, but Moira's alert intelligence grasped its powerful possibilities. He had not fought through those bitter years of war against Washington in North America, and been Adjutant-General under Cornwallis at the age of 26, without realising that the British Army was far from perfect. He put our minister to work in a laboratory in the Tower of London and undertook to pay a substitute to man the pulpit at Belhelvie. Within a year Forsyth had developed a lock with almost infallible detonation and which was unaffected by any weather. Furthermore it was not difficult to convert a flintlock gun to this new system. During this time his experiments were shrouded in deep secrecy. He dealt almost entirely with Lord Moira, and little was put on paper. They started to agree the basis of his remuneration, which was to be the equivalent of the saving of powder for a certain period, when Lord Moira was replaced in office by John Pitt, 2nd Earl of Chatham and brother of the great William Pitt. Because there was almost nothing on paper, the Board of Ordnance knew little except that there was a Scottish clergyman, carrying out experiments in the Tower, with whom no binding arrangement had been made. The new Master-General curtly told Forsyth to leave the Tower and remove his "rubbish". He went with dignity. After several months of waiting he got some money for his expenses, but none for his replacement at Belhelvie.

Our minister had been shabbily used, but he was at least free again and he wasted no time in taking out a Patent, on July 4th, 1807. He entered partnership with James Watt, the inventor of the steam engine. They put the famous gunsmith, James Purdey, to work in manufacturing the percussion lock. It was alarmingly expensive. The lock alone cost more than a first-class flint gun, but it soon won admirers. Mr. H. Baring, M.P. (father of the first Lord Cromer) an expert and tireless shot, became an early enthusiast. In a letter to our minister on February 1st, 1814 he predicted that "in a few years nothing else will be used by sportsmen in this country. I have shot with your guns for the last four years entirely. . . . I shoot every day it is possible to go out from the beginning of the season to the end, and I am often in the predicament of firing my gun, as often as my barrels will bear to be fired on one day." Parliament then was less demanding, and there was no autumn session. The famous Colonel Peter Hawker, the author of one of our few shooting classics and champion of the flint gun was converted. In a diary entry, of a sturdy July 9th, 1811, the Colonel describes taking a boat to shoot cormorants. He writes of them—"They dive so quick that if you fire at one on the water, he will generally be down at the flash. . . . I was told by the boatman that a man completely outmanoeuvred them (a few days since) by one of Forsyth's patent locks, which never failed to kill them on the water."

It was to solve that precise problem that our minister had himself to work in his smithy at Belhelvie manse. But now he breathed a larger air. His experiments had led him to a discovery of international importance. A letter appeared in the *Gentleman's Magazine* in 1817 "expressing grave concern about the Mr. Forsyth's patent detonator lock", and ending with this paragraph. "If, moreover, this new system were applied to the military, war would shortly become so frightful as to exceed all bounds of imagination, and future wars would threaten, within a few years, to destroy not only armies, but civilisation itself. It is to be hoped therefore that men of conscience, and with a reflective turn, will militate most vehemently for the suppression of this new invention.

I am Sir, yours etc.

AN ENGLISH GENTLEMAN."

Men of influence saw it, tried it, and passed on the word. The American minister described his later years, with a wild flight of fancy regarding the game resources of the parish.

"More years went by, quietly and cheerfully. The minister, no longer young, spent one decade upon another in proclaiming the Good News from his pulpit, in going his parish rounds, and doubtless in seasonable sallies among the game—ducks, geese, shore-birds, grouse, partridges, pheasants, hares, black-cock and even deer. . . . that abounded along the surf, the moors, or in the forests of the Grampian foothills behind Belhelvie's farms."

The Army's resistance to change was slowly broken down. The new weapon was given its first serious test in 1834 at the Ordnance Department at Woolwich. In that same year Forsyth was given a LL.D. by his old university and not by the University of Glasgow as many have said. In 1840 the Black Watch were issued with the new musket and a year later it was tested for the first time in battle at the capture at Amoy in the First China war. Lord Gough's despatch in the London Gazette (October 8th, 1841) tells the story.

A Company of Sepoys, armed with flintlock muskets, which could not go off in the heavy rain, were closely surrounded by some 1,000 Chinese, and were in some imminent peril, when two companies of marines armed with percussion cap muskets were ordered up, and soon dispersed the enemy with great loss.

Two years later the Government gave up manufacturing flint firearms.

Forsyth's friends pressed him to claim on the Government. He refused initially. But the Press started a newspaper campaign on his behalf. The matter was brought up in the House of Commons in 1840 and Lord Brougham advised the presentation of a petition. This was duly done on July 14th, 1840 by Mr. Alex. Bannerman, M.P. for Aberdeen. For nearly two years nothing happened and then the Treasury gave him a gratuity of £200. In the autumn of 1843 the matter was reconsidered and a further £1,000 made its way North. It ended by being shared among his relatives, £500 to his niece, £250 to his grand-nephew and £250 to his sister's husband. For he had died on June 11th, 1843, little noticed by the Government of a country that he had served so well. Two years earlier almost to a day, his parishioners had given him a public dinner and a piece of plate inscribed "as a mark of regard and esteem for his unwearied services as their pastor for upwards of fifty years." In all likelihood that meant more to him than any other tribute or the recognition of his country's Government. After all he had set out to get the better of the duck who dived at the flash of his flintlock, and the weather that sometimes spoiled his priming. He had succeeded. That he had revolutionised the armaments of his country's Forces was interesting, but incidental. Recognition came after his death. He became the first private citizen ever to be commemorated by a medallion in the Tower of London. At Bisley each year there is a competition for a silver medal which commemorates him, the gift of the Armourers Company, and there is a prize in his honour at our own Wappinschaw every year.

More than a century later Lieutenant-Colonel Calvin Goddard of the United States Army, an expert in firearms and their development wrote the final postscript on Alexander John Forsyth—

> To this sport-loving Scottish clergyman the world is indebted for an invention hardly less far-reaching than that of gun-powder itself.*

* *Encyclopedia Britannica,* 1945 Edition.

21 *A Sword in India*

WHEN the dead hand of the York Buildings Company was withdrawn, in the 1780s, new faces came to the parish. Among them was Harry Lumsden, an advocate of Aberdeen, who acquired Belhelvie Lodge. Few families have given more splendid service to Britain in arms than the Lumsdens. One of them fell at Flodden in 1513. A coat of mail at King's College is said to have been worn by one of them a century earlier at the Red Harlaw, one of the bloodiest battles in history. It settled for ever that the Lowlands of Scotland would not be ruled by the Highlands. This Harry Lumsden's third son, one day to be Colonel Thomas Lumsden, c.b., served with great distinction as a lieutenant in the Pindari Campaign of 1818 and 1819, under the Marquess of Hastings, who recognised the high quality of his services. Not for the first time had this enlightened Marquis appreciated a Belhelvie man. It was he who had set up our minister, with accommodation to carry out his experiments in the Tower of London, some fifteen years earlier.* As a captain, Thomas Lumsden fought in the first Burmese War and was one of three officers chosen to convey the ratification of the subsequent treaty to Amerapura. Lieutenant Henry Havelock, who was with him, was one day to earn immortality as the commander of the force that relieved Lucknow. Thomas Lumsden retired in 1842 to die at Belhelvie Lodge thirty-one years later. He used to describe Belhelvie to his old comrades as "just a suitable chateau for a worn-out old ramrod to wind up his days in." He left strong sons to carry on his name in India. His younger brother William made a fortune in India in the Bombay Civil Service, such a thing being then legitimate, and acquired Balmedie in this parish. You pass beside the grey stone wall that borders his well-treed policies, as you leave Balmedie village going north on the Ellon road. These Lumsdens were not the first of the parish, by any means, to make the long journey to India. Robert Turner of Menie, a close neighbour to Balmedie, had sent four of his five sons to the Honourable East India Company's service, at the beginning of the century, and India claimed them all. John and Robert had died of sickness, William had fallen in battle, and Alexander died of wounds. Only George was left. He saw service at the Cape of Good Hope, Orthez and Toulouse, as well as taking part in the Peninsular War, and survived to become a lieutenant-general, K.C.B., and Colonel-Commandant of the Royal Artillery.

Perhaps our connection with the Indian sub-continent has ended with the last owner of Belhelvie Lodge who spent a lifetime soldiering in India and Burma, and commanded the Chin Hills battalion in the last war. We gave a lot to India and Pakistan over more than a hundred and fifty years, for one small north-eastern parish.

One of the attractions of soldiering in India, in the nineteenth-century, has been the fact that promotion was by merit alone. The practice of obtaining commissions by purchase which, like pocket boroughs, was not quite so indefensible as it sounds, was not done away with until Cardwell became Secretary of State for

---

* Hastings died in 1826 after a splendid career as a soldier, a statesman and an administrator. He died somewhat impoverished in spite of the great position that he had held, largely because his ideas of hospitality entailed putting a book of signed cheques in each guest's bedroom.

War in 1868, and brought in his reforms which substantially shaped the British Army of today.

In the year of 1843, which was the year that our famous minister died, two stalwart young men of the parish, sons of Colonel Thomas Lumsden of Belhelvie Lodge, were twenty-two and fourteen years old respectively. Harry, the elder, had been born during a gale in the Bay of Bengal on the Honorable East India Company's Ship *Rose*. Because of some aberration of bureaucracy Stepney became his native parish. He had been sent to Britain from India at the age of six, and educated at Bellevue Academy in Aberdeen until the age of 16, when he had returned to India to be commissioned in the Bengal Native Infantry.

Already at twenty-two he was a seasoned veteran, with the March on Kabul behind him. He had already formed a close friendship with the great John Nicholson, who was to fall at the taking of Delhi fourteen years later. He had just been promoted lieutenant. India and the world were in front of him, and Belhelvie in the background, and he loved them all.

Two years later he was severely wounded in the Sutlej Campaign at the Battle of Sabraon, fighting against the Sikhs, who at all times have been among the greatest warrior races of the world. A year later he was chosen by another great man of India, Henry Lawrence, to be his assistant. He was coming to be regarded as a natural-born Frontier officer and was, moreover, a master of languages. History was being made at a gallop. Until then the gunfire that rolled along the frontier hills had been that of the flint-lock rifle, little different from those that Marlborough's soldiers had used at Blenheim in 1704. But the new percussion lock rifle was taking its place. A weapon that hardly failed to fire once in a thousand rounds, was utterly unaffected by the weather, and owed its origin to the smithy in the garden of the manse at Belhelvie.

Henry Lumsden was on the way up. Lawrence took him to Kashmir, and then, at a very early age, he received his first important independent command. Lawrence sent him with three-thousand Sikhs and six guns to bring the hillmen to heel in a wild part of the Border. Seven thousand of them faced him, but he deftly forced the passage of a tributary of the Jhelum and, in two actions, forced the hillmen to surrender. The thanks of the Government were delivered to him and he was charged with the formation of a Corps of Guides for Frontier service, initially of a hundred horse and two hundred foot. They were chosen from the fiercest and most intractable men on the Frontier, and were dressed in khaki, which no Indian Army troops had, at that time, ever worn. Their discipline was inflexible, training was thorough and recruitment purposely limited. The prestige that this force built up they still enjoy, on the Frontier and far beyond it. They first saw action when his cavalry distinguished themselves at the siege of Multan destroying a force of Sikhs on the Khyber Border, and for the second time, this remarkable subaltern received the thanks of his Government. He seemed indifferent to danger, impervious to hardship, and possessed of a charmed life. He was mentioned in despatches at Gujerat, which ended the Second Sikh War as Sobraon had ended the first. His Corps of Guides was now raised to four hundred horse and six hundred foot. Lord Dalhousie, the Governor-General of India wrote of him—

> A braver or better soldier never drew a sword. The Governor-General places unbounded confidence in him and the gallant body of men he commands.

And thus after fifteen years of India and with all this achievement behind him he returned for three years' leave at Belhelvie, with the rank of subaltern. The Panmure estates had passed to the Dalhousie family, and but for the confiscation after the Fifteen Rebellion this same Lord Dalhousie would, in all probability, have owned our parish. Had he done so there might have been no land for the Lumsden's to buy.

On May 11th, 1850 his deeds and those of the Guides began to reach the papers in Britain. He wrote to his mother, "I am delighted to find that the good people of Aberdeen approve of the conduct of the Guides at Sangao (a mountain fort at 3,000 feet). But as I have got hold of as fine a set of young lads in the Corps [it was now officially the Corps of Guides] who don't care a pinshead for being shot at, I consider that a Belhelvie man who could not . . . go ahead with them, deserves to be kicked out of the parish". Harry's life was the Frontier, and his beloved Guides. At home among men chosen for their fierce slant of character, he lived their life, in a world where a burning sun shimmered on the bare rocks by day, and nights were bitter cold. It was life lived in the smell of sweat and horses and leather and dry country.

Impatient of officialdom, he evaded any promotion that might take him away from the life and strife of the Frontier. Just before the Indian Mutiny of 1857, he and his brother Peter, and a certain Dr. Bellew, were sent on a mission to the Amir of Afghanistan at Kandahar. The purpose was to see that the annual payment to the Amir was used for the improving and maintaining of his Army. The party was accompanied by a small handful of the Guides and they reached Kandahar after a more than usually hazardous journey, to find it in a state of anarchy as a result of a grinding famine. They had hardly settled down before the news of the Mutiny was brought to them, and they were ordered to stay at their posts at Kandahar at all costs. One letter after another reached Lumsden telling him of the spread of the Mutiny, the defection of troops, and the slaughter of Europeans. Many were the voices who urged on the Amir to proclaim a Holy War, to slay these infidels within the city for a start and then go south through the passes into India holding high the Green Flag of the Prophet. These three steadfast men with their tiny handful of soldiers, month after month succeeded in seeming cool and confident and unafraid. Letters from the south told of the growing gathering of mutineers at Delhi, as every Regiment that mutinied went to swell the rebel army there. The loyal troops marched on Delhi but had to wait for considerable reinforcements before they could attack. Cawnpore fell. But Lucknow held. Then at last came the letter that Delhi had been captured, but that the great John Nicholson had fallen while Henry Lawrence lay dead at Lucknow. News came that their younger brother, William Lumsden, had been killed with the 1st Punjab Regiment in the storming of Delhi, and their cousin John Tower Lumsden of Auchindoir and Clova and of the Bengal Army, had led the 93rd Highlanders to which he was attached, through the breach, to fall, claymore in hand. He and Harry had played together as boys. The old keeper at Clova, John Ledingham, had walked forty miles to see him off on the steamer at Aberdeen. "Noo, Johnnie," he is believed to have said to the young man, "gin ye gang to the wars, mind me, and haud well ahint the dykes." And now Johnnie lay dead beside one of the most historic dykes on earth, the walls of Delhi. Six hundred Guides had been there and three hundred and fifty killed or wounded, but not a man had deserted to the enemy. Harry Lumsden's self-control can never have been more severely tested, as it was at that time at Kandahar, facing not only the day to day peril of himself and his immediate followers, but knowing that his Guides were in action without him. He now returned to them, and led them in the Waziristan Campaign a year later, from which he returned with a gash in the arm from the dagger of an assassin.

But now it was a new India. The Act for the Better Government of India 1858 was passed. The Honourable East India Company, after more than two hundred years of existence came to an end. Many whom he had known and served, like Lawrence and Nicholson, were dead. The governor-generals who had marked him for preferment, Dalhousie and Canning, had retired. He spent his last two years commanding the Hyderhabad contingent and returned home in 1869. He was still on the Army List, but was never employed again. His service came to an end in 1875 as lieutenant-general and a K.C.S.I., and he settled down at Belhelvie Lodge. He was far too big a man to be bitter. He coolly analysed the new India and his own career, saying "I cannot complain, for I have had my share of luck but kings apparently have risen in the East who know not Joseph." His army nickname had been Joe. He has been described in his heyday as "tall and powerful, a good rider, an excellent shot, and skilled with all weapons. He was an ideal Frontier soldier, unequalled in his knowledge of the Pathans and his influence over them."

He spent his last years very pleasantly at Belhelvie Lodge. Among its group of outbuildings stands the mews that he built for his hawks. Another one was his gun room, his photographic dark-room, and his wood carving shed. He was remarkably good at all his hobbies. A life-long falconer, he carried his hawk on the right hand as they do in the East, which is the opposite of our custom in Europe. His wood carvings were exhibited in London, and one can see a few of them today at Belhelvie Lodge. There is a particularly good one of a wild boar. He was a superb shot, and was one of the team of twelve guns at Broomhead Hall in Yorkshire on September 14th, 1872, killed 1,313 brace of grouse in a day's driving, which was then a record. He seems to have been a very gentle and charming man in his old age. Like our minister, if he found anything to be worth doing it was worth doing well. Both had a sense of humour. Henry Lumsden once came into his dark room to find that his ducks were paddling in the bath of chemicals in which he was developing photographs. Another story tells how a keeper from a next door estate proudly showed him a large hawk that he had just shot, with Jesses on its legs, not knowing that it belonged to the Belhelvie Lodge establishment. But there was no complaining, no explosion. He had long left behind him what Wavell used to call "the privileged irascibility of senior officers." And thus he passed his last years happily. He died just before the Guides celebrated their half century since their creation at his hand.

His brother Peter, who had been on the Kandahar mission with him rose to great heights in the new India, having taken part in the China War and the occupation of Peking in 1860. He was quartermaster-general in India from 1868 to 1873 and adjutant-general 1874 to 1879, when he became chief-of-staff India and then A.D.C. to Queen Victoria. He returned home in 1893, having been for the last ten years on the Council of India as a full general and a G.C.B. He settled down in Banffshire at a small estate, and like his brother, had two decades of happy retirement, dying within a week of the Armistice being declared in 1918.

They built firm foundations for those that followed them. As the Queen's Own Corps of Guides the regiment fought in the Second Afghan War in 1878 and continued on the Frontier, until they served abroad in the First World War. Britain left India and that sub-continent divided itself, and its two new nations went to war with each other. The Guides were of the Pakistan Army. They had said goodbye to their old station at Mardan in 1939 and the Guides cavalry parted with their horses two years later. But they did not forget them for they won the Pakistan Polo tournament in 1962, and are the only regiment in their Army to have produced its own polo team since the foundation of Pakistan. They had become a tank regiment, then an armoured car regiment, and are now a tank regiment again. The Guides infantry are now 2nd Frontier Force (Guides). Both cavalry and infantry fought with their old valour in the Indo-Pakistan War of 1965, a war that the admirers of these two great countries watched with the deepest regret. They emerged from it rich in battle honours.

They are well past their century now but they have never forgotten their founder. Fighting men do not forget a man of whom it was said, "a braver, or a better soldier never drew a sword."

Epilogue

I had to bring this book to a halt somewhere, although there were other distinguished men of Belhelvie about whom I could have written at length—two eighteenth-century provosts of Aberdeen, for example. And it would have taken a full chapter to have done justice to the career of that famous soldier of Wellington's army and Colonel Commandant of the Royal Artillery, Lieutenant-General Sir James Turner of Menie. It may seem to some that this Aberdeenshire parish is entirely unrepresentative in having made so much history. But it is not unique by any means in this county. If you doubt me, study the achievements of the sons of the parishes of Strathdon, Rhymie and Strichen to take only three. We go on quietly making history. But if we ever lose the desire to go out into the world to seek our fortunes, history will take no more interest in us.

Index